The Workhouse System 1834–1929

The Workhouse System 1834–1929

The history of an English social institution

M.A. CROWTHER

Batsford Academic and Educational Ltd

London

DEDICATION
In memory of
WILLIAM BROUGHTON WORDEN
AND
PROFESSOR JOHN PARKER

© M.A. Crowther 1981
First published 1981

Photosetting by Thomson Press (India) Ltd., New Delhi.
and printed in Great Britain by
Billing & Son Ltd., London, Guildford & Worcester

for the publishers
Batsford Academic and Educational Ltd
an imprint of B.T. Batsford Ltd
4 Fitzhardinge Street
London W1H 0AH
ISBN 0 7134 3671 9

Contents

Figures in the text

Acknowledgements

For permission to consult and to quote from manuscript sources, I should like to thank the following: the British Library, for John Burns MSS; the University of Birmingham, for Chamberlain family papers; the Public Record Office for Ministry of Health records; Kent County Council; The Greater London Council; The Principal Archivist, Nottinghamshire Record Office. I am grateful to the archivists and librarians in these and the other institutions who have helped me, but I should like to mention in particular Miss E. Melling of the Kent County Archives and Miss E.L. Plincke of Bromley Public Library.

For permission to quote at length from copyright material I am indebted to the following: Mrs Margaret Asher for Richard Asher's *Talking Sense* (Pitman Medical); Andre Deutsch Ltd., for Bella Aronovitch's *Give it Time: An Experience of Hospital*; Professor Peter Townsend for his *The Last Refuge* (Routledge & Kegan Paul). I should also like to thank the British Federation of University Women and the Trustees of the Theodora Bosanquet Bursary for enabling me to spend some time in London for research purposes.

Many colleagues have contributed directly and indirectly to the writing of this book, but I should like to mention in particular Professors R.H. Campbell, S.G. Checkland, M. Jeanne Peterson and M.I. Thomis, who assisted me with their expertise in specific areas. Dr Esther Welbourn patiently answered my queries on medical matters. Karl Figlio, Rosalind Hargreaves, Ludmilla Jordanova, Gillian Sutherland and Pat Thane all helped to expand my field of vision. I hope they will accept the result charitably.

To Dr Anne Digby, a fellow long-term inmate of the pauper palaces, I owe a special debt for her meticulous criticism and encouragement.

Abbreviations

Add. MSS   Additional Manuscripts, British Library
BMJ   British Medical Journal
Ec. Hist. Rev.   Economic History Review
GLC   Greater London Record Office, County Hall, London
HJ   Historical Journal
HMSO   Her Majesty's Stationery Office
KCA   Kent County Archives, County Hall, Maidstone
LGB   Local Government Board
MH   Ministry of Health Records, Public Record Office
MoH   The Ministry of Health
NPLOA   National Poor Law Officers' Association
NRO   Nottinghamshire Record Office, County House, Nottingham
PLB   Poor Law Board
PLC   Poor Law Commission
PP   Parliamentary Papers, House of Commons

A note on terminology

The names of the authorities and officials responsible for Poor Law administration changed several times, and the following guide may be useful:

1. From 1834 until 1847, the Poor Law was administered by three *Poor Law Commissioners*, assisted by their Secretary (Edwin Chadwick), and a small staff of about nine clerks. *Assistant Commissioners* had the duty of local inspection. The Poor Law Commission was not directly represented in Parliament, and had no official spokesman; after the scandal of Andover workhouse in 1845, the Commission was fatally weakened.

2. From 1847 until 1871 the *Poor Law Board* was the responsible authority, having been created by an Act of Parliament to replace the Commissioners. The Board was a cypher and never met, but its president was a member of Parliament. The chief executive officer was the civil servant who was permanent Secretary to the Poor Law Board, but as political convenience dictated these appointments, much of the actual administration during the Board's life was done by one of its senior clerks, Sir Hugh Owen (sen.) The titles of the Assistant Commissioners changed to *Poor Law Inspectors*. The size of the Inspectorate fluctuated between ten and 20, depending on the financial policies of the time; it became slightly more specialized in this period, with the appointment of two Inspectors with special responsibility for Poor Law schools.

3. From 1871 until 1919 the responsible authority was the *Local Government Board*, created to handle a wide range of affairs, particularly public health. Poor Law administration became a department of the Board, whose president was usually a member of the Cabinet. At first there were three joint permanent secretaries to the Board, but these were soon replaced by a single secretary, who was the main driving force of the administration. The Inspectors were now called *General Inspectors*, and there was also a Chief Inspector. More specialized Inspectors were appointed. The task of school inspection ceased in 1904, but in 1906 there were 13 General Inspectors, two

Medical Inspectors, and three women Inspectors for children in foster homes. The staff was increased by appointing Assistant Inspectors, who usually hoped for promotion to General Inspector.

4. From 1919 until 1929, Poor Law administration was under the *Ministry of Health*. The Ministry assumed most of the functions of the Local Government Board, but the *Minister of Health* had more senior Cabinet rank than his predecessor. The Poor Law department was less important to the Ministry than it had been to the Local Government Board, owing to the growth of new departments for national insurance and public health. There were still General Inspectors for Poor Law purposes, but medical inspection of Poor Law institutions was taken over by the Medical Officer of Health's department.

These various titles obviously create difficulties, and the method here adopted follows that of the Webbs. The different administrative bodies are referred to as the *central authority*, and the inspectorate simply as *Inspectors*, unless a specific reference is being made.

Introduction

On a winter's day early in 1860, Charles Dickens visited Wapping workhouse. The first room he entered was the 'foul ward', in which, some on bedsteads and some on the floor, lay women in all stages of illness. The reticence of the period prevented Dickens from stating directly the nature of their affliction, but anyone familiar with workhouses would have known that the usual occupants of the foul ward suffered from venereal disease, or skin ailments caused by living in filth. Only the workhouse offered shelter to such women if they had no money, for the nature of their illness deterred the charitable, and the free hospitals of London had few places for them. A casual observer might have seen the women only in the mass, embodying the worst degradation in his society, but even in these circumstances Dickens was able to distinguish some traces of personality.

> None but those who have attentively observed such scenes, can conceive the extraordinary variety of expression still latent under the general monotony and uniformity of colour, attitude and condition. The form a little coiled up and turned away, as though it had turned its back on this world for ever; the uninterested face at once lead-coloured and yellow, looking passively upwards from the pillow; the haggard mouth a little dropped, the hand outside the coverlet, so dull and indifferent... these were on every pallet; but when I stopped beside a bed, and said ever so slight a word to the figure lying there, the ghost of the old character came into the face.[1]

The historian must envy the novelist his freedom to conjure up that 'ghost of character' from the anonymous poor. Any book which deals, as this one does, with the most helpless members of a past society, runs the risk of turning them into an abstraction, of stripping them of their humanity. It is difficult enough to write working class history, and its historians have tended either to search for working class heroes, or to turn the whole class into a heroic figure ennobled by endurance and achievement. Yet in history, the working class has a sense of activity and purpose, which are the two qualities most lacking in that large section of it which was at one time or another forced to seek refuge in the workhouse. Legally, any man who accepted relief from the poor

1

rate became a pauper and lost his status as a citizen, signified by his being denied the right to vote,[2] but there was a great difference between being paid enough to subsist outside the workhouse, and being maintained within it. The workhouse pauper might often have been more comfortable than many working people in their own homes, but he lost all independence. He is not an active figure in the class struggle: instead he has given up the fight and accepted such crumbs as the enemy will offer. In the view of posterity he becomes like the children in the mines or the women in the sweat-shops, a passive emblem of the misery of the nineteenth century.

The history of an institution like the workhouse is history without heroes. It must necessarily be the history of a relationship between those who dispensed relief and those who received it, but it remains to be seen whether, lacking heroes, it still requires villains. A generation has now grown up which has no recollection of the Poor Law except from tradition, but the idea persists of the workhouse as a place where the poor were barbarously treated. Dickens himself is partly responsible for this view, even amongst those who have never read him: Oliver Twist lives on in popular versions, ever asking for more. Mr Bumble and the guardians who almost made Oliver a chimney sweep still represent the callous Poor Law administration, and Oliver himself the oppressed poor. *Oliver Twist* appeared in 1837: nine years later a Select Committee confirmed that paupers in Andover workhouse had been reduced by hunger to gnawing the rotting bones which they had been set to pound. It is not enough to argue that Dickens was describing an unreformed workhouse of the type which existed before the 1834 Poor Law Amendment Act, and that Andover was an example of the evils of uncontrolled local administration: the point was that such things continued to happen even after Poor Law reform. It is no wonder that the workhouse of the popular imagination is the workhouse of the 1840s, although the workhouse survived even after the Local Government Act of 1929 which ended the power of the Poor Law guardians.

Yet Dickens was a journalist as well as a novelist, and his writings provide two separate views of the workhouse. He concluded that Wapping workhouse was as well and kindly run as it could be, given inadequate buildings and the poverty of the local ratepayers. His suggestion was for the richer sections of London to contribute towards the expenses of the poorer; although he preferred private charity to poor relief, he was apparently prepared to accept that the workhouse could be improved, not simply abolished. Yet neither the symbolic workhouse in *Oliver Twist* nor the actual Wapping workhouse is 'typical' of a Poor Law which produced many diverse institutions.

It would be easy to write a history of the workhouse which concentrated on the scandals, just as it would be easy to write a scandalous history of hospitals, prisons, asylums, public schools, or any institution where one group of people has a fair amount of arbitrary control over another; but in workhouses, as in the other cases, it would not be reasonable to describe only the evils and forget the developments which turned workhouses from deterrent institutions into instruments of social welfare. For many years workhouses had to combine the functions of schools, asylums, hospitals and old people's homes, as well as being the last refuge for the homeless and unemployed. It cannot be claimed that these duties were always effectively performed, but it was the workhouse which provided the experience of managing the more specialized state institutions of today. The workhouse was the first national experiment in institutional care; many mistakes were made, and both deliberate and unintentional cruelties were perpetrated, but in trying to remedy these, the state was led into creating the specialized institutions which eventually replaced the workhouse.

The New Poor Law of 1834 made the workhouse a place of unresolvable tension, as all its critics have noted. How could an institution simultaneously deter the able-bodied poor while acting as a humane refuge for the ailing and helpless? The law was based on a hard belief that the deserving and the undeserving poor could be distinguished from each other by a simple test: anyone who accepted relief in the repellent workhouse must be lacking the moral determination to survive outside it. During a century of increasing prosperity, this notion wavered and changed, though it has never disappeared. The categories of 'deserving' gradually widened, and were removed from the workhouse. Separate schools, separate hospitals, asylums for lunatics, old age pensions, health and unemployment insurance, successively peeled layer after layer of the 'deserving' away from the workhouse. By the 1920s the remaining inmates were the most 'undeserving' and the most helpless—vagrants, unmarried mothers and the aged poor. Many guardians continued to operate hospitals associated with the workhouse, but these had lost much of their terror, and were being used by people who were not destitute. The deterrent 'bastiles'[3] of 1834 had been much deflected from their purpose by the time Neville Chamberlain was planning to incorporate them into a scheme for county hospitals. This process of change is the central theme of this book.

Workhouses have usually been regarded as uniquely reprehensible, and studied in terms of their repressiveness, or, in decline, as part of the 'break-up' of the Poor Law. This ignores the continuity of the workhouses even after the abolition of the Poor Law. Not only the buildings, but the officers, the administrators, and many of the habits developed over the previous century survived well into the period of the Welfare State. The influential work of Erving Goffman suggests that all residential institutions, whatever their purpose, have many features in common, especially the need to regulate the lives of the inmates into a common discipline.[4] Workhouse discipline was in some ways exceptional because intentionally deterrent at first, but workhouse history must be studied in the context of other, less controversial institutions. It is tempting to compare the workhouse with the prison, but it should also be compared with the lunatic asylum, the charitable home, and the hospital. The repressive features of the system were not all peculiar to the Poor Law, but were found in other institutions of the time. This is not an apology for the Poor Law, for no historian can be unmoved by the unnecessary suffering it caused, but it must be seen over a longer period of time and in a wider context. To reject the workhouse may be to reject not only the implications of the Poor Law, but to reject residential institutions as such. Some present-day social theorists have followed this reasoning to the point where they seek non-institutional solutions not only for the problems of unprotected childhood and old age, but also for crime, illness and insanity.[5]

In spite of all changes in policy, workhouse life seems to be a continuum, with similarities not merely between one institution and another, but over long periods of time. Modern observers try to explain these similarities by studying the institutions as enclosed worlds, regardless of their intended functions. Goffman, who coined the phrase 'total institutions' to describe these enclosed worlds, was most concerned with mental hospitals, but refers also to prisons, barracks, boarding schools, concentration camps and even nunneries. He does not, of course, maintain that all institutions are the same, but that they have similar attributes.[6] Fundamentally, all require that a relatively small staff exercises control over larger groups of inmates; that inmates accept the formal rituals of the institutions, but that they also develop their own codes of behaviour, attempting to recreate some of the habits of the outside worlds in an artificial environment. Incarceration in most types of institution has usually been seen as evidence of the inmate's social failure. In Goffman's words:

> The interpretative scheme of the total institution automatically begins to operate as soon as the inmate enters, the staff having the notion that entrance is *prima facie* evidence that one must be the kind of person the institution was set up to handle. A man in a political prison must be traitorous; a man in a prison must be a lawbreaker; a man in a mental hospital must be sick. If not traitorous, criminal, or sick, why else would he be there?[7]

The pauper could join this list of deviants; if he were not a social failure, why else would he be in the workhouse? He was immediately labelled both by the staff and the rest of society. Hence inmates attempted, within a narrow range of possibilities, to regain some kind of position and respect, and in particular, to reassert their individuality. Goffman goes further than this: he argues that the very adjustment of the inmate to the institution makes it harder for him to return to the outside world. Institutions breed dependence, as the behaviour of some habitual criminals and mental patients seems to indicate.

Goffman's views arouse controversy. Those who can see no alternative to institutions for the helpless or the criminal nevertheless have to defend them in Goffman's own terms. The size of institutions, their openness to public scrutiny, the training and numbers of staff, the relative freedom of inmates, all may be offered as alternatives to Goffman's bleak vision; but all these arguments tacitly admit that under certain circumstances institutions do lapse into Goffman's stereotypes. The historian is tempted to project this model back into the nineteenth century and see the workhouse as an early kind of total institution, for it has many of the characteristics which Goffman defined. And yet to the inmates no two institutions were exactly alike. Solzhenitsyn makes the point in a famous novel: the Stalinist prisons are the seven circles of hell, all part of the same system of 'social control', but an immeasurable distance separates the relative comforts of a privileged prison in Moscow from the appalling brutalities of a labour camp on the Tundra. A group of prisoners is about to be removed from Mavrino prison in Moscow back to the camps. One of them insists, 'There's no such thing as a *good* prison,' but the rest know that what awaits them is incomparably worse, that in future 'they would dream nostalgically of Mavrino as of a golden age.'[8] The history of enclosed institutions must encompass this paradox, and

Goffman's ideas are examined in the historical context, to provide a framework rather than a set of rigid definitions.

Workhouses differed from modern institutions in one important respect—their localism. Even in Goffman's American institutions, which are state-run, local differences are outweighed by standardized professional training. The people in charge of institutions are likely to be members of a skilled profession, but professionals did not control nineteenth-century workhouses, each of which was part of a small unit of local government. The notion of 'social control' is a trite but indisputable explanation of the workhouse system; but the kind of control exercised by guardians who were variously shopkeepers, landed magnates, coalmine-owners or industrialists, was never uniform.

The Poor Law also offers a striking example of central policy contending against local independence. Its history must avoid generalizations which give no idea of the great differences of practice in the localities, but also avoid the maze of colourful yet disconnected details in which this subject abounds. Source material is voluminous and confusing, and the thousands of volumes of correspondence between guardians and Poor Law authorities survive as memorials of these struggles. The huge bulk of documents, in the Public Record Office and in county archives, daunts the single researcher. No historian can consult more than a small number of them, and he will not know whether the area he selects is exceptional. My aim in this book has been to sample the different types of record available, and to write a general history which tries to show the diversity and social significance of these institutions. I have relied also on work by local historians to provide comparisons. Conditions within workhouses were affected by the size of the union, the wealth of the ratepayers, the calibre of the guardians, and the activities of local pressure groups. An institution's size vitally affected its administration: small rural workhouses naturally had different problems from large urban ones, but local and personal factors could sometimes outweigh these. The great workhouses of London and the industrial cities could be models of organization, part of a growing civic pride, or sink-holes for an impoverished and indifferent community.

This is not a history of the New Poor Law, but of a central part of it. Workhouses were intended to replace all other forms of relief, not only for the able-bodied poor, but by stimulating thrifty habits to protect workers against sickness, bereavement and old age. This hope was never fulfilled, and the number of people receiving relief in money or goods outside the workhouse was never less than twice the number of inmates. In years of distress like the 1840s, the outdoor poor outnumbered workhouse inmates by more than seven to one. People on 'out-relief' experienced even more diverse treatment than inmates, and the central authority rarely noticed their condition. Unless they died of absolute want (a rare occurrence), they received less attention than the workhouse inmates, for whom the authorities hoped to provide uniform standards. Guardians had virtually unfettered discretion over outdoor relief, unless they illegally tried to give it to able-bodied people. Nor did the outdoor poor, so much a part of the common scene, attract the eye of press and public as often as did workhouse scandals. It was a significant shift in attitude when the Royal Commission of 1905, unlike that of 1832, began to consider how the lot of the outdoor pauper might be improved, thus revealing how far short the workhouses had fallen from their original aim of discouraging pauperism. This, however, is a history of institutions rather than of the relief of poverty as a whole.

At this point also, the English-based historian must usually confess that the affairs of Scotland and Ireland do not concern him: I must make the same apology, because, unlike Wales, the differences in theory and practice between theirs and the English law are too great for a study of this size. Even to define a 'workhouse' needs care, for many other institutions grew from it, such as the separate infirmaries and district schools, to provide more expensive and specialized attention for certain types of pauper. I have considered some of these in their relationship with the parent workhouse, but fuller information is available elsewhere.[9] The workhouse, unlike the other Poor Law institutions, has become a myth. The rotting bones of Andover still occupy a central place in its history, but can they be replaced by anything more savoury?

In 1929, just as the Act of 1834 was to be superseded by a new framework of local government, Sidney and Beatrice Webb published their two-volume history of the New Poor Law. It has lately become rather fashionable to disparage the Webbs, usually over minor inaccuracies, and indeed because they wrote with specific reforms in view, they directed their history to a political end. Yet criticism of the Webbs is often tinged by a natural envy of the resources they commanded—their first-hand knowledge of the Poor Law, their private means, their self-assurance, their social contacts, their research assistants—not to mention the combined power of two formidable minds. The present historian can only follow this austere pair with respect.

I

ADMINISTRATORS

1

From the Old Poor Law to the New

After a sustained political crisis, the Great Reform Act was passed in 1832, making a moderate concession to the fact that the wealth of Britain was now being generated in the towns rather than the countryside. The countryside itself was still in an uneasy state, and had in the previous two years experienced a series of labourers' riots, with the burning of ricks and destruction of agricultural machinery. One of the first acts of the Whig government which had passed the reform was to bow to a long-felt pressure and attempt to change the laws which governed the relief of the poor.

The Royal Commission appointed to investigate the Poor Law was faced with unravelling legislation of more than two centuries, local acts affecting certain parishes, and almost unfettered local discretion in administration, all of which made both the theory and the practice of the Poor Law very complex. The Commissioners, or rather, the dominant figures of Nassau Senior and Edwin Chadwick, were fortunate in possessing that ability characteristic of political economists of their day: to reduce the most disorderly social problems to their simplest essentials. They believed that they were clearing a jungle of evil growths, from which would emerge the original intentions of the Poor Law: these they dated at 1601, 'the 43 Elizabeth', in which was affirmed the obligation of each parish to relieve the aged and helpless, to bring up unprotected children in habits of industry, and to provide work for all those capable of it who were lacking their usual trade. The men responsible for carrying out the law were the parish overseers, elected annually by the parish vestry, and serving unpaid and often unwillingly in dispensing bread or money, and supervising the parish poorhouse.

Not surprisingly, the preoccupations of the Tudors and the Royal Commission were entirely different, in spite of the effort made in the Commissioners' report to convince the public that their recommendations were reviving a worthy statute which had fallen into corruption and abuse. To both, the able bodied dependent poor were a source of concern, but the 'unemployed' who most agitated the Tudors were not those settled poor who found themselves temporarily without their normal labour in a hard winter or a depression of trade: the main problem was the large number of roving vagabonds and beggars who offered a threat to civil order. The Elizabethan law assumed that the settled poor would accept such work and relief as the parish provided; it was not expected that the offer of work, in their own homes or a parish house, would be felt as harsh and punitive by the poor. One of the aims of the law was to prevent the poor becoming detached from their place of origin, and to discourage them from vagrancy. Legislation of 1607 set up county Houses of Correction where work was given as relief to the unemployed at the local rates of pay, and where work could be enforced on the idle and vagabond, but the element of punishment soon became stronger, and the houses became an early form of gaol, quite separate from the parish workhouse.[1] The law distinguished between the settled and the wandering poor.

The Commissioners of 1832 confronted a different type of able-bodied pauper. They barely mentioned vagrants in their report, but were preoccupied instead with inadequately paid labourers in counties where the poor rates were used to supplement wages. Able-bodied labourers also believed they had an automatic right to parish relief when temporarily out of work. The system came to be known as 'Speenhamland' after the Berkshire parish where, in 1795, the magistrates had decided to supplement wages on a scale which would vary with the price of bread. The Commissioners blamed the Speenhamland magistrates unfairly, for the system had not originated there, but such practices certainly became more common as wages failed to keep up with rising food prices during the French wars.

The Commissioners argued that under this system, the pauper claimed relief irrespective of his merits; large families received most relief, and this encouraged improvident marriages; women claimed relief for their bastards, which encouraged immorality; labourers had no incentive to work hard and be thrifty when they saw that the most worthless idler in the parish could get more from relief than could be earned through honest labour. Employers, realizing that their workers were subsidised from the poor rate, kept wages artificially low. The Poor Law demoralized the labouring classes and interfered with their natural relationships both with their employers and with their families.

The pauper did not respect his employer when he knew that wages would be supplemented by the parish; he was discouraged from providing for his family and his aged parents when he knew he could throw them upon the rates. Although the Commissioners did qualify their language, for not all parishes suffered in this way, the total effect of their report in 1834 was emotive. The Old Poor Law was undermining the prosperity of the country by interfering with 'natural' laws.

It appears to the pauper that the Government has undertaken to repeal, in his favour, the ordinary laws of nature; to enact that the children shall not suffer for the misconduct of their parents, the wife for that of the husband, or the husband for that of the wife: that no one shall lose the means of comfortable subsistence, whatever be his indolence, prodigality, or vice: in short, that the penalty which, after all, must be paid by some one for idleness and improvidence, is to fall, not on the guilty person or on his family, but on the proprietors of the lands and houses encumbered by his settlement. Can we wonder if the uneducated are seduced into approving a system which aims its allurements at all the weakest parts of our nature—which offers marriage to the young, security to the anxious, ease to the lazy, and impunity to the profligate?[2]

As this shows, the language of the report was charged with moral judgements.

The Commissioners offered many answers to these apparently overwhelming problems, but essentially they required that parish administration, with all its potential for inefficiency and corruption, be replaced by a more unified system under the regulation of a central board. The workhouse was to be at the centre of the new system. No longer a mere receptacle for all kinds of paupers, the workhouse was to be supervised by the central board, and run by a staff of professional officers. The board should be able to unite several parishes in order to build an efficient workhouse if the existing parishes were too small for the purpose. The ultimate aim was that 'ALL RELIEF WHATEVER TO ABLE-BODIED PERSONS OR TO THEIR FAMILIES, OTHERWISE THAN IN WELL-REGULATED WORKHOUSES (i.e., PLACES WHERE THEY MAY BE SET TO WORK ACCORDING TO THE SPIRIT AND INTENTION OF THE 43 ELIZABETH) SHALL BE DECLARED UNLAWFUL...'[3]

Many historians have attacked the Commissioners both for their assessment of pauperism in the 1830s, and their recommendations. Their criticisms undeniably applied more to the agricultural than the industrial counties, for relief in aid of wages was almost unknown in industrial areas. The Commissioners investigated the agricultural southern counties more than the cities or the north, but their methods were dubious. Mark Blaug argues that the report was 'wildly unstatistical,' and that it ignored evidence which the Commissioners themselves had collected. The Commissioners had sent out a questionnaire to which about 10 per cent of the 15,000 parishes in England and Wales had replied. If the Commissioners had framed their questions more carefully, and scrutinized the replies thoroughly, they might have realized that the 'Speenhamland' system was declining, and that most agricultural parishes were really paying a kind of family allowance to maintain the large families who could not earn enough to keep themselves. At a time of agricultural depression and low wages, such help was essential.[4]

Further evidence suggests that in the years after the French wars, the southern counties had to pay more poor relief, not because of their administrative methods, but because of the depression and the nature of the labour market. It is still a matter of debate whether bread scales were being more widely used in these years, but in any case, the poor rate was rising as fast in parishes in the south-east where there was no bread scale, as in those where it was used. Parishes had their own notions of how relief should be given, usually related to the number of children in a family, and possibly also to the amount the whole family could earn; but in the 1820s falling wages forced more labourers to apply for help. The vestry sometimes had a rough and ready system under which they gave more relief to the 'deserving'. It seems that few parishes gave relief according to a regular scale, for they knew as well as the Commissioners that this encouraged paupers to demand their 'rights'.[5] In the south, although the laws of settlement probably did not discourage emigration as much as the Commissioners believed, labourers did not wish to move a long distance from their native place. If there were no large town nearby to draw them away, the ever-growing population remained on land which offered full employment only at harvest time.

The able-bodied male pauper may have been less of a problem than the Commissioners implied, for the bulk of relief must have gone to the sick and aged, and particularly to children. The average expectation of life for the labouring classes was much lower than it is today, which meant a high proportion of widows and orphaned families. Widows with young children frequently depended on poor relief, for women's wages (even where work was available) were rarely sufficient to support a family. J.D. Marshall argues, admittedly of an earlier period (1802–3), that probably no more than 20 per cent of the pauper population were able-bodied men, even in the counties worst affected by pauperism.[6] This is a speculative subject because there are no reliable statistics, but agricultural employment notoriously fluctuated with the seasons. Parishes had more able-bodied applicants in the winter months when work was slack; summer wages could not tide a family over the whole year.

Historians have not been as certain as the Commissioners that poor relief encouraged the huge expansion in population from the end of the eighteenth century. Other explanations offer themselves, not least the growing national income, which made it possible for the country to sustain more people. Poor relief may have helped to diminish mortality, especially infant mortality, by sustaining the rural population in years of hardship, but even wages subsidized with poor relief did not give families more than a subsistence income.[7] Poor relief was usually as parsimonious as possible—hardly an encouragement for the poor to breed recklessly, and families with young children were likely to be the most impoverished. The Poor Law was supposed to encourage bastardy too, and it does seem that the illegitimacy rate rose during the eighteenth century: but this began well before the period of Speenhamland. Peter Laslett's research suggests that bastardy was highest in the northern counties of England, where Speenhamland did not operate, and where presumably no more generous relief was given to bastard children than in the south.[8] Most rural parishes did not give unmarried mothers enough relief to support their children altogether, as the questionnaire showed; this scarcely encouraged vice. Sexual standards cannot be tabulated like wheat prices, but rather than the moral standards of the poor having declined after 1795, it is likely that the standards of the upper classes hardened. Traditional village habits, including the anticipation of marriage, became opprobrious.[9]

The Commissioners assumed, at a period of agricultural depression, that work would always be available to the able-bodied labourer who was denied outdoor relief. They knew this would cause difficulties, and planned to sponsor emigration from overpopulated parishes and to simplify the laws of settlement: labourers would diffuse neatly to places where labour was scarce. Yet it was not easy to transform a farm labourer into a factory hand, even if he could be persuaded to leave familiar places, and industrialists in any case were often more interested in child workers, who were tractable and cheap. Political pressure did not leave the Commissioners enough time to sift their own evidence before the lengthy report was printed; but several passages in it were repeated almost verbatim from Senior's communications with members of the government in 1832, before much of the evidence had been collected. The social philosophy of the report was already commonplace amongst political economists of the time, and Chadwick and Senior had probably agreed on its substance well in advance: the questionnaire was intended to prove their point.[10]

The Commissioners did not necessarily ask their questions dishonestly; rather, they were working at a time when collection of evidence on such a scale was unknown, and they were unaware of some of the pitfalls. They have been criticized for the wording of question 24: 'Have you any, and how many, able-bodied labourers in the employment of individuals receiving allowance or regular relief from your parish on their own account, or on that of their families: and if on account of their families, at what number of children does it begin?' Apart from its inscrutable grammar, this confuses outdoor relief to the able-bodied with allowances to large families; one type of relief subsidized the employer, the other aided a vulnerable group. A wage which would support a family with two children might not support four, and many parishes recognized this by giving some aid on behalf of the third and subsequent children. The Commissioners would not have distinguished between these two types of relief because both were equally bad: to subsidize any member of a family would break the necessary bonds of family responsibility. Against the mounting pressures of a newly industrialized society they defended the traditional view of the family as the unit of social care: the young must support the aged, the parents their children. To interfere with this upset not only political economy but morality.

Even modern statistical techniques would not have helped the Commissioners to translate some of the replies they received from local overseers, vestry clerks, magistrates and clergymen, many of whom misread questions or did not bother to answer them. Even worse, the respondents happily discussed matters of which they knew little: several answers from the northern counties speculated on the cause of the agricultural riots of 1830, which had affected only the south. There were 53 questions for rural and 64 for urban parishes, many of them requiring detailed knowledge. Even a well-managed parish did not always keep careful records of the ages and occupations of its paupers, and the larger the parish, the more vague the replies were likely to be. On being asked the ages of paupers on outdoor relief, their sexes and occupations, the Lambeth vestry clerk replied tersely that they were labourers, and that the adults were all ages from 16 to 84.[11]

Long-felt doubts shaped the Commissioners' views of the nature and purposes of the Poor Law. Over the past century, opinion had alternated between those who saw poor relief as a necessary extension of Christian charity, and those who wished to abolish it altogether.[12] By 1832, the high cost of poor relief reinforced the demand for total abolition: the influential work of Malthus added to this that poor relief merely encouraged improvident paupers to breed.[13] The Commission of 1832 was the most important of several parliamentary inquiries after the Napoleonic wars; most of these inquiries favoured greater restriction, if not abolition, of relief. Total abolition was not politically feasible; it was inconceivable to throw so many people on their own resources or to make private charity responsible for them. The Commissioners' solution was intended as a compromise, the effects of which would be gradual, and, in the words of one historian:

> The extraordinary fanaticism associated with the doctrine of the workhouse test in the nineteenth century . . . sprang from the resolution it offered of the conflict between the necessity and the undesirability of a Poor Law.[14]

Abolition of outdoor relief to able-bodied labourers the Commissioners considered practical, though they were prepared to leave it to the new central authority as to how and when this would be enforced. The deterrent workhouse system would be a 'self-acting test', which would not abolish relief, but would ensure that only the truly destitute and helpless would receive it—the rest would have to find work. The old and infirm, the orphan and the widow would not be denied relief, but the Commissioners hoped that even these would ultimately be removed from the Poor Law. If the able-bodied labourer feared the workhouse, he would provide for his old age; he would join savings banks and benefits clubs to provide for his family. In time, new provident habits amongst the working class would save them from dependence on the parish, and private charity could cope with the residue whom thrift had not been able to protect.

In devising the workhouse system, the Commissioners had no particular animus against the poor. They argued that unscrupulous farmers and employers forced down wages below the 'natural' market level and kept a pool of surplus labour in both the town and the countryside, knowing that labourers could be turned away from work and on to the rates whenever it suited business. The poor rates also gave middlemen a cheap supply of out-workers, for many industrial concerns still depended on domestic workers who could be laid off in hard times. The Commissioners believed that men would cope best when unfettered by artificial devices like relief in aid of wages. They hoped to end pauperism: it is less certain whether they hoped to cure poverty. In the 1830s the fatalism of an agricultural society had not yet given way to the optimism of an affluent industrial economy. Poverty, as most writers on the subject realized, was relative: the poorest English labourer was not expected to sink to the same level as the French or Irish peasant, for the English labourer subsisted on bread, and despised the Irishman who ate potatoes. In England, a subsistence income included providing the pauper with bread, some kind of clothing and shelter, fuel, perhaps, and the services of the parish doctor. The peasantry in most of Europe would not have expected as much. The Commissioners, standing between the old and the new societies, thought that poverty, as distinct from pauperism, was inevitable, and not the proper object of poor relief:

> ... in no part of Europe except England has it been thought fit that the provision of relief, whether compulsory or voluntary, should be applied to more than the relief of *indigence*, the state of a person unable to labour, or unable to obtain, in return for his labour, the means of subsistence. It has never been deemed expedient that the provision should extend to the relief of *poverty*; that is, the state of one who, in order to obtain a mere subsistence, is forced to have recourse to labour.[15]

Here the Commissioners quoted almost entire the words of Bentham 40 years before,[16] but they did not accept the bleak Malthusian argument that population would always press, if unchecked, on the means of subsistence. The country *had* sustained great population growth, and the Commissioners concluded that the economy could absorb all the people who were able to work. If the able-bodied labourer received no poor relief, he would have to work harder to compete on the labour market, his productivity and his wages would rise, and he would become more comfortable.[17] Like Bentham and Adam Smith, the Commissioners seem to have believed that a life of modest contentment was possible for the labouring class. There was no Malthusian 'surplus population' which could not be fed. If fear of the workhouse forced the labourer to give up drinking and other unthrifty habits, the Commissioners could foresee a period of rural bliss. Chadwick described what he had seen at Cookham, a model parish which had imposed task work on the able-bodied at very low wages. Perhaps this was the desired standard:

> I visited several of the residences of the labourers at their dinnertime, and I observed that in every instance meat formed part of the meal, which appeared to be ample, and was set forth in a very cleanly manner... I noticed some very trim hedges and ornaments in the gardens of the labourers, and it was stated to me that nothing of that sort had been seen in those places before the parishes had been dispauperized. Mr Knapp, the assistant overseer, stated that the labourers were no longer afraid of having a good garden with vegetables and fruit in it; they were no longer 'afraid of having a pig', and no longer 'afraid of being tidy'. Before the changes took place he had been in public-houses, and had seen paupers drunk there...[18]

This passage also illustrates a less familiar theme of the Commissioners' report—their belief that they were reinforcing traditional values. The report and the subsequent act have been seen as an example of the violent intrusion of capitalism into the 'moral economy' of the countryside. Previously the labourer had been guaranteed a subsistence; now he was offered the punitive workhouse. Employers of labour had finally renounced all responsibility for their workers. Thus the Poor Law is seen as part of the growth of capitalism and of a market economy. The farmer, like the industrialist, was producing for the market, and in his search for profit was prepared to abandon any care for the poor: such an interpretation causes a leading Marxist historian to argue, as Engels did, that the Poor Law was a piece of naked class legislation, 'perhaps the most sustained attempt to impose an ideological dogma, in defiance of the evidence of human need, in English history'.[19]

This assertion is true. The Poor Law Commissioners believed strongly in individualism and in forcing labourers to make their own way. They did not intend to pander to employers, but their report underwrote some of the worst excesses of *laissez-faire*. Yet this tells only part of the story: the curious thing is that the Commissioners also believed that their methods would re-establish in the countryside traditional values which they thought the Old Poor Law had destroyed. The report was an ill-assorted mixture of the new individualist philosophy and rural paternalism. The labourer was to be independent of the ratepayers, but financially and socially dependent on his employers. If employer and labourer could not rely on any outside agency to supplement wages, the former would resume his paternalist duties, the latter would become more deferential. The Commissioners fell into the classical error of contemporary political economists: they believed that in a free market economy the employer and the labourer would bargain on equal terms.

Hence the Commissioners recommended centralism, but the parish was still the unit of responsibility, and each had to pay for the maintenance of its own poor. The Commissioners believed that parishes, acting on motives of individual interest, would be better guardians of the rates than any larger aggregate. The Commissioners hoped simultaneously to encourage the uprooting of agricultural labourers to work in the new towns, and to maintain in the countryside a comfortable standard of living and the mutual dependence of master and man. Their report was presented, not as an attempt to cast the labourer adrift, but to force him back into reliance on his master, who would in turn have to pay him the market wage or lose him.

It has been noted that the weakness in the Commissioners' reasoning here was their misconception of what the 'market wage' really was, and their misplaced hope that the labourer could be easily shifted into the towns—not to mention their rosy view of the life that would await him there. Yet the picture they drew of a revitalized agricultural community, together with the seductive argument of reduced poor rates, may explain the remarkable lack of opposition which the Poor Law Amendment Act encountered in both houses of Parliament. The landowning class which still dominated Parliament was not interested only in reducing the poor rate, for the landowner bore indirectly the burden which fell on the tenant farmer, the shopkeeper, and the householder. Landowners were more concerned with the recent upheavals in the countryside. The Poor Law Commissioners were anxious to establish a connection between the riots and the maladministration of the Poor Law; indeed, the rural discontent had been a strong motive in setting up the Commission in the first place. The Commissioners asked their correspondents in agricultural parishes what they believed to have been the cause of the rioting; unfortunately for their arguments, only 40 parishes out of over 500 who replied were prepared to blame it directly on the Poor Law, while a further 29 attributed it to the Poor Law combined with other causes.[20] Most parishes blamed the Beerhouse Act, which had caused a proliferation of a low public houses, or foreign agitators, or, more commonly (and more rationally), low wages and the depressed state of agriculture. The Commissioners, of course, were not discouraged, in that they blamed both the riots and the low wages on the Poor Law, and their Assistant Commissioners produced many alarming accounts of 'discontented and turbulent' paupers. Paupers, they argued, had come to look on outdoor relief as a right, and considered themselves entitled to it even if they did not work. Because the parish paid them, they were insubordinate to the farmer, and would resist any attempt to force an adequate day's work out of them. The Assistant Commissioner in Dorset, D.O.P. Okeden, was particularly given to this view, although Dorset had not in fact been heavily affected by rioting. Okeden sensed trouble, however:

> Industry fails, moral character is annihilated, and the poor man of 20 years ago who tried to earn his money and was thankful for it, is now converted into an insolent, discontented, surly, thoughtless pauper, who talks of 'right' and 'income' and who will soon fight for these supposed rights and income, unless some step be taken to arrest his progress to open violence.[21]

Riots and the Poor Law were not arbitrarily connected. In times of trouble the parish workhouse and the overseers were natural targets for discontent. In East Anglia, rioters in 1816 had marched on the magistrates to demand that outdoor relief be increased, with cries of 'Bread or Blood'.[22] In the early 1830s the followers of Captain Swing had in 13 parishes attacked the poorhouses and in Selborne and Headley had actually destroyed them, while overseers had been intimidated.[23] The Commissioners could therefore argue that the law, by giving the labourer 'a sort of independence' from his employer, made the labourer riotous and his employer irresponsible. The pauper was discontented in proportion to what he received in poor relief or from reckless private charity.[24] If the labourer were driven back into employment by the threat of the workhouse, his sense of social deference would be restored.

The Commissioners here confused the symptoms and the causes of the problem. Only the Poor Law stood between the labourer and starvation in times of depression, and he naturally vented his hostility on the dispensers of relief, especially if they were locally thought to be mean. The poorhouse which, apart from the church, was probably the only public building in a small parish, was also the obvious place to attack: it was a useful symbol of class hostility. But the underlying cause of the hostility was not poor relief but low wages. In any case, the Swing rioters attacked not only the overseers, but anyone in the parish who happened to be unpopular, and who could give them money and food. Indeed, as the *Quarterly Review* argued, almost a lone conservative voice, the Poor Law might equally well have discouraged revolution by preventing the labourer from falling into the dreadful distress which had provoked the revolution in France.

The weakness of the Commissioners' arguments did not reduce their attraction to a Parliament full not of thrusting industrialists, but of landowners. The promise of low rates and a return to agricultural peace was alluring. No one made the point more blatantly than Henry Brougham, the Lord Chancellor. Introducing the Bill in the Lords, he began with a warning of the impending 'agrarian war', and attacked the Poor Law as the foundation of class hostility. The labourer, 'secure in the protection of the law . . . demands his allowance not as a man, but as a master'. Brougham's views on indiscriminate relief were worthy of Gradgrind ('any hospital for the reception of foundlings . . . is a public nuisance'), and in a florid passage he eulogized the bucolic past, when labourers lived in the same house as their employers:

> They were on the kindest terms with the master; they formed part of the same family; the master was more like the head of a patriarchal family, and the labourers were like his children.[25]

The new law implied a return to these lost days, just as the Commissioners had romanticized the '43 Elizabeth'. The historian may assume, according to his lights, that Brougham was indulging in a piece of hypocrisy specifically designed to attract a landowning audience, and will point out the incongruity of such language from an urban radical whose ideas are often seen as typical of orthodox political economy. John Henry Newman, the embodiment of passionate medievalism, saw Brougham as the very essence of the debased utilitarianism of the nineteenth century. Nostalgia from Brougham is suspect: his speech, and the Commissioners' emphasis on paternalism, may perhaps be dismissed as political gambits. Yet many radicals had a strong streak of rural romanticism: while praising progress and efficiency they hankered after a system of social relations which was dying.[26] The unlikely combination of forces which took the bill through the Commons attests its attractions to radicals and conservatives alike: it was proposed by Lord Althorp, an aristocratic Whig, seconded by George Grote, a middle-class radical, and supported by both Whig and Tory peers in the Lords. That the landowners believed they were passing not a radical but a backward-looking measure, is affirmed by Lord Althorp's biographer:

> The measure, indeed, was so conservative in its complexion that the Whigs were aware that in undertaking it they must not look for mere party support, and might have to depend on the Tories, whose connection generally with the landed interest made them the chief gainers by the new law.[27]

The framers of the law thus believed that they could encourage the growth of an industrial economy, while at the same time shore up the patriarchal society which that economy was eroding. The purposes were incompatible. The deterrent workhouse could not be used to revive the old society; rather, it added to the bitterness of the new. It was not by means such as this that the golden age could be recaptured. Enclosures, emigration, labourers' wages paid by the day, agricultural depression, had all contributed to the change in rural society, but the Commissioners paid little heed to these things, and tried to force the labourer back to his employer by ending his parish relief. The Commissioners tried to impose an unworkable ideal on the countryside, driven as much by impractical nostalgia as by capitalist urges.

In other ways the Commissioners' exaggerated hopes left problems for the future. The cost of poor relief was not growing faster than the population, nor than the national product in the 1820s. The trouble was that the cost fell unequally: parish responsibility for the local poor meant that impoverished parishes had a heavy burden while wealthier ones escaped more lightly. The complex and antiquated system of assessment forced householders with small means to pay relatively heavy rates, while absentee landlords and large commercial enterprises escaped payment. Because the Commissioners concentrated on the free movement of labour and the workhouse test, they largely ignored the problem of equalizing the rates. They hoped pauperism would disappear, making rate reform unnecessary, and so they rejected the idea of a national charge for the poor.[28] Later administrators solved the problem piecemeal: in 1865 the unions rather than the parishes were made to bear the cost of pauperism, and in 1929 the county and borough councils took over from the unions. Meanwhile, government gradually accepted certain expenses, such as old age pensions, as a matter for a national administration. The story of the reform of the rating system requires an historian with superhuman patience. Yet the unequal burden of poverty between one part of the country and another has never been fully shared, despite the Commissioners' belief that the deterrent workhouse was the answer.

If the Commissioners exaggerated the benefits to be gained from their proposals, did they also exaggerate the horrors of the old workhouses in order to enhance the prospect of reform? The conclusion must be that, although the Commissioners used their evidence selectively, they did not have to invent their descriptions of filth and misery. Outdoor relief was, in a way, an abstract concept. Its evil effects could be discerned only through hearsay and the subjective comments of observers. Workhouses were altogether more tangible objects of investigation.

By the end of the eighteenth century, about one fifth of all paupers on permanent relief were in workhouses. Most communities of market-town size had a workhouse; there were about 3,765 by 1803, while an uncounted number of others made arrangements to lodge some of their poor in neighbouring workhouses.[29] Numbers of workhouses were not accurately estimated, partly because some of the local overseers hesitated to dignify with the title 'workhouse' the small and unregulated building which they hired to house a few of their paupers. The Commissioners' correspondents from rural parishes revealed a considerable and important confusion between the terms 'workhouse' and 'poorhouse'. To the question, 'Have you a work-house?' the parish of Broxbourne cum Hoddesdon (Herts) replied: 'No workhouse; but we have a poorhouse, which is a complete nuisance, a harbour for idleness, and under no control.'[30] Binfield (Berks) replied:

> Not a regular *workhouse*. We have a poorhouse, under the care of a master and matron. The inmates are six men, all past 70, and eight women, of whom four are past 70, two of them being wives of the old men, two more past 50, and the two others past 40. Three Boys aged 16, ten and nine. One young Child.[31]

To these two parishes, a workhouse clearly implied a regulated institution in which people of working age were set to labour. A poorhouse was either an institution for the old and helpless, like that at Binfield, or an unregulated receptacle for all kinds of paupers. Yet many other parishes used the term 'workhouse' when it was clear that few of their inmates were capable of work. Throughout the eighteenth century the two terms had been used indiscriminately, along with 'house of industry', or even 'hospital'.[32]

The Commissioner's report described two types of workhouse. In the first, the common unregulated poorhouse, was a mixture of all kinds of paupers in a state of filth, oppression, and debauchery. Since most parishes had small populations, few could afford to keep more than a small, undivided building. The often-quoted words of the Commissioners have affected all histories of the old Poor Law: the inmates were

> a dozen or more neglected children . . . about 20 or 30 able-bodied adult paupers of both sexes, and probably an equal number of aged and impotent persons, proper objects of relief. Amidst these the mothers of bastard children and prostitutes live without shame, and associate freely with the youth, who have also the examples and conversation of the frequent inmates of the county gaol, the poacher, the vagrant, the decayed beggar, and other characters of the worst description. To these may often be added a solitary blind person, one or two idiots, and not unfrequently are heard, from among the rest, the incessant ravings of some neglected lunatic.[33]

The larger workhouses in cities, the Commissioners argued, also became depots for immigrants and vagrants, and attracted prostitutes and criminals with the loose discipline and ample food.

The second type of workhouse was rare but important. In certain parishes, far-sighted men had tried to prevent pauperism by making relief less attractive, and had experimented with deterrent workhouses. In Nottinghamshire, reformers like George Nicholls (later appointed as one of the three members of the central board) had tried to combine reduced outdoor relief with a strict workhouse discipline. The technique seemed to produce a marked reduction in the poor rates. The Commissioners relied heavily on evidence of this type, and proposed to make these conditions uniform throughout the country, but they did not judge wisely. Nottinghamshire was not a heavily pauperized county, and industry was steadily drawing labour away from agriculture. Relief in aid of wages had been given to framework knitters after the depression of 1819: it was a new 'abuse' which the reformers had ended without difficulty, and not as essential to the local economy as it was in the south of England.[34] Yet as subsequent events in Nottinghamshire showed, the system could not cope with industrial slumps, while in southern England labourers did not have the safety net of nearby industrial employment when agriculture was depressed.

The Commissioners exaggerated the horrors of the unregulated poorhouse and the virtues of the deterrent workhouse, but they rightly pointed to the possibilities of exploitation under a system of uncontrolled local discretion. Vile, insanitary sties like the workhouse at Bristol supported the argument that the old workhouses were not merely inefficient, but inhumane. The suffering received no care, the children no education; while at worst the pauper could be literally starved. If the workhouse were farmed out to a contractor who engaged to support the paupers at a fixed sum per head, he could profit from their deprivation.[35]

The Commissioners attacked the old system not only for cruelty, but for misplaced kindness. If paupers were lodged at the parish expense without being obliged to work, the house became a magnet for the idle and disorderly poor, who oppressed the helpless. In fact, it is difficult to say how many workhouse inmates were capable of work: replies to the Commissioners' questionnaire suggested that few were between 16 and 60 years old. Town workhouses, with many 'casual' paupers who stayed for short periods, were in a different class, but even these seem to have held mainly the sick and infirm. Of the 1015 inmates in St Pancras, and the 688 in Shoreditch, very few were able-bodied, though some 'refractory' paupers were boarded out elsewhere. Liverpool, in spite of its restrictions on outdoor relief and its position as a seaport, had only 12 per cent able-bodied people among its 1661 inmates.[36]

Rural workhouses did not want to admit people who could work, except for the special case of large families. These were always a problem, and some parishes took them into the house, allowing the father to continue his usual work outside. (Even Malthus had admitted that a family with more than six children was a kind of Act of God, requiring special assistance from society.) The Commissioners' statistics did not show whether younger inmates were physically fit, but they relied on more colourful evidence from the Assistants. In Gravesend a group of benevolent ladies had set out to reform the young women in the workhouse:

Hitherto they (the workhouse officers) had purchased the most gaudy prints for the females, and ready-made slop shirts for the men in the house, whilst the young women were lying in bed idle . . . A general order was given that the hair of the females should be braided, and put under their caps, and no curls or curl-papers seen. We got the whole of the young females clothed in the manner we designed in two months during the first year. This was done by their own labour . . . One effect of this partial discipline in the house was that in almost two months about one half of the workers left.[37]

It seemed that under the old system paupers were alternately pampered or mistreated.

Throughout the eighteenth century the functions of most workhouses had fluctuated. Some vestries had hoped to make their houses self-supporting, or even profitable, by putting the inmates to work under a businessman contractor, who would maintain them for a fixed sum and take the profits of their labour. An act of 1722 permitted vestries to deny relief to any pauper who refused the workhouse and its labour, but like much other Poor Law legislation, the Act was not enforced. Some parishes even restricted their workhouses to able-bodied inmates and children who could be made to work. Dr Body's research on Dorset shows that larger parishes like Blandford preferred to relieve the aged and sick in their own homes, while the able-bodied went into the house, where they were employed at button making, and later in the spinning and weaving of linsey.[38] Even before 1722 the workhouse at Wisbech (Cambs) excluded paupers incapable of work.[39]

The vision of the workhouse as a profitable institution was never realized, and became more unlikely as the Industrial Revolution advanced. Sometimes the work made a small profit, but not enough to make the house self-sufficient. Many contractors allowed paupers small sums to encourage their work, and Dr Body maintains that some Dorset workhouses in the area of the Bridport textile industry may have been self-sufficient for a short period while that industry boomed.[40] But paupers were usually most experienced in the local handicraft, and if many of them sought relief, it probably indicated that this craft was already depressed. If a man could make a living from spinning, he would not go into a workhouse to spin. If a local trade were doing well, the workhouse might earn something by employing the elderly, the infirm and the children, but these workers suffered first in a depression. Local people feared competition from cheap workhouse labour, while the Webbs argued that paupers worked slackly because their livelihood was assured.[41] In 1803, about £40,000 was spent on employing workhouse paupers in England and Wales, and they earned about £70,000, but this was nowhere near self-sufficiency.[42] Guardians usually fell back on unskilled tasks such as stonebreaking, which was not as profitable as the older, but obsolete, skills.

The idea of the self-supporting workhouse died slowly, for it had been popularized by Jeremy Bentham in his plans for the great 'panopticon.' In this polygonal building of Bentham's imagination,

2,000 paupers of all ages would sleep in cells observed from a central block. All outdoor relief would be superseded by these institutions, where the paupers, strictly segregated according to age and morals, would work according to their ability.[43] The children would be educated for a well-paid occupation, and the sick properly treated. The panopticon, Bentham believed, would ultimately end all beggary, vice and crime; but by 1811 the government had lost interest in the plan, first projected in 1797. In 1832 the Commissioners did not plan the workhouse as a large manufactory, instead they argued that since the able-bodied would seek work outside, workhouse labour would be for discipline rather than profit: but many local authorities still hoped to cut their costs with workhouse labour, and the subject was acrimoniously debated.

By the end of the French wars, the workhouses seem to have become mainly asylums for the helpless poor and rarely employed the able-bodied; aged people and children predominated in them. Evidence from Cambridgeshire, Dorset and East Anglia suggests that rural parishes had abandoned their attempts to set inmates to work, and were likely to give outdoor relief to anyone capable of earning.[44] Large urban workhouses were more likely to provide work for the inmates, for the vestries found it economical to employ paid officers to supervise the tasks. Deterrent work also commended itself to city authorities faced with rapid population growth, as in Liverpool, where the vestry adopted the workhouse test very early in order to discourage the influx of destitute Irish. In 1723 they discontinued outdoor relief in favour of parish work, a policy which rarely lapsed. The work—oakum picking, tailoring, weaving, building and other trades—sometimes made a profit over the cost of materials, but deterrence was its chief purpose.[45]

If by 1832 the purpose of many workhouses was to provide refuges for the helpless, few historians have claimed success for them. Workhouse conditions varied immensely, and the same workhouse might experience fluctuations from year to year, depending on the honesty of officials and the zeal of vestries and magistrates. No one has seriously questioned the Commissioners' revelations of the foul conditions in many workhouses: but there were also some well-regulated institutions which attempted to provide specialized treatment for their inmates. St Marylebone had pioneered dispensaries and hospitals for the sick poor, with professional medical attendants and nurses, while many town parishes had separate institutions for children (central London parishes were legally obliged to send them away from the city), and some rural parishes fostered children in labourers' homes. Yet these types of 'separate treatment' could easily be corrupted: children's homes or foster parents did not necessarily provide better care than the mixed workhouse.

A well-regulated workhouse offered the poor cleaner lodging and better food than they had in their own wretched dwellings, yet the poor in any district suffered the vagaries of fortune and the changing ideas of successive local authorities. The essential weakness of the old system was its fluctuation and lack of distinct purposes. No local historian has discovered a workhouse which was consistently run in the interests of its inmates, nor one which did not suffer at some time from the dishonesty of paid officials or the parish authorities. A well-regulated workhouse might be endangered at any time from a new and more parsimonious vestry, and in the economic distress which followed the French wars, parsimony was often uppermost in local administration. The Royal Commission hoped to prevent the workhouses from falling below a certain standard which should not offend the humanitarian principles of the time: in spite of many problems of enforcement, the new system did introduce a kind of safety-net for the workhouse pauper which had not existed under the Old Poor Law.

The great variety of workhouses under the Old Poor Law prevents a general judgement from being made on them. Comparatively speaking, they acted to prevent the worst extremes of social suffering. Filthy, unplanned and unsupervised the worst may have been, but they can hardly have been worse than the erratic system of charity in eighteenth-century France, where an even more impoverished rural economy forced thousands to beg and wander, and the authorities then punished them viciously for it in the galleys or the disease-ridden *dépôts de mendicité*.[46] The English paupers fared better, on the whole, than the *pauvres misérables*, but by 1832 the Commission could argue that many workhouses were an affront to decency. It is now necessary to observe the ways by which the newly created authority, the three Poor Law Commissioners at Somerset House, tried to create this new institution, which should simultaneously relieve the helpless, deter the idle, set children on the right path, encourage thrift and temperance, reduce crime, improve agriculture, raise wages, and heal the growing divisions in the social order.

2

The Coming of the Bastiles

The early years of the New Poor Law arouse that peculiar fascination which comes with watching an elaborately devised machine fail to start. The three Commissioners and their indefatiguable secretary, Edwin Chadwick, devised lengthy and complex regulations which were to embody the principles of the law: most were to remain empty theories. Some unions received the new system peaceably, some violently, but in both cases the practice fell short of the Commissioners' hopes. The law had been intended to impose order on the chaotic regionalism of poor relief; instead, the law was bent to conform with local conditions. The new workhouses were supposed to be governed on a uniform principle, but most unions insisted on retaining old habits, and some even refused to provide a suitable workhouse altogether. The Commissioners themselves were bedevilled by internal discord, for Chadwick, selfless and enthusiastic devotee of the New Poor Law, could not agree with two of the men who had been appointed over his head. In 1845 the Poor Law Commission was broken by the Andover scandal, and the Parliamentary committee which investigated Andover also exposed all the tensions in Somerset House.[1] Chadwick had already been edged out of all responsibility by his superiors, and the Assistant Commissioners were divided in their loyalties. The Commissioners were replaced by a Poor Law Board of pragmatic men rather than ardent theorists.

The years of the Poor Law Commissioners were years in which the workhouse myth was created, and in which the workhouses gained their reputation as places of oppression. John Walter, editor of *The Times*, led a vigorous propaganda warfare against them. An implacable opponent of bureaucracy, he printed stories accusing the Commissioners of jobbery and the guardians of gross inhumanity towards paupers, while other anonymous pamphlets accused the Commissioners of all manner of crimes. Although the House of Commons had accepted the

New Poor Law with little opposition, some members began to resent the Commissioners' threat to local independence. The poor themselves were ready victims of alarm and rumour. Many believed the current stories that the guardians would be able to refuse all relief, that the bread which was taking the place of money doles for the outdoor poor was poisoned, that the children of the poor would be forcibly taken away from them. Of the workhouses even more terrifying rumours circulated, of floggings, starvation, cruel separation of mothers and infants, and of dying men torn from their relations. Above all, it was feared that the dead did not have decent burial. One Inspector reported from Kent in 1839:

> A short time back, it was circulated in this county that the children in the workhouses were killed to make pies with, while the old when dead were employed to manure the guardians' fields, in order to save the expense of coffins.[2]

The historian, confronted with this mass of rumour and half-truth, separates fact and fiction with difficulty. The opponents of the law undoubtedly helped to spread malicious and unfounded tales about the workhouses. Some stories were fabricated, others wildly exaggerated a grain of truth. In any case, many rumours could not be traced to a particular source: most of the tales in the *Book of the Bastiles* gave no names, dates, or places. For the same reason, it was hard for the Commissioners to refute them. David Roberts has examined 21 of the lurid stories reported in *The Times*, and found that only five of them stood investigation by the Commissioners.[3] Roberts argues that the historian does not need to unravel all these matters, because even if the allegations were true, guardians who allowed offences were flouting the Commissioners' will, not obeying it. The Commissioners certainly did not countenance flogging or starvation, but on the other hand, they not only failed to detect many cases of cruelty, but ignored certain kinds of incident. Roberts also accepts too readily the Commissioners' inquiries, as published in the Parliamentary papers. *The Times* may have been too quick to condemn, but the Poor Law Commissioners also had a strong interest in disproving complaints. They sent their Assistants to hold an inquiry, but the word of officers and guardians would be believed rather than that of paupers—who were usually the only witnesses to workhouse abuses.

The Bath case (1839), in which the master was actually found guilty of a misdemeanour, is a good example. It arose in typical fashion after a quarrel between workhouse officers: the chaplain and a dismissed clerk accused the master of numerous offences, from irregularities with the accounts to interfering with female paupers. D.G. Adey, the Assistant Commissioner, investigated only two of the charges, because the guardians had dismissed the rest as hearsay. He found that the master had indeed locked up Rebecca Collet, a woman believed to be pregnant, in a damp 'black hole' overnight in November, without bedding. Rebecca Collet claimed to have miscarried afterwards, but could not prove she had been pregnant: but everyone had thought her pregnant at the time of the offence. Roberts mentions that the case was 'proved', but not that the Commissioners took no action. They decided merely to caution the master, firstly because Rebecca Collet was (in Adey's words) a 'low prostitute' who had been fighting with another pauper, and secondly because Robert Weale, another Assistant Commissioner, knew the master personally and spoke up for him. Instead, the Commissioners dismissed the chaplain at the guardians' request, for showing a 'rancorous and ungovernable temper', although there had been some truth in his allegations. An undoubted offence was thus played down because committed on a disreputable pauper.[4] The master resigned a few months later because the guardians tried to discontinue a payment of £26 per year which they allowed him for hiring a clerk; he had not hired a clerk, but done the extra work himself and pocketed the money. Financial irregularity upset both guardians and central authority more than did excessive severity.[5]

The short list of proven cases is damning enough: for instance, the master of Blean workhouse locked a little girl in the mortuary overnight as a punishment, and the master of Hoo indecently flogged women and children. Only a few unions created public scandals of this dimension, and in most cases the officers were forced to resign their posts after inquiry. Were these isolated incidents, a relic of more anarchic days, or did they reveal defects in the whole system?

Three main charges against the Poor Law stand out: the refusal of any relief to the destitute, resulting in death and misery; the voluntary sufferings of the honest poor who preferred their wretched independence to the degradation of the workhouse; and the horrors perpetrated on those who entered it. The first two may be dealt with briefly. Cases of the destitute being denied relief still occurred, like that of the young woman in labour who finally bore her child in a cab after having been turned away from several London workhouses and charity hospitals.[6] Vagrants and strangers were particularly liable to be refused relief, but their case was clearly one where the law was not being properly operated: guardians and officers who refused to aid destitute strangers were acting illegally. Irrespective of their place of settlement, all paupers in urgent distress had to be relieved at any workhouse to which they applied, and they must be aided until they could be returned to their place of origin. The 1834 Act had not stated this sufficiently, but in 1837 the Commissioners ruled that no tramp or 'causal' should be refused a night's lodging if he were without money. Since the Commissioners had power to dismiss any officers who offended against this provision, officers soon learned there was no point in denying relief: they left it to the guardians to decide the applicant's future in the long-term. Although guardians did sometimes illegally refuse relief during the nineteenth century, the question rapidly resolved itself into whether guardians were justified in offering the workhouse rather than outdoor relief to a particular applicant, since this was the main area of discretion. The honest poor, it was said, really did prefer to starve rather than enter the workhouse, and this charge long outlived the Poor Law Commissioners. It will be discussed in detail in Chapter 9.

The question at this point is how far the early workhouses met the expectations of their founders, and how justified was their reputation for cruelty. Like definitions of poverty, definitions of cruelty are of course relative, and will change from generation to generation. In the early Victorian period, as in most periods, different types of cruelty were simultaneously tolerated by some sections of the community and condemned by others. In 1834 executions were still carried out publicly, severe floggings were used as a matter of course to discipline men in the forces and boys in public schools; the movement to prevent young children from working in dangerous and unhealthy occupations had just begun. Amongst all classes of society, treatment of children ranged from the utmost severity to total refusal to inflict punishment. In the prisons, experiments were made in keeping the prisoners isolated and in total silence; a method which was praised as a means of regenerating the individual and execrated as unworthy of a civilized society. Drunkenness, wife-beating and tormenting of animals were common in sections of the working class, but by no means exclusive to them. In such an age it is difficult to place the 'cruelty' of the workhouse in perspective, especially as there were many sober people who argued that a temporary 'cruelty' is appropriate if it achieves some lasting good: such a man was Edwin Chadwick and so were many of the Assistant Commissioners. At this point the academic and the popular historian usually part company. Whereas in popular history the scandals still occupy the largest space, the academic historian has tended to assume that the workhouse was cruel by accident rather than intention.[7]

Both the popular and the academic versions can distort the history of the workhouse. The former lingers obsessively over the 1830s and 1840s, branding a whole century of administration with the problems of the first years, while the latter minimizes some of the evils. It is convenient to dismiss the starving paupers at Andover or the little girl in the Blean mortuary, because these were not really 'typical' of the workhouse system. A compromise is put forward by Ursula Henriques, who argues that the real cruelty of the workhouse lay in its psychological constraints (which were referred to at the time as 'discipline'), and that as this discipline was a conscious device of the Poor Law Commissioners, they may be charged with mental, if not physical cruelty.[8] It will be seen, however, that there were other features of the system, such as the officers' working conditions, which made physical cruelty inevitable from time to time, and which were the unintentional products of the administration devised by the Commissioners.

The historian must in fact contend with two kinds of myth: the gross and salacious stories fostered by the anti-Poor Law campaigners, and the myth which was deliberately encouraged by the Poor Law Commissioners themselves, in their attempt to make the workhouses seem repulsive. To understand this paradox, it is necessary to explain how the law worked, and how the workhouses came into being. Here there is at once a sharp contradiction between the claims of the Poor Law Commissioners in their annual reports, affirming their success in achieving administrative unity, and the patent diversity of practice in the unions. Annually the Commissioners explained their principles, described the new regulations, and claimed that these were being applied to the whole country without difficulty. The testimony of men like Sir John Tylden, chairman of the Milton Union in Kent, confirmed their statements: he wrote to them in 1836 that the labourers in his district, fearing the workhouse, were finding employment, and that 'their moral habits are decidedly improved'.[9] This praise was the more ironical in that Milton had seen some of the worst anti-Poor Law rioting in Kent, and Edward Carleton Tufnell, the Assistant Commissioner for that area, had in fact provided the Commissioners with a list of guardians, including Tylden, who could be relied on to provide favourable reports for publication.[10]

Responsibility for paupers was shared by three groups: the Commissioners, the guardians, and the salaried union officers. Their relationship was complex. The Commissioners had only limited powers over the guardians, for the law had not been designed to undermine local authority: the Royal Commission had hoped that the building of new workhouses would be compulsory, where needed, but the framers of the Act gave the Commissioners power only to restrain, not to command. The Commissioners could prevent rates being spent on guardians' feasts, or on outdoor relief to the able-bodied, but they could not compel guardians to spend. Guardians could be made to close an insanitary institution, but could not be forced to spend more than £50, or one-tenth of the average annual rate, on improving it. The ratepayers could demand that the guardians spend more on the workhouse, but no instance of this has yet come to light. Even such coercive powers as the Commissioners possessed had to be operated through the cumbersome process of a writ of mandamus, which they tried to avoid except in the most extreme cases.

Many of the Act's supporters had expected an immediate fall in poor rates, but they were not satisfied by what ensued. At first the financial position was satisfactory; the rates did fall for a short period, helped by a good harvest and relative trade prosperity, while the percentage of paupers in the population had been falling even before 1834. The fall continued until the mid-1840s, from an estimated 10.2 per cent in 1831 to 5.4 per cent in 1837, and although the proportion rose slightly in the 1840s, it never again reached the levels of the early 1830s.[11] The total cost of poor relief also fell, from nearly £7 million in 1833 to £4 million in 1837.[12] This seemed to justify the Commissioners' confidence, but the trend did not continue.

Although the Commissioners hoped to reduce expense by ending all outdoor relief to the able-bodied, they also threatened to commit the unions to heavy expenditure. Their chief priority, once a union had been declared, was to persuade the guardians to build a new workhouse, for few existing workhouses seemed suitable. The Commissioners insisted on salaried officers to run the workhouse, to administer outdoor relief and investigate applications. Guardians hoped to see the able-bodied poor vanish, but to achieve this they had to vote a large lump sum for a new building or for renovating an existing one. Admittedly, the money would come from loans and be paid for gradually out of the rates, but it was a much larger sum that many guardians had ever needed to raise before. They feared that the cost of the new building would force up poor rates, and had to be convinced that a short-term expense would produce a long-term advantage.

Since the Commissioners could not coerce, they had to cajole. In counties where the gentry eagerly awaited the New Poor Law, there was little difficulty. The chief persuaders were the Assistant Commissioners, whose role in these years was not only to carry out central orders, but to suggest improvements and negotiate with local interests. The inspectorate was a new feature of British administration. These were not the first, for they had been preceded by the factory inspectors, but unlike most other inspectorates, they had to construct as well as report. They had to decide which groups of parishes should be united, and what the property qualification of guardians should be. They had to convince local dignitaries that it was worth surrendering some traditional independence in order to destroy pauperism. They had a salary of £700 a year with expenses, and their posts inevitably went to men of gentlemanly background with influential friends. There were 15 Assistant Commissioners in 1835—most of them from the landed gentry, younger sons of substantial families.[13] They enjoyed higher pay and prestige than the other inspectors, and this reflected the delicate and onerous nature of their task. Not only their connections had secured them positions, for Chadwick was anxious to select men who were attached to the principles of the law, and several of them had already collected evidence for the Royal Commission.

The Assistant Commissioners went into the countryside as missionaries, with the advantage of being able to speak to the local gentry as equals. This was particularly important in deciding the shape and size of Poor Law unions, for many landowners wished to retain control by drawing the union boundaries around their own territory. If their tenants were elected to the boards of guardians, their own influence would not be destroyed, and they could also sit on the board as ex-officio guardians, the magistracy having been given this privilege in rural unions. The Assistant Commissioners dealt with the larger landowners where possible, for many of these favoured the new law, unlike the suspicious groups of farmers who expected to have their ricks burned by disgruntled paupers, or who rightly thought that building a new workhouse would be an expensive business. Hence in Northamptonshire the Assistant Commissioner divided the unions to suit the interests of local magnates;[14] in the south Tufnell negotiated with Lords Shaftesbury, Salisbury and Sydney to ease the adoption of the law; Edward Gulson in Nottinghamshire enlisted the aid of the Dukes of Rutland and Newcastle; and on Tyneside, Sir John Walsham was able to use his personal connections with the gentry.[15] Consequently, many unions fell into most inconvenient shapes and sizes which told heavily on travelling officials like the medical and relieving officers. The poor themselves might have to walk many miles to have their cases considered by the guardians in the workhouse board room. Tufnell complained that his predecessor had devised the Maidstone union 'like a comet with a tail of parishes ten miles long'.[16]

Once the union was declared, the Assistant Commissioners pressed the guardians to review its workhouse accommodation. Almost at once there was a departure from the advice of the Royal Commission, which, although it had advocated the deterrent workhouse, gave few precise details. The new central authority was to devise 'wholesome discipline', but the Commission had not intended that the poor should be housed under a single roof: guardians should keep more than one institution for the sake of both economy and efficiency. The report suggested at least four separated buildings, one for the aged, one for children, and the others for the male and female able-bodied paupers.[17] Because different types of supervision would be needed for each class, nothing would be saved by placing them in one building, indeed, it would be cheaper to use the existing parish poor houses rather than invest in expensive new ones. The early minutes of the Poor Law Commissioners show some confusion over this. They considered using any existing large parish workhouse for the able-bodied poor of the whole union, 'whilst the aged, infirm, and children, may be more satisfactorily provided for in buildings of a less expensive description, but better adapted for their accommodation'.[18] Failing such a workhouse, the Commissioners thought that the small parish workhouses could be used to 'constitute . . . the wards of one common workhouse'. This idea was only transitory, and the Commissioners were soon urging the guardians to build new, single workhouses in all unions which had no large building. The 'general mixed workhouse' had been adopted, and the first report of the Commissioners noted Sir Francis Bond Head's comment that in Kent and Sussex he was persuading the guardians to adopt the 'same low, cheap, homely building' as a model rural workhouse.[19]

Yet the creation of the general mixed workhouse is still a mystery. Why did the Commissioners abandon the idea of separate institutions in favour of a system which has since been universally decried? Once the principle of a single building was accepted, it proved difficult to adapt in later years when demand was growing for specialized treatment of different classes of pauper. The Webbs blamed Head, one of the most active and dashing of the Assistant Commissioners. He believed not only that a single workhouse would be more economical to run, but, significantly, that it would be a more impressive symbol of the New Poor Law:

> The very sight of a well built efficient establishment would give confidence to the board of guardians; the sight and weekly assemblage of all servants of their union would make them proud of their office; the appointment of a chaplain would give dignity to the whole arrangement, while the pauper would feel it was utterly impossible to contend against it.[20]

Head argued that the Assistant Commissioners could more conveniently inspect one central workhouse than several scattered ones; since the inspectorate was reduced to nine in 1842, this point is valid. Separate workhouses also made administrative difficulties; since families had to be admitted and discharged together to prevent the head of the family absconding, the workhouse officers would waste time in collecting the family from different institutions.[21]

Nevertheless, it was not Head's influence alone which produced the general mixed workhouse. Professor Finer absolves Chadwick from all blame, for 'He had conceived of the workhouse system as a set of specialized schools, hospitals, asylums, almshouses, not as the promiscuous barracks that his superiors approved.'[22] The continuous quarrel between Chadwick and his superiors may have forced him to yield to their pusillanimous and economical views. Yet there is no evidence that Chadwick fought against the general mixed workhouses, and the comments which he made against the system date from some 30 years later, and from second-hand reports of what he said.[23] In the first year of the Poor Law Commission, Chadwick's influence was still strong amongst the Assistant Commissioners, and two of his staunchest supporters, Tufnell and Kay-Shuttleworth, strongly advocated the single workhouse. The only proviso the three men made was that children ought to be put in a district school, but even here they emphasized that a single building would be more economical and efficient. In any case, there was a logical fallacy in having separate buildings, because able-bodied pauperism would soon disappear. The single building under one administration would be more flexible if the numbers of paupers in different groups should fluctuate. Chadwick's private papers suggest that he accepted the general mixed workhouse as a transitional stage in the Poor Law, and by 1838 he was hoping to supersede it by county institutions for the aged, the sick and other special cases, on the same plan as the district schools for children.[24] But by this time he was losing his power.

Chadwick and the Assistant Commissioners must have appreciated the administrative difficulties of separate workhouses, given the economical management which they all favoured. Otherwise it is hard to explain the Commissioners' pressure on those unions which did attempt to follow the recommendations of the Royal Commission, as evidence from Kent and Sussex shows. Nine unions retained two or more of the parish workhouses and segregated the paupers, but Head and Tufnell pressed them to conform, arguing that poor rates were lower and the cost of administration less in unions which had adopted the single workhouse.[25] Tufnell also believed that labourers were less likely to riot against the Poor Law if they knew that families would be under the same roof, even if in separate wards: in Horsham riots had broken out (he claimed) when the poor discovered that pauper families were to be split up and sent to different parishes.[26]

Chadwick was more concerned with forcing recalcitrant northern guardians to end outdoor relief to the able-bodied: this, not, the question of the single workhouse, was the main issue between himself and the Poor Law Commissioners. Outdoor relief could not be stopped until an efficient workhouse had been provided, and since many northern districts did not have suitable buildings, the erection of a new workhouse was a desirable sign that a rebellious board had capitulated to Somerset House. This was to be welcomed even if it fell short of the ideal. George Nicholls may also have influenced the system, for in his previous career as an overseer he had successfully instituted a central workhouse test in a group of parishes which became part of the Southwell union. Some Assistant Commissioners had not favoured the general mixed workhouse, but were soon overborne. Charles Mott, who had advocated the practicality and cheapness of separate workhouses in 1834, was in 1839 unsuccessfully urging the single workhouse on northern unions. William Day, a country squire who had managed eight workhouses in the Uckfield union, objected to the single building when he became an Assistant Commissioner, but was overruled by Tufnell, and the Uckfield guardians built a new single workhouse. Day himself had the thankless task of trying to impose the system on riotous Welsh parishes, and was later dismissed from his post as a scapegoat for the 'Rebecca' riots.[27] Other Assistant Commissioners found existing workhouses in poor repair, and argued that a multiplicity of institutions would make their own work of inspection more difficult.[28]

At the heart of the question are Head's previously quoted comments on the importance of the 'sight of a well built efficient establishment'.

It was plain that one building would be a more potent symbol of the new law than a series of familiar parish poorhouses. The essence of the single workhouse was its novelty, its mystery, and its formidable appearance. Head himself had not actually planned large workhouses: he sketched a plan for a rural workhouse which was square, with dormitories only 15 feet by ten, because, as he argued 'well built, substantial rooms being a luxury, as attractive to the pauper as food and raiment'.[29]

Head's plan was not adopted, but the more substantial workhouse proposed by the architect Samuel Kempthorne was favoured in many rural unions. This had some obligation to the panopticon principle, with a central observation tower, although the design was cruciform. A rectangular boundary wall enclosed the cross, to give four separated courtyards for the different classes of pauper. The observation tower was not always built, but the master's quarters were usually placed at the centre to give rapid communication with all the wards.[30] The workhouse was surrounded by high walls, and in many early buildings the windows were barred and so high over the dormitory floors that the inmates were unable to look out. The Commissioners hoped that the building would be enclosed 'to prevent casual communication from without, and egress from within'.[31] This new construction, which in many rural unions would be the largest public building, was bound to have a powerful effect on the local population. Thus the Commissioners accepted that the large *single* building was itself an essential part of deterrence.[32]

This argument must also refer to the famous notion of 'less eligibility' which pervaded the New Poor Law. This phrase is sometimes misinterpreted as meaning that the inmates were to be worse treated than the poorest independent labourer, and that workhouse conditions must necessarily be harsh. The Royal Commission is then criticized for not realizing that the condition of the poor was so appalling that it would be impossible for a responsible society to countenance anything worse. Finer, for example, argues that less eligibility was an 'abstraction', based on inadequate knowledge of rural wages, but also that Chadwick interpreted it in a psychological, not physical, sense.[33] In fact the Royal Commission was well aware of the problem, and plainly stated that 'less eligibility' was to rest on discipline rather than material conditions, as the following passage shows:

All labour is irksome to those who are unaccustomed to labour;

and what is generally meant by the expression 'rendering the pauper's situation irksome', is rendering it laborious. But it is not by means of labour alone that the principle is applicable, nor does it imply that the food or comforts of the pauper should approach the lowest point at which existence may be maintained. Although the workhouse food be more ample in quantity and better in quality than that of which the labourer's family partakes, and the house in other respects superior to the cottage, yet the strict discipline of well-regulated workhouses, and in particular the restrictions to which the inmates are subject in respect to the use of acknowledged luxuries, such as fermented liquors and tobacco, are intolerable to the indolent and disorderly, while to the aged, the feeble, and other proper objects of relief, the regularity and discipline render the workhouse a place of comparative comfort.[34]

In 1834 the Poor Law Commissioners reaffirmed this, almost to the letter.[35]

The early administrators did not contemplate workhouses which were badly built, insanitary, overcrowded, dark or unwholesome, as were the dwellings of the poor. Nor did they wish the paupers to be as scantily fed, clothed, and warmed, as the poorest labourers. Given that the Commissioners' standards were, in contemporary terms, relatively high, they then faced the problem of making the workhouses repellent to the poor. Hence arose the obsession with workhouse discipline, the enforcing of a monotonous routine, which occupied the administration throughout the life of the New Poor Law. The old parish poorhouses were too close to the community, and would not serve to enforce this discipline. Day argued that the single workhouse would be too prominent and that the poor would be tempted to attack it, seeing in the destruction of one building the destruction of the system; but other Inspectors rightly judged that the poor were too weak to resist. In this context the often-quoted words of Kay-Shuttleworth, that the appearance of workhouses ought to be 'as prison-like as possible' must be understood, and also Tufnell's comment that 'at present, their prison-like appearance, and the notion that they are intended to torment the poor, inspires a salutary dread of them'.[36]

At this stage the enduring priorities of the workhouse system emerged. Separation was to be enforced between the different ages and sexes. A school must be provided for the children. The able-bodied must be set to work and given plain, frugal, but sufficient food. Tobacco and spirits must be banned. The sick should have separate wards, and cleanliness, order and ventilation were to be enforced, not merely because of hygiene (though this was important to the Commissioners), but because they were essential to discipline. When a pauper entered the workhouse he was to be bathed, and his clothes and property taken from him, and not to be returned until he left. He was to be put into workhouse uniform, and not to leave the workhouse without permission. Clearly there were many similarities with the prison system, except that the pauper could discharge himself at will. But Goffman has noted that many types of 'total institution' observe such rituals when a new inmate is admitted, in order to diminish his individuality.[37]

The Commissioners devised a sevenfold classification:

Aged and infirm men
Able-bodied men and youths over 13 (increased to 15 in 1842)
Boys aged from seven to 13
Aged or infirm men
Able-bodied women and girls over 13 (increased to 16 from 1842)
Girls from seven to 13
Children under seven

The Webbs, whose lifelong interest it was to separate the poor into numerous classes to be dealt with by different authorities, were perhaps unduly severe on this system: for it had no separation on moral grounds, no regulations for infants, and although it was assumed that the sick would have a ward to themselves, no segregation for the insane or infectious was enjoined, nor that special consideration be given to pregnant women.[38]

Nothing caused more public hostility than the separation of married couples in the workhouse, though the regulations did allow guardians to provide married quarters for elderly couples, the Commissioners noting that it would no doubt be uneconomical. This separation was seen as fundamental to discipline, but the Commissioners were suspected of having a sinister Malthusian desire to prevent the poor from breeding. Rather, the Commissioners assumed that since the pauper had renounced the obligation to support his family, he should be separated from them; but deprivation of normal sexual relations was of course a prime deterrent as well. These arguments applied less to aged couples, but again logical problems arose: outdoor relief was not forbidden to the aged, and so the workhouse was supposed to be offered to those old people whose destitution was the result of improvidence:

Even with the aged and infirm (the Commissioners argued) the extent to which any assurance of support is held out, to that extent precisely are the incentives to provident and industrious habits in early life destroyed.[39]

To separate such old couples, they thought, was no injustice, and the residuum of irreproachable or very infirm old people might be allowed the married quarters. In any case, the Commissioners claimed that 'efficient' guardians had practised such separation long before 1834.[40]

The problem did not seem large, for on 1 January 1851, married couples of all ages made up only 5 per cent of the workhouse population.[41] Perhaps guardians were succeeding in deterring them, but, more probably, they were giving outdoor relief to married couples on various pretexts.[42] On that day there were ten times as many wives of able-bodied men being relieved with their husbands outside the workhouse as within it, and the figures do not show the marital status of couples where the husband was not able-bodied. As the ratio of indoor to outdoor paupers was approximately 1:7 at that time, it seems that a married couple had a higher chance of being relieved outside the workhouse than other types of pauper. If one partner were able to look after the other, it was easier and cheaper to give outdoor relief than to take them both into the workhouse.[43] Nevertheless, so strong was popular feeling that regulations for aged couples were relaxed in 1847, and couples over 60 were not to be refused a room together if they requested it. Guardians did not always inform them of this right. On 1st January 1853, 299 of these couples had shared accommodation, and 578 had been separated (16 of them for health reasons or at their own request).[44] By 1863, 180 unions still made no special provision for them.[45]

It was even more harsh to separate mothers and children, especially as many inmates were widows or unmarried mothers. On 1 January 1852, children with one parent in the workhouse made up 19 per cent of the workhouse population.[46] The regulations allowed mothers to sleep with children under seven, and to have reasonable access to them, but some guardians separated mothers and young babies so that the mothers could be put to work. St Marylebone even enforced premature weaning, to the great danger of the babies.[47] Yet the system caught the guardians in a dilemma: if they allowed children into the women's wards, critics accused them of 'contaminating' the young by association with adult paupers. If they separated mothers and children they were accused of cruelty.

The Commissioners devised elaborate rules for the punishment of paupers who committed workhouse offences, including being noisy or dirty, refusing to work, swearing, malingering, attempting to enter the quarters of another class of pauper, and disobedience. Punishments ranged from making the pauper wear special clothes to reducing his diet for 48 hours, but serious offenders had to be sent before a magistrate. The aim of the regulations was twofold—to discipline the pauper and to control the workhouse officers, who must not reduce diets below a stated amount, flog adults, or confine paupers in punishment rooms for excessive periods. Girls could not be beaten, and boys under 14 only if a certain time had elapsed after their offence. The medical officer had to consent to the punishment of the old or the pregnant. In view of the long history of workhouse abuses under the Old Poor Law, these regulations controlled officers as much as paupers.

Other petty regulations resembled the prison system: silent meal-times, and control over visitors and mail. All these commandments fostered the workhouse myth, although they were far removed from daily life in most workhouses. Paupers were supposed to be clean, orderly, hard-working, silent, obedient and amenable to religious influences. Officers were to have all these virtues and to be honest, efficient, and to keep accurate accounts. The ideal was unworkable without powers of enforcement which did not exist, for the workhouse lacked the ultimate authority of the prison: paupers could not be detained in it against their will. Only friendless children and the certified insane could not leave, nor was there anything to prevent the ordinary inmates discharging themselves for a few hours only. As soon as these rules were presented to the localities, trouble broke out.

The story of the reception of the New Poor Law is an oft-told tale, and will not be repeated here in detail.[48] The Commissioners expected trouble in the heavily pauperized unions which had given generous outdoor relief, and warned the Assistant Commissioners that 'to introduce the workhouse system in all its rigid simplicity, suddenly and at once, would be most unjust and highly impolitic, even if it were safe or practicable.'[49] Instead, a labour test would be an interim measure, allowing able-bodied paupers to do hard labour in return for a subsistence allowance for their families. But the Commissioners miscalculated: it was not the heavily pauperized agricultural unions in the south and East Anglia which could resist the workhouse test, but the less pauperized industrial unions, where outdoor relief was given to the unemployed in times of trade depression. Here the violent but short-lived anti-Poor Law campaign began.

Resistance to the Poor Law took three main forms: riots amongst agricultural labourers; refusal of guardians in some areas to implement the Act; and, most effectively, steady resistance of guardians all over the country to implement the details of the Law, even if they accepted it in principle. The first two types of resistance did not last long: by 1846 the most recalcitrant unions, Rochdale, Oldham and Ashton, had been forced into outward conformity, though Todmorden was still refusing to build a workhouse. Popular resistance in the south and in East Anglia had been put down without difficulty. In a few places the Commissioners' powers were more limited—the Gilbert Act unions and parishes where a local Act was in force. The Commissioners could not alter the boundaries of these local administrations without their consent, and part of the responsibility for the poor still remained with the authority appointed under the local Act. Hence some important towns such as Bristol, Liverpool and Manchester, together with much of London, retained their old governors, but they had to conform to the regulations of the central authority. Yet in a longer perspective of the Poor Law, violent resistance had less effect than the stubborn maintenance of local customs even in the most conformist unions.

After a brief outbreak of rioting, Kent and the southern counties were apparently quiet, but even these welcoming guardians did not necessarily uphold the law. East Kent seemed the most docile area, for Head had persuaded all the guardians to send representatives to a conference which fixed scales for outdoor relief and a uniform diet for the workhouses. Head resigned from his post in a satisfied mood, sending to the guardians the last of many circulars in his habitual military tone:

> You are now sufficiently armed to protect the Poor Rates of your Country, to repel every species of attack upon them, to detect every case of imposition to crush every attempt of intimidation and force [into employment] as soon as you shall deem it necessary all those who would indolently hang on their Parishes for support.[50]

This optimism proved inflated. More than any other part of the country, Kent managed to reduce outdoor relief to the able-bodied, but even in Kent some unions gave outdoor relief to fathers of large families rather than take the whole family into the workhouse; and they gave outdoor relief in severe winters.[51] The Commissioners often referred to Kent as a model county, but although the guardians did not directly oppose the Commissioners, the regulations were constantly undermined. Guardians refused to build new workhouses, or, if they did build, tried to spend too much or too little on it. They tried to dismiss efficient officers, or they wanted to retain officers whom the Commissioners had detected in misdemeanours. They did not segregate workhouse wards, or they segregated them so rigidly that families suffered excessively. They were too mean, or too generous, with the workhouse diet. They paid their officers pitiful salaries, or they appointed their own relatives to official posts. Boards fell into the hands of political cliques, or were composed of farmers who refused to attend regularly. They were too kind, or too severe, to the paupers: they wanted to give luxuries such as tea and beer to the aged, and to impose harsh penalties on unmarried mothers. The Commissioners tried to set a common standard, but were never unquestioningly obeyed. All this may be discussed later in a more detailed account of workhouse life, but it should indicate that not even the 'model' unions conformed in all respects.

The Assistant Commissioners also found that apparently docile unions rejected the 'frills' which central authority considered essential to the success of the law. This included plans for separate schools. Only in a few large unions were district schools built, although guardians could amalgamate for the purpose. Tufnell tried ineffectually to persuade unions in rural Sussex to combine:

> The objections to it were various. One guardian said that if the junction took place the contracts for provisions, clothing &c would probably be taken by some one out of the union to the manifest loss of the union tradesmen; another said the management would all fall into the hands of the *ex officio* guardians; a third said that I wanted to give the children a classical education; a charge of which I profess my entire innocence; a fourth said to teach writing to the children, especially to the female children, was of no use.[52]

The remote Cornish hamlets also successfully resisted the workhouse. In five unions the guardians, frightened by popular disturbances, refused to provide adequate workhouses: the Commissioners did not press them as few paupers were involved.[53] Until the 1920s some of the Cornish workhouses resembled the poorhouses of the Old Poor Law, with little segregation and few paid officers. Wales also offered resistance, both open and covert. Merthyr Tydfil refused to operate the workhouse test before 1853, and continued illegally to pay the rents of outdoor paupers.[54] The Welsh gentry had little interest in the Poor Law, and left its administration to the small farmers in the rural unions. The guardians' own standard of living was low, and they resented 'luxurious' workhouses: they also circumvented the unfortunate Assistant Commissioner, William Day, by speaking Welsh at their board meetings in his presence. In 1842–3 the Rebecca riots in South Wales were ostensibly directed against turnpikes, but the rioters sacked Carmarthen workhouse as well. The Commissioners could not exert much influence, and the Welsh workhouses remained mainly small almshouses, not intended for the able-bodied. Cardiff received the new law with more enthusiasm, for it had many immigrant paupers, but otherwise Welsh guardians avoided the workhouse test, believing that their parsimonious outdoor relief was the best way to keep rates down.

Many local histories reveal similar refusals of guardians to obey instructions. Shropshire boards persistently opposed the Commissioners, and local rather than central issues determined the treatment of the poor.[55] Nottinghamshire, once lauded for its workhouse management, rapidly degenerated. Inevitably, the model workhouse of yesterday tended to become the overcrowded den of the present. The Southwell workhouse, once the scene of George Nicholls' experiments, deteriorated because the guardians would not spend on it: in the 1840s it was overcrowded, insanitary, and poorly furnished.[56] In Nottingham a new workhouse was sorely needed, for the old one was grossly inadequate by 1838, but the guardians, reft by political faction, refused to build a new one. When Nassau Senior visited it, he commented that it was one of the worst he had ever seen, with sometimes seven or eight children sleeping in one bed.[57] In Coventry the guardians spent £1,000 on heating and repairs and implemented a strict regime, but only after epidemic disease in 1838 had killed 63 of the 228 inmates.[58]

Events in the north of England were particularly interesting, not only because of several violent and bizarre incidents, but because the Poor Law intersected wider political issues. The men who led the anti-Poor Law campaign were already known in the factory reform movement. Richard Oastler, Parson Bull, Joseph Rayner Stephens and John Fielden occupy a larger place in the history of the nineteenth century than their part in the anti-Poor Law campaign. Their political methods—public meetings, vigorous propaganda and violent speeches—were adopted by the Chartist movement, which many of their followers were to join. Yet in the 1830s the middle-class leaders and the northern working class were able to combine against the Poor

Law: both frugality and humanitarianism were affronted by it. In parts of Lancashire and the West Riding the ratepayers deliberately elected guardians who would refuse to implement the law because it was irrelevant to industrial conditions. In times of slump it was impossible to take all unemployed families into the workhouse, while to wait until the unemployed became destitute, as the law demanded, would make it harder for them to recover when trade picked up. The guardians refused to build new workhouses, and Dr Boyson has described the circular argument of the Clitheroe guardians:

> When there was distress and pressure of numbers upon the workhouse accommodation, the guardians rejected the building of a new workhouse because of heavy rates, and when times were good and there were few workhouse inmates the guardians rejected a new workhouse as unnecessary.[59]

In Cumberland and Westmoreland the law affronted Tory paternalism in some unions, but R.N. Thompson argues that the opposition was based less on principle than on practical objections to changes in the existing system. Since these unions ran their Poor Law administration economically, they resented having to pay for 'southern' mismanagement. Each parish could develop its own specific objections, from refusal to amalgamate with a neighbouring parish, to the self-interest of those who were handling the workhouse contracts. Only three of the 12 new unions in these counties agreed to build new workhouses, for the old ones were believed to be sufficient.[60]

In the North East the law met with little resistance, for in many parishes the vestries already operated strict policies on outdoor relief, and the new guardians welcomed the law as a means of encouraging labourers in independence and thrift. In any case, the economy of the North East was not as unhealthy in 1830s as that of Lancashire or the West Riding, where the handloom weavers were suffering their long decline. On Tyneside and in County Durham guardians and Commissioners appeared to be in harmony, aided by the good personal relationships which Sir John Walsham had in those parts. But even here areas of disagreement emerged, though not violently. On Tyneside the guardians ran the workhouses perhaps more leniently than the Commissioners approved, though the diet in the North East was admitted to be of a superior standard, justifying greater workhouse liberality. Since there were few able-bodied people in the workhouses, the Tyneside guardians refused to admit that the workhouse conferred a social stigma.[61] In County Durham the early harmony began to crack in the 1840s with economic recession: here the guardians began to run the workhouse even *more* harshly and frugally than the Commissioners desired.[62] Nor would the Durham unions agree to spend more than small sums on workhouse renovation.

On the whole the northern guardians did not think of the workhouses as a deterrent: they believed them to be almshouses for the aged and helpless. Where guardians did try to implement the law, they were menaced by public demonstrations in Lancashire and Yorkshire, and at Bradford had to be protected by troops when rioting broke out. Fielden led a rate revolt in Todmorden, and in Huddersfield Oastler and his supporters successfully defied the Commissioners for over a year. The public outcry in these parts caused the Commissioners to act more cautiously than Chadwick approved, for Chadwick blamed the unrest on the benighted self-interest of guardians who wished to keep their local powers of patronage, and on publicans and tradesmen who thrived by supplying provisions to outdoor paupers. He was not entirely mistaken, for several northern towns, including Leeds, were run by political cliques who used the guardians' powers to further their own interests;[63] but Chadwick was blind to the underlying social problems which made the workhouse test irrelevant. In spite of a visit which he paid secretly to the north in 1841, he remained convinced that the workhouse test ought to be applied. The more realistic Commissioners, however, refused to coerce the northern guardians. Severe depression in the manufacturing towns in the early 1840s made the workhouse an even less plausible solution to economic problems. Not until 1852 were the northern unions directed to apply a labour test if the able-bodied sought relief, and even then outdoor relief was not entirley prohibited as it was in the south.

These troubles had serious consequences for the workhouse system in the north. The Commissioners may have affronted many people's standards of humanity in trying to end outdoor relief, but in workhouse management they were often more humane than the northern guardians. Some union workhouses in Lancashire and Yorkshire were sordid dens, and the guardians were both sentimental and parsimonious. The aged had a better diet, more liberty and less supervision than if strict principles had applied, but where considerations of larger expense arose, the inmates fared worse than in southern unions. Some of the buildings were old, decaying, filthy, badly ventilated and with poor sanitation: in times of slump they rapidly became overcrowded. The guardians took little interest in medical care, nursing, or education, and left much to the masters' discretion.

Poor conditions in these workhouses reflected the Commissioners' weakness, for it has been estimated that in about half the workhouses of the textile districts, strict classification was not possible.[64] Inmates did not necessarily object; but laxity could bring disease.

After the Commissioners refused to countenance the appalling parish workhouses in Todmorden, the guardians closed them but refused to build any workhouse at all. Paupers who could not be given outdoor relief were boarded in neighbouring unions, at a distance from their friends. Bolton workhouse was notorious:

> There is no classification; males and females occupy the same airing grounds and even the same privies. There is no bathroom for cleansing, no probationary ward for receiving the paupers on their admission, which renders it impossible to prevent the spread of any contagious disorders. There is no adequate accommodation for the sick poor; and in short the workhouse in its present state cannot be conducted with proper discipline and economy.[65]

The Assistant Commissioner who wrote these words possibly exaggerated in order to show the rebellious guardians in the worst light, but given the guardians' reluctance to spend on improvements, the description is probably fair. Not until 1854 did the Bolton guardians agree to build a new workhouse. They did not object to children sharing beds with adults, nor to several children sharing the same bed, for they argued that these were common habits amongst the poor; but the Commissioners expected workhouses to be better than lodgings in the slums.

From the more prosperous 1850s the northern unions capitulated and began to build new workhouses, though they did not end outdoor relief to the able-bodied. By the 1870s the northern workhouses were often vast, impressive institutions, fit to stand beside the new town halls and the heavy architecture of the wealthy industrial towns. Then the central authority tried to restrain expenditure on these expressions of civic pride; but in the 1840s it was the Commissioners who urged expense, and the guardians who rejected it. This was to become a recurrent feature of Poor Law administration: in times of hardship the workhouse was the first to suffer economies. Cutting outdoor relief was impolitic, not only because allowances were already low, but because in times of depression the poor could become dangerous. Workhouses could be neglected with impunity, renovations skimped, staff numbers and salaries kept down. Such circumstances always threatened the indoor poor, for where guardians were overfrugal, neglect and cruelty could occur.

Yet the guardians represented the ratepayers who elected them. Poor householders as well as rich ones paid poor rates, and the poor themselves often opposed workhouse expenditure.[66] Although each parish paid to maintain its own poor until 1865, the 'establishment' costs of the union fell on all the parishes: they had to pay for the workhouse building and the salaries of its staff. Each parish paid according to its average pauperism in the preceding years, a system designed to magnify discontent. Parishes with few paupers resented paying anything towards a workhouse they hardly used, while poor parishes resented having to carry a heavier burden than their rich neighbours. Hence the phenomenon which arose in many of the 'comet-like' unions consisting of one or two towns and a tail of rural parishes. Rural guardians attended board meetings infrequently, but came in force whenever an important financial decision was to be made, usually to block expenditure. The Commissioners themselves were partly to blame for this: in the early years when towns were less amenable to the new law, they had deliberately swamped the urban vote by attaching rural parishes whose representation was disproportionate to their population.[67]

Nevertheless, by 1840 the Commissioners had promoted much new building. 271 unions had plans for new workhouses, 85 more had hired or converted old ones, 34 had bought suitable buildings, and 24 had substantially converted old buildings. This was a great expense by the standards of the time:[68]

16 unions were spending up to	£2,000
63 between	£2,000 and £4,000
84	£4,000 and £6,000
69	£6,000 and £8,000
29	£8,000 and £10,000

Six other unions were spending even more: Lambeth had committed £23,905 for buying land and altering the old workhouse, but even small unions like Bath and Newton Abbot were spending around £12,000. Between 1840 and 1857, another 83 unions spend nearly a million pounds between them on new workhouses, an average cost of £11,602 per workhouse. In fact 54 of these unions were spending less than £1,000, but a few city workhouses were spending large sums, including £59,215 for the City of London and £120,121 for Liverpool, then the largest provincial workhouse in the country.[69]

All this took place even before the northern unions had begun to build new workhouses. Some of the money came from Treasury loans, but mostly the unions borrowed from insurance companies on the security of the poor rates. Workhouses did not have an edifying reputation, but insurance companies knew that this type of public investment was a safe home for their funds. Some unions sold former parish property to raise money, but the workhouses still represented a large public investment. The figures above are an underestimate, as they show only tenders approved by the central authority: once guardians started building, they usually found they had to spend more than they had intended. The unions built for present rather than future needs, and many workhouses were overtaken by events. Not only was the population still expanding rapidly, but certain towns experienced a disproportionately large share of that expansion. There was no way of foretelling that in a few decades some of the rural workhouses would be half empty, while London would be continually struggling to house its helpless poor in overcrowded institutions. The Commissioners believed that pauperism would decline, and this logically excluded provision for large buildings; but rapid developments in sanitary and medical knowledge meant that modest institutions built in the early days of the New Poor Law would soon seem inconvenient and unhealthy.

After the first few years the central authority stopped trying to impose a rigidly uniform system of poor relief. They still aimed at uniform standards, but hoped to achieve them through lengthy private correspondence with each union. The new law had met with diverse response in the localities, and diversity remained its dominating feature. Nevertheless, the myth of a monolithic Poor Law structure had been created, and was still fostered by the central authority. Against this complex background the cruelty of the New Poor Law must be judged. If the Commissioners' regulations were obeyed, the pauper would live in semi-penal conditions, separated from his family; but his children would be educated, his diet sufficient, and his body reasonably warm and comfortable. The workhouse would be cleaner and less overcrowded than his own home. In attempting to diminish the workhouse's attraction, the Commissioners laid down rules which were intolerably mean-spirited. Tufnell, who devoted his life to the education of pauper children, who ignored the argument than paupers ought not to be educated when the independent poor were not, and who with Kay-Shuttleworth began one of the first experiments in teacher-training, was yet able to write complacently:

At Seven Oaks . . . a farmer entered the workhouse, found fault with the dietary, and gave ten pots of beer to the inmates. Upon discovering this, I instantly issued a summons requiring his presence at the next bench of magistrates, who fined him £6.[70]

This attitude sums up the New Poor Law. In major questions the Commissioners were more progressive than many guardians, but they believed that comfort must be tempered with 'discipline', to be achieved only by a niggling attention to detail. On the other hand, a pauper in one of the northern workhouses where the Commissioners' writ did not run, was likely to have more of the comforts dear to the poor—some liberty of movement, a more varied diet, tea (and sometimes beer), and easier access to his family and the opposite sex. If, however, he were sick, infirm or insane, he was less likely to have the care which the Commissioners thought necessary, and might have his health and life endangered in an insanitary institution. By present-day standards, the chief cruelty lies in the attempt to incarcerate people who needed an institution for no other reason than poverty. For those who could not manage outside an institution—the infirm, the deserted children, the sick and the insane—the Commissioners tried to provide some basic protection which had not existed before. If they failed, it was because of their lack of power rather than their overbearing authority. Yet, as will be seen, they created problems by their own use of the workhouse myth, and their regulations gave to officers of workhouses a temptation to tyranny, petty and otherwise, which was not always resisted.

3

From Workhouse to Institution

The Poor Law Commissioners had created the public image of the
deterrent workhouse, and their successors, the Poor Law Board, also
fostered it. In 1871 the Local Government Board assumed responsibility for the Poor Law: at first the traditional policy of deterrence was
paramount, but the Board soon found that it needed to soften, if not to
obliterate, the workhouse's grim reputation. The Royal Commission
of 1832 had been so concerned with deterrence that they had barely
considered the workhouse's other function as a receptacle for the
helpless poor. The Local Government Board had to give far more
attention to the care of the sick and helpless. A series of institutions for
different classes of the poor was beginning to supplement the general
mixed workhouse, which itself began to be termed 'a place of safety'
for certain paupers. A second Royal Commission on the Poor Laws,
summoned in 1905, was far more aware of the conflicting purposes of
the workhouse system. They agreed that the mixed workhouse could
not deal effectively with different social problems, and recommended
specialized institutions, run by trained staff, in which each class could
be appropriately treated. Deterrent institutions should be offered only
to the 'residuum' of incorrigibles such as drunkards, idlers and tramps,
who ought not to be able to leave voluntarily.

Between the two Commissions had occurred a shift in attitude,
not only towards poverty and pauperism, but towards the role of
residential institutions in society. The Commissioners of 1832 had not
been simply moralistic in their explanations of pauperism, but believed
that administrative errors in the Old Poor Law demoralized hard-
working labourers while encouraging the idle. Pauperism was thus a
mixture of environmental and personal factors, but the Commissioners
shared the boundless Benthamite optimism that malleable human
material could be transformed by administrative changes. The
deterrent institutions would cause a moral reformation amongst the

54

poor, and when all the mechanisms of thrift had been encouraged, even the aged and helpless would have no need of the workhouse, because they had insured against it. The institution, like the Marxist state, would presumably wither away.

Senior's Commission wished to return the labourer to sturdy independence, but could not state with confidence that poverty, as opposed to pauperism, was curable. By 1905, however, it was possible to believe that not merely pauperism, but poverty itself, could be eradicated. There was, of course, no consensus on this. The economic optimism of the high Victorian age was now modified by anxiety about the slackening growth rate. The easy Benthamite confidence in the plasticity of human nature had been qualified by Darwin and by Galton. To those who believed in eugenics, it seemed that social evils, far from being curable by administrative reform, were genetically influenced, and that the criminal, the lunatic, the 'incorrigible' pauper, would pass their tainted blood from generation to generation unless strong action were taken against them. Yet to those who lived in the late nineteenth century, the growing wealth of Britain was obvious, expressing itself not only in social organization but in many articles of everyday life. For those who took the trouble to observe, it was plain that this affluence had its boundaries: about one third of the population still lived on, or below, the level of subsistence. In spite of this, the man who had carefully tabulated the nation's poverty spoke optimistically, and Rowntree's words are not unrepresentative of his generation:

> The dark shadow of the Malthusian philosophy has passed away, and no view of the ultimate scheme of things would now be accepted under which multitudes of men and women are doomed by inevitable law to a struggle for existence so severe as necessarily to cripple or destroy the higher parts of their nature.[1]

The Royal Commission of 1905 would not have disputed these words. The disagreements between the two factions of the Commission, the Majority with its leanings towards the Charity Organization Society, and the Minority influenced by the Webbs, are well documented, and have obscured the considerable areas of agreement. If poverty were a diminishing problem, then administrative solutions seemed even more feasible than in 1832. The Commission was divided mainly on the nature of the administrative solution, with the Majority favouring a reformation of the existing system, to incorporate voluntary charities as well as public assistance, while the Minority desired more redical change and more government interference. The Commission did not, however, dispense with the need for deterrence. In a world where poverty was diminishing, pauperism could seem even more blameable, and so both reports criticized the self-inflicted pauperism of the drunkard and the idler. The Minority wished to 'break up' the Poor Law and to replace it by a series of authorities which should deal with each type of social problem separately. The Majority also believed in segregation, but considered the Poor Law capable of providing it, with help from voluntary organizations.

The Commission of 1832 had made the workhouse the central solution to the problem of pauperism: the Commission of 1905 replaced it by preventive measures of another kind. The Majority hoped to encourage thrift and voluntary insurance; the Minority to provide a range of means-tested social services and to combat unemployment at its source. Residential institutions, however, retained an important place in both schemes, and the Commission did not disagree over them. Institutions were now seen as the only desirable places for the treatment of certain social and medical conditions—the distinction between the two was not always clearly made. For the chronic sick there would be long-stay hospitals; for the mentally deficient, asylums; for children, special homes; for the vagrant or the 'residuum' of incorrigible unemployed, labour colonies. Institutions, rather than the homes of the poor, should offer 'continuous care and treatment' to people who needed them; in some cases even without the consent of the paupers. Formerly, institutions had the rather negative function of deterrence; but by the 1890s social reformers were investing them with a more positive purpose. Under the original scheme of the Poor Law, a man could refuse to enter the workhouse if he could survive outside it—indeed, the whole aim was to encourage him to do so. The Majority Report thought tentatively of forcible incarceration of certain social groups, while the Minority was not tentative but emphatic:

> The Local Health Authority should be granted compulsory powers of removal and detention, similar to that which it now possesses in respect to certain infectious diseases, with regard to all aged and infirm persons who are found to be endangering their own lives, or becoming, through mental or physical incapacity to take care of themselves, a nuisance to the public.[2]

> ... the Maintenance and Training Division should also establish one or more Detention Colonies, of a reformatory type, to which men

would be committed by the Magistrates, and compulsorily detained and kept to work under discipline, upon any such offences as Vagrancy, Mendicity, neglect to maintain family or to apply for Public Assistance for their maintenance if destitute...[3]

The Minority therefore wished to incarcerate not only those who were, in the old sense, 'a burden on the rates', but those who had not asked for relief, and whose style of living was felt to cause public scandal.

This shift in attitude towards institutions, from the workhouse whose main function was to deter, to the many-faceted, compulsory and curative institutions of the later nineteenth century, is not easy to explain. Other residential institutions, such as lunatic asylums and hospitals, also reflected this changing attitude. In the eighteenth century, institutions were usually considered a last resort. Charity hospitals were for the poor—the rich paid to stay out of them. The insane might be committed to a private madhouse, their maintenance paid for from the poor rate, but many more were left to roam unattended, while the rich paid for private keepers. By the end of the nineteenth century, however, institutions had become a universal panacea. The change may be partially tested in one of its aspects—the number of people who died in institutions rather than in their own homes. The Local Government Board collected such statistics for the period 1871–1906.[4]

Deaths in public institutions as a percentage of all deaths in England and Wales, and in London

Deaths in workhouses and other Poor Law institutions

	1871	1881	1891	1901	1906
England & Wales	5.6	7.0	7.1	8.1	9.7
London	11.3	13.2	14.9	18.9	20.9

Deaths in hospitals

	1871	1881	1891	1901	1906
England & Wales	2.6	2.8	3.5	5.5	6.6
London	6.5	7.4	8.9	11.3	14.3

Deaths in lunatic asylums

	1871	1881	1891	1901	1906
England & Wales	0.8	1.0	1.1	1.5	1.9
London	0.4	0.3	1.8	2.3	3.1

Thus by 1909, 18.2 per cent of all deaths in England and Wales occurred in public institutions, a proportion which had doubled in 30 years. In London the figure was much higher, 38.3 per cent, which suggests that the proportion depended on the number of available hospital places. London far surpassed the rest of the country in hospital provision, and its capacity increased faster in the period 1870–1920 than ever before or since. Most of the increase was in the general hospitals, including Poor Law infirmaries.[5]

This was an important social change: death was being removed from the home to institutions. The insane, also, were more likely to be committed to asylums for treatment instead of being left at large. This movement coincided with the development of psychiatric medicine as a specialized profession, and the asylum doctors made strong (if frequently unfounded) claims for institutional care as a cure for insanity.[6] Since the arrival of cholera, local authorities had gradually acquired powers to remove certain infectious patients compulsorily to the hospitals. For those who believed in the value of institutions, it was not a great step to commend them for unmarried mothers, harmless imbeciles, vagrants and the 'morally unfit'. The aim of the institution was not now to frighten them into independence, but to keep them from harming themselves and disg acing the community.

The material results can still be seen in many places, in the massive investment of bricks and mortar which are the legacy of the period. The decades between 1860 and the Great War were the age of institutions on a scale rarely known before. Professional journals such as *The Builder* published the architect's plans not only for new town halls, but for hospitals, lunatic asylums, prisons and workhouses. The trend was usually towards fewer but much larger institutions, for just as the union workhouses had replaced the more numerous but smaller parish poorhouses, so the county gaol and the county asylum replaced small local buildings. In 1827 the nine county asylums held an average of only 116 patients each, and private madhouses supplied much institutional care: by 1910 there were 91 county asylums, holding an average of 1072 patients each.[7] Huge model prisons like Pentonville replaced the modest eighteenth-century gaols. Except in rural areas where population was declining, the workhouses continued to expand, not only to hold the larger population, but because of the widespread belief that residential buildings were desirable and necessary. As the hospital functions of the workhouse became more important, guardians had to invest heavily in specialized buildings.

The effects on Poor Law finance soon became clear. High rates of pauperism in the late 1860s had caused the President of the Poor Law Board, G.S. Goschen, to urge stricter application of the workhouse test in order to reduce the cost of outdoor relief; but the cost of institutions soon dominated Poor Law expenditure. From the mid-1870s, the indoor, not the outdoor poor, put the heavier burden on the poor rate, and the cost continued to rise. Political opinion always responded more easily to short-term fluctuations in the numbers of outdoor poor, and to absolute rather than relative figures. Sporadic rises in outdoor pauperism, with peaks in the years of recession 1879–80, 1887–8, 1895–6 and 1905–6, created disproportionate alarm, and disguised the fact that outdoor pauperism was steadily declining. Even in the difficult year 1905 there were only 16.3 outdoor paupers per 1,000 population, whereas in 1871 there had been 39.1.[8] By 1914 there were only 10.5 per 1,000 as old age pensions began to take effect. Because the population was still increasing, the actual numbers of outdoor poor did not fall noticeably until just before the war, but even so, the average annual figure for the decade 1895–1904 was over 13 per cent lower than the comparable figure for 1875–1884.

By comparison, the proportional number of the indoor poor not only kept pace with the increase in population, but occasionally outstripped it. Inmates numbered between six and eight per 1,000 between 1870 and 1914, reaching a peak of 7.8 per 1,000 in 1910.[9] But these figures did not account for vagrants in the casual wards nor pauper lunatics in asylums, who would have together raised the proportion by some 14 per cent. In absolute terms the effect was marked. Whereas in 1875–84 the Poor Law authorities had to house an average of 167,740 paupers, in 1895–1904 the figure was 209,308, an increase of 24 per cent.[10] In the first decade of the twentieth century it cost more than three times as much merely to provide food, clothing and fuel for an indoor pauper as for an outdoor one, but these basic costs were less important than the ever-increasing expense of maintaining the institutions and their staff. Although the outdoor poor continued to absorb the interest of politicians and reformers, the indoor poor required most finance. (See Figures 1 and 2).

The Poor Law authorities were continually requiring more space for indoor paupers, at a time when the rising standards of treatment made institutions out-of-date almost as soon as they were built. Although costs in the building trade, particularly for labour, did rise in this period, higher standards were the major reason for expense. The solid, ornate Victorian buildings expressed the affluence and self-confidence of that generation. The prison vied with the town hall in grandeur, and even the workhouse, one of the most lowly institutions, could seem a 'palace' merely by virtue of its size. The 'pavilion' principle of hospital

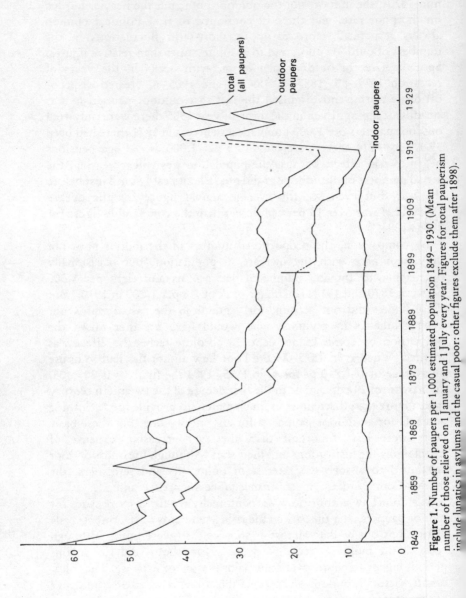

Figure 1. Number of paupers per 1,000 estimated population 1849–1930. (Mean number of those relieved on 1 January and 1 July every year. Figures for total pauperism include lunatics in asylums and the casual poor; other figures exclude them after 1898).

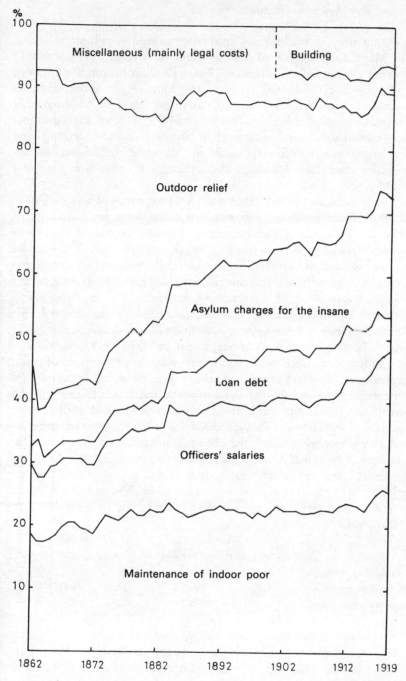

Figure 2. Distribution of expenditure on poor relief in England & Wales 1862–1919.

building affected workhouses infirmaries as well as voluntary hospitals. Many doctors believed that light and ventilation were essential to prevent the spread of infection. Hence pavilion hospitals were huge and sprawling, with high ceilings and long, echoing corridors, so soundly constructed that many are still in use. The new buildings of St Thomas's hospital in London (completed 1871) were amongst the most famous and most costly examples of this type of construction. Even the largest new workhouses could not compete with these, but the humbler Poor Law buildings also reflected a desire for space and ventilation.

The workhouses of the 1860s and 1870s were part of a second wave of workhouse building, and most of them were in the towns or suburbs. In areas of diminishing population, some of the 1830s workhouses now seemed too big for the community. The original 'pauper palaces' of East Anglia, now half-full, remained unspecialized: sometimes guardians let them fall into disrepair, and the paupers occupied one wing of a crumbling building. Yet in some towns Goschen had to check extravagant expenditure on architectural details such as 'granite columns, terra-cotta mouldings, encaustic tile pavements, Portland stone decorations, and so on'. The 1905 Commissioners added that since architects were paid a proportion of total expenditure, they had every incentive to overspend, while the medical officers also pressed for the most modern and lavish facilities in the infirmaries.[12] Majority and Minority both recommended smaller, more specialized institutions. They assumed that once adequate measures to reduce poverty were taken, the need for institutions would diminish, but here they erred. Once a public institution began to offer more specialized and expensive treatment than many people could afford privately, the need for institutions would grow. The cost of a new bed in a workhouse or infirmary in 1885–89 may be compared with that in 1900–1904.[13]

	1885–9		1900–1905	
	no. of new beds	cost per bed	no. of new beds	cost per bed
workhouses, including				
workhouse infirmaries	1873	£69.2.0	1893	£222.10.0
Separate infirmaries	484	£70.2.0	2272	£158. 4.0

Guardians' expenditure on buildings and the interest on building loans also show the trend towards larger institutions. Poor Law returns before 1900 did not distinguish building costs from other expenditure, but repayment of loans rose from under 3 per cent of

Poor Law expenditure in 1869 to 8 per cent in 1899, and remained at this level until 1914. In 1900 the cost of buildings and repairs took up another 8 per cent of the total expenditure. The guardians spent over £2 million a year on buildings and repairs from 1903 onwards.[14] Most of this went on infirmaries, but there were also new administrative blocks, nurses' homes, children's homes, and other specialized institutions.[15] From 1863 unions could raise cheap loans from the Public Works Loan Commissioners. Such expansion expressed a new belief in the curative, rather than the deterrent aspects of residential institutions.

At the same time, institutions inspired charitable enthusiasm: charitable subscriptions financed the growing voluntary hospitals and other well-publicized experiments in residential homes, such as Mary Carpenter's houses for 'children of the streets,' and the even larger venture by Dr Barnardo. Institutions had an inexhaustible sentimental appeal. They were visible signs that charity was 'doing good'; the best of them were clean, orderly, fit for ladies to visit, and quite unlike the homes of the poor. The zeal which drove Octavia Hill or Mrs Barnett into the slums of London was perhaps harder to acquire than the taste for visiting a neat institution, at designated hours, where the inmates could be afterwards left under the control of the staff. Many institutions housed children, the sick, or the elderly, who seemed the most fitting recipients of charity. It is harder to explain the attraction of institutions, both for curing and punishing, to social reformers of the time. Faith in well-run institutions linked the most disparate bodies—both sections of the 1905 Commission, the Salvation Army, the Charity Organization Society, and many religious organizations.

Official surveys continued to widen the class of potential inmates of institutions. In the 1890s the aged poor were the subject of Parliamentary committees and a Royal Commission (1895). This Commission reaffirmed what had usually been Poor Law practice, if not open policy, that the elderly should not be sent to workhouses if they could look after themselves: but for old people needing special care, institutions were necessary. The Commission criticized the harsh conditions in some workhouses, and recommended that institutions for the old should not be deterrent, but should actually encourage the helpless to enter in order to enjoy better facilities than in their own homes.[16] A decade later another Royal Commission inquired into the treatment of the feeble-minded and recommended special institutions for them, not under the control of the Poor Law authorities, though the 'unimproveable' cases, they significantly added, could be left in separate workhouse buildings.[17] In 1906 a departmental committee on vagrancy tried to sift out the 'worthless' from the 'curable' vagrant: the latter was to be found work, the former detained in a labour colony. Elderly vagrants should be encouraged to settle in workhouses; feeble-minded ones should be committed to institutions.[18]

This trend towards incarceration is not easy to explain, especially as institutions began to usurp the honoured position of the family. Large institutions were obviously quite opposed to the principle of the family: the inmate was not only separated from his relatives, but the family had to defer to the institution's staff. The debtors' prisons had been perhaps the last British institutions which allowed whole families to remain together. Yet the Victorians venerated family life, and had to offer exceptional reasons for disrupting it. The institution was supposed to offer a substitute for family care to the friendless old person and the orphaned young; but it also separated members of the family from one another. In 1834, Chadwick believed that inability to support one's family was sufficient to justify separation in the workhouse, in spite of public hostility: by the end of the century separation had to be justified in a different way. In the early 1860s Mary Carpenter had thought even an inferior family life better than any institution, but to the Royal Commission of 1905 the institution was not merely a substitute for family life, but sometimes superior to it.[19]

The central authority, which had begun by fearing that the workhouses would be more attractive than the homes of the poor, made a positive virtue out of this from the 1870s. If the institution were superior to the impoverished home, then the workhouse must be continued as a focal point of administration. Henry Longley, who like the other Inspectors demanded a more severe policy on outdoor relief, expressed this feeling. He derided guardians who disliked sending families to the workhouse because it broke up the home:

> [this] assumes . . . that the applicant has a home at all, or such a home that its loss will be otherwise than to the ultimate benefit of himself and his family . . . A change of home, which is a serious matter to the rural poor, is a matter of constant occurrence with the poor in London.[20]

Although the Inspectors still believed in 'less eligibility,' the idea was now highly confused: Longley was actually defending the workhouse because it was *more* eligible than the homes of the poor.

The British, on the whole, had been slow to create institutions.

Since parish autonomy survived into the nineteenth century, it kept public building on a small scale, unlike those institutions in countries where government authority was more centralized or the religious establishment more hierarchical. Eighteenth-century France had developed large hospitals, refuges, foundling homes and gaols: both Church and State were directly concerned with them. Michel Foucault, in his influential works on prisons, hospitals and asylums, has shown how institutions developed the same principles of 'discipline'—the monotonous routine which should ensure the inmate's total subjection. Foucault ascribes this process to the most significant changes in European thought and the nature of the power structure. The criminal was no longer to suffer excruciating torture, the lunatic no longer to be kept in chains; but the power exerted over them was more subtle and insidious. The dominating classes no longer ruled by naked force but by discipline: previous methods of control had attacked the body, but the new methods conquered the mind. The Enlightenment, so often described as humanitarian, merely replaced physical with mental subjection.[21] Hence arose that phenomenon which has been noted concerning the workhouses, but which applies to penal institutions also: that the destitute and the criminal might be offered a better standard of living in an institution than the labouring poor could achieve outside it. In return for material provision, all independence was surrendered.

D.J. Rothman has considered other explanations for these developments in the United States, where institutions also grew, though on a more limited scale than in Britain or Europe. The growth of institutions, Rothman believes, was encouraged by a new secular belief that social problems were curable, not God-given and to be patiently endured. Almshouses were to rehabilitate the idle; prisons to reform the criminal; asylums to cure the insane. There was a boundless faith in the possibilities of scientific treatment and a correct environment in altering the individual, as in Bentham's panopticon. Rothman, unlike Foucault, is more concerned with the divergence between theory and practice. A grand theory, such as the separate or silent system for convicts, rarely worked in practice, given the constraints of finance and the efforts of the inmates to frustrate it. Hence the institutions degenerated into mere receptacles: they housed, but made little effort to treat or cure the socially deviant and helpless. Incurable, chronic cases filled the asylums; violent or habitual criminals the prisons. The poorhouses, as in Britain, housed mainly the long-term, helpless paupers. Even the most elaborate systems of discipline had little effect on this kind of inmate. Rothman argues that the institutions had been intended to correct family life: if deviance or poverty could be explained as a result of family breakdown, then the humane but severe institution was a model of what parental discipline ought to be. But order, control and discipline cease to be agents of reform and become ends in themselves.[22]

A more traditional argument asserts that institutions become popular simply because they are effective. Hospitals cured instead of killing; the comfort and treatment in homes and hospitals was greater than most people could afford in their own families.[23] The lunatic asylums began to defeat their own purposes as they grew larger, for staff could not give individual attention to the inmates, but even in these overcrowded institutions the standards of comfort were higher than in the homes of the poor. Hospitals became popular even before medical science was revolutionized in the late nineteenth century: more effective surgery and improved hygiene lowered their mortality rates. The workhouses lagged behind other institutions in physical standards, but even these were constantly improving, at least in the towns. The poor were suspicious of institutions, but nevertheless supported them: new hospital beds were filled as soon as available; pressure on asylums and charitable homes continued to grow. Even the workhouse responded to this new belief in institutional care.

Hegemony, materialism, a substitute for family discipline, are concepts which provide an overall explanation for the development of large institutions. The significance of the change will be overlooked if not seen in an international context. It is plain that the reform of the workhouse system in 1834 accommodates well to Foucault's arguments. The discipline which could be seen as far more humane than that of the eighteenth-century poorhouses, was a carefully calculated method of subjection of the unruly classes, and the Parliament which passed the 1834 Act accepted it as a measure of control in times of social upheaval. Nor is the secular intention of the workhouses in doubt. Although, like prisons and asylums, they incorporated a religious element in their discipline, the purpose of the institution was social rather than spiritual. The souls of convicts and workhouse inmates were indeed to be saved, but the proof of salvation was to be seen in the reward to society. Equally, the workhouses penalized inefficient families for their failure, while offering them a more comfortable environment than their own homes.

The empirical historian will not wish to pursue these comparisons further than the evidence will bear. While they provide a useful explanation for international changes, they will not account for the intricate differences between the institutions of different countries, nor the precise reasons for the development of a particular institution at a particular time. Although institutions of all kinds developed certain common features of administration, it is artificial to consider in the same breath institutions which were intended to deter the populace from entering them, such as prisons and workhouses; and those which were intended to be curative, such as hospitals and asylums. Nor does the 'social control' theory of institutions adequately explain their development, for administrators were often divided amongst themselves, and inmates showed a surprising ability to subvert the routine of the institution, as will be discussed later.

The historian may observe the institutions from a distance and note remarkable similarities between them: under the microscope the differences are equally striking. The inmates themselves understood perfectly the distinctive features of their own institution. For vagrants, who could wander between one workhouse and another, there was an elaborate system of comparisons, circulated by graffiti and word of mouth. The historian may see casual wards as uniformly repressive, but the tramp who scrawled the following on the wall of the ward at Whitchurch knew better.

> The governor's name is Sutton
> The pauper's diet is mutton
> But you must not be a glutton
> When here you lodge;
> You had better go to Andover
> Where you can live in clover
> A far better dodge.[24]

Habitual offenders also knew that one prison was not the same as another, and that it was necessary to exploit the nuances of the system. Both the near and the distant perspectives must be considered. The rest of this chapter will therefore concentrate on those features which were peculiar to the English experience, and which produced a changed attitude towards the workhouse.

Charitable influences

One of the earliest pressures on the workhouse system was the work of individual reformers and charitable groups outside the Poor Law administration. Workhouses, like many Victorian institutions, attracted reformist pressure groups. In some ways these groups inherited the mantle of the anti-Poor Law campaign; they extolled the virtues of paternalism and private charity above the 'cold' official relief policies. Charles Dickens, with his great popular following, achieved as much as any one person could in arousing sympathy for workhouse inmates. His early novel *Oliver Twist* pleaded for the workhouse child; in 1857 *Little Dorrit* did so for the aged pauper. In *Our Mutual Friend* (1865) old Betty Higden trudged herself to death to avoid the workhouse and a pauper funeral. In private life, Dickens supported many charitable institutions, acting as almoner to the heiress Angela Burdett Coutts; he was fascinated by schools, prisons, hospitals and asylums. Valuing personal charity above the impersonal public relief, he praised institutions which tried to treat each inmate individually, whereas the workhouse crushed the personality. Thus he describes the old pauper Nandy, in a coat 'that was never made for him, or for any individual mortal', living in the Old Men's Ward 'in a grove of two score and nineteen more old men, every one of whom smells of all the others.'[25] The 'good' institutions, like the Children's Hospital in Great Ormond Street, showed up the deficiencies of the bad.

Other reformers accepted the necessity of institutions, and hoped to bring the workhouses up to the standard of the best charitable institutions. Hence Florence Nightingale extended her strictures on hospital nursing to workhouses, and in 1865 her disciple Agnes Jones was allowed to work with trained nurses in Liverpool workhouse infirmary, a scheme financed at first by a local philanthropist.[26] Miss Nightingale had a plan for London which would have provided separate infirmaries for the sick poor; while after unfavourable publicity for workhouse infirmaries in *The Lancet*, an 'Association for the Improvement of the Infirmaries of London Workhouses' was set up in 1866.[27]

Charity was not permitted to enter the workhouse without a struggle. The Royal Commission of 1832 had not objected to charitable effort on behalf of the helpless inmates, but the Poor Law Commissioners disliked all public intrusion into the workhouse because of the possible disruption of 'discipline'. Louisa Twining, a daughter of the family of tea merchants, went in the early 1850s to visit an old acquaintance in the Strand workhouse, and was so distressed by what she saw that she wished to organize regular charitable visits. She intended at first to interest the old people by conversation, Bible readings and sympathy, but her plans also extended to practical help. She was affronted not only by dirt, poor food and lack of comfort, but by the utter monotony of workhouse life. Charity could provide cushions, better blankets, armchairs, books and amusements for the elderly, and toys for the children, as well as comforts for the sick. Miss Twining founded the Workhouse Visiting Society in 1858, 'to promote the moral and spiritual improvement of workhouse inmates... and provide a centre of communication for all persons interested in that object.'[28] At first both guardians and the Poor Law Board refused the offer; Miss Twining had to exert all possible influence, and the Board grudgingly recognized the society. Local guardians could ignore it, but many saw the wisdom of supplementing the rates by charitable gifts.

The Workhouse Visiting Society had a comparatively short life, but it left behind a habit of workhouse visiting which spread into the provinces. It also produced successful offshoots, in which Miss Twining was interested. In 1861 Baroness Burdett Coutts gave funds for a home in London to train workhouse girls as servants and to care for them between jobs; for the Society believed that workhouse children must be prevented from looking on the workhouse as their natural home in times of trouble.[29] The Poor Law Board distrusted the home, though some guardians found it useful. In the late 1860s the Society offered places to 'refractory' workhouse girls who were in danger of becoming permanent inmates, and found employment for unmarried mothers. R.G. Lumley, one of the Board's assistant secretaries, objected because the guardians continued to support these women in the charitable homes, at a cost of four or five shillings each per week:

> The practice of mixing up charity with pauperism by taking *paupers* from the W.H. but keeping them still *paupers* in the Homes is a pitiful course of action, & so far as the small amount of it extends, has a mischievous effect.[30]

The Board reluctantly allowed the expenditure, probably because many ladies of the society were of high social standing and not to be flouted. Mrs Senior, daughter-in-law of Nassau Senior, herself helped to found the Metropolitan Association for Befriending Young Servants (MABYS), to provide care for workhouse girls after they had gone out to work. In 1879 legislation allowed guardians to support the funds of MABYS and other charitable organizations which co-operated with the Poor Law.

MABYS operated only in London, but the Girls' Friendly Society, run by the Church of England, offered similar help in the provinces. E.M. Ross calculates that by 1880 it took care of about 2718 girls from

374 unions: unlike the London body it was interested only in 'respectable' girls.[31] Local charities were often willing to given concerts, books, newspapers and outings to deserving inmates, and made their lives less dreary. Dr Boyson describes how, from 1858, a local subscription took the Burnley workhouse paupers annually to Blackpool, 'and if the day was wet they sang Temperance melodies in the Blackpool Primitive Methodist Sunday School'.[32] By the 1880s, such outings were both more general and more hedonistic, as in this description of the Skipton workhouse outing:

> The party started in four brakes... Cracoe, the first stopping place, was reached by 10.15, and here refreshments were served to the 'trippers' by willing hands. At Burnsall this process was repeated but it was at Appletree [wick] that the meal of the day was partaken of.. the host and hostess of the New Inn having prepared a spread which could hardly fail to entice any appetite however epicurean... and the men who were considered suitable to wash down the solids with a draught of ale were allowed to do so... the journey was resumed to Bolton Abbey, and here another substantial meal was awaiting the party at the Red Lion Inn. This over, the customary thanks to the donors of the treat, and to the Master and Matron, were heartily returned, the company... also giving the workhouse master a special cheer for not attempting, though a teetotaller himself, to deprive the old men of their customary glass of beer.[33]

After 1862, guardians could send certain inmates to charitable institutions, and pay for their maintenance. Roman Catholics wished to take pauper children into their own residential schools; but here the prejudices as well as the finances of guardians were likely to be a hindrance. Some guardians subscribed to send handicapped children to special institutions, even though their maintenance cost more than in the workhouse. By 1885, about 7 per cent of all pauper children were in non-pauper institutions (excluding lunatic asylums): by 1908 the proportion was 15 per cent.[34] As usual, all depended on local decisions, and some guardians had no compunction in keeping handicapped children in the workhouse.

Another charitable venture, the Brabazon scheme, tried to keep elderly and handicapped inmates active and self-respecting by training them in handicrafts, which could then be sold to obtain comforts for the makers. Begun by the Countess of Meath in 1882, the scheme spread to 177 unions by 1900.[35] Lady Meath offered eight London workhouses £50 annually each for the raw materials, and lady visitors supervised the work.[36] Like most charitable reformers, Lady Meath ignored the able-bodied inmates; and stricter guardians also deprived them of the outings, special dinners and entertainments allowed the other inmates. The Workhouse Visiting Society did try to reclaim 'refractory' women, and Josephine Butler found an outlet for her incipient feminism by visiting the prostitutes in the oakum sheds of her local workhouse. Emma Sheppard, another propagandist of workhouse visiting, drew an affecting picture of her own approach to this group:

> I found about ten wretched degraded looking women crowding round the fire; several in bed, one... who hid her disfigured, diseased face, under the bed clothes from me. I went up to them, laid my hand on a shoulder, and said: 'My poor women, is it true that if I offer to come in and see you now and then, you would treat me with abuse and coldness? Can this be true of English women to an English lady?' They rose, turned round, and with a respectful curtsey, said, 'Oh! do come to us, nobody seems to come for us; we would kindly welcome you.'[37]

Charity was of course erratic, and tended to make even more arbitrary distinctions between the deserving and the undeserving poor than did the guardians. Nevertheless, the agitations and appeals of charitable groups helped to keep the workhouse in the public eye, and to expose its deficiencies long after the anti-Poor Law campaign had subsided. Charitable reformers insisted on judging the workhouses by charitable standards which attacked the whole conception of deterrence under the Poor Law.

As will be seen in Chapter 7, the comparison between voluntary and official solutions to poverty also helped transform workhouses into general hospitals towards the end of the nineteenth century. Since the voluntary hospitals excluded so many categories of the sick poor, including chronic and long-term patients, the Poor Law was compelled to make up the deficit. Yet the great charity hospitals provided a yardstick by which to measure the Poor Law infirmaries, and although the infirmaries were usually sadly deficient by comparison, reformers like Florence Nightingale were able to use this example to influence the Poor Law authorities. Thus charity provided a stimulus to the Poor Law, both because charity would not assist all who needed help, and because its own institutions set the acceptable standard.

The problem of deterrence

From the 1880s, social attitudes towards poverty, and particularly unemployment, began to change. Economic factors assisted this change of mood: years of prosperity in mid-century were followed by depression, and 'unemployment' was used to describe a social problem rather than an individual failing. Traditional attitudes of course survived alongside new ones,[38] but in the 1880s workers' demonstrations no longer aroused fear of revolution, but stimulated charitable donations and other panaceas: consequently, the able-bodied poor began to escape from the Poor Law system.

In industrial unions the Poor Law Board had permitted the labour test which allowed outdoor relief in return for work such as stone breaking or oakum picking—a tacit acknowledgement that the workhouse test could not solve large-scale unemployment. In 1886 Joseph Chamberlain made the first effort to remove such relief from the Poor Law by encouraging town councils to provide relief work for the unemployed. His recommendations, largely unobserved, nevertheless tried to separate the concept of unemployment from that of pauperism. If the able-bodied male could be offered aid without deterrent tests or the stigma of pauperism, why should deterrence still apply to the helpless poor who could not avoid the workhouse? The statistics of pauperism gave no accurate picture of the age or health of people on relief, and the 'able-bodied' category was probably much exaggerated.[39] Nevertheless, by any contemporary interpretation, the able-bodied were a small proportion of the pauper host. In the 1860s, able-bodied men accounted for just over 5 per cent of indoor paupers, and usually under 5 per cent of outdoor paupers. Even during the Lancashire cotton famine, when outdoor relief was given to unemployed factory workers, the proportion of able-bodied men on outdoor relief was only about 6 per cent of the national total. Able-bodied women were usually twice as numerous, mainly because of the large numbers of destitute widows with children, but these were not such a sensitive political subject as able-bodied male paupers.[40]

Defenders of the Poor Law argued that the very absence of able-bodied male paupers demonstrated the success of the workhouse test.[41] Thomas Mackay, prolific author on Poor Law affairs, argued that any relaxation of the workhouse test would immediately cause an increase in able-bodied pauperism and discourage thrift. The most famous mouthpiece for these views was the Charity Organization Society, which tried to separate the deserving from the undeserving poor by means of intensive personal investigations. The Society hoped to prevent wasteful duplication of charitable resources by ensuring that the worthy poor received appropriate aid, while the undeserving might be left to the Poor Law.[42] The COS, while neither popular nor large in membership, managed to influence the administration of several important unions, and is rightly seen as a pioneer of the modern casework system; yet it was also a bastion of traditional Poor Law notions, seeing deterrence as the nation's chief defence against the 'residuum' of incorrigible paupers.

Popular and sentimental writings of the time, however, persisted in concentrating not on the able-bodied whom the workhouse was supposed to deter, but on the workhouse's actual inmates: the old, and the helpless. In the 1850s Emma Sheppard wrote of the aged inmates:

> the listless look—the dull vacuity—the lack of all interest, except for the petty details of tea versus gruel—potatoes versus rice! The only object from their windows of moving interest the parish hearse preparing to take away some of their former companions.[43]

Fifty years later Rider Haggard turned aside from African romances to describe an East Anglian workhouse:

> The poor girls, with their illegitimate children creeping, dirty-faced, across the floor of brick; the old, old women lying in bed too feeble to move, or crouching round the fire in their mob-caps... The old men, their hands knobbed and knotted with decades of hard work, their backs bent... come here at last in reward of their labour.[44]

The popular press of broadsheet ballad and penny novelette had always described the workhouse in terms of fear and pity: in the later nineteenth century the pity spread to a wider section of the middle-class press.

The more the workhouse was seen as an institution for the aged and helpless, the harder it was to justify a policy of deterrent discipline. In the 1890s the researches of Charles Booth and the report of the Royal Commission on the Aged Poor made plain how many of the population entered the workhouse in old age. Of those aged between 70 and 75, 88 out of every 1000 were in the workhouse: for those who survived longer, the probability of pauperism was even greater.[45] The Local Government Board's preoccupation with able-bodied paupers indirectly encouraged the workhouse's reputation as a refuge for the helpless, especially in London. In the early 1870s the Inspectors were striving to reduce outdoor relief by a strict application of the workhouse test. They feared that the large and chaotic London workhouses were still too attractive to incorrigible loafers; hence the Board encouraged an experiment in Poplar whereby the inmates were separated into different categories and sent to neighbouring unions, leaving only the able-bodied in Poplar workhouse. Here the labour test was to be enforced, diet and discipline to be more severe than in other workhouses. Any spare capacity in Poplar workhouse was offered to other London unions, who could give their able-bodied poor an 'order for Poplar,' as a more efficient deterrent.

The Poplar experiment continued for about 20 years, before Poplar became famous for a different type of administration, and was followed by similar arrangements in Kensington, Birmingham, Manchester and Sheffield.[46] The Webbs deplored the results, for, they argued, the genuine loafer never entered a test workhouse, but remained outside to sponge on society and become a nuisance to the police, while the test workhouses contained inadequate men of all ages for whom the strict discipline was inappropriate.[47] The point is, however, that in these large cities the ordinary workhouses became even more firmly associated with the aged and helpless poor. If the incorrigibles (however defined) could be sent to special institutions, then a deterrent policy for the ordinary workhouses was less defensible. The Board was long reluctant to acknowledge this, but finally did so in a circular of 1895:

> ... Whilst workhouses were in the first instance provided chiefly for the relief of the able-bodied, and their administration was therefore intentionally deterrent, the sick, the aged, and the infirm now greatly preponderate, and this [has] led to a change in the spirit of the administration...[48]

In a more wealthy society, punitive measures against the poor seemed less necessary. From about 1860 the rateable value of property rose faster than the cost of poor relief,[49] but regional variations obscured the issue. Agricultural areas such as East Anglia, which felt the 'Great Depression' most severely, had falling rateable values: in 1896 the government was forced to allow rate relief on agricultural land. In many towns, however, the value of land constantly increased. Any effort to make public institutions more comfortable was bound to be expensive, and some parts of the country were more ready to meet this expense than others. It had seemed in 1834 that unions would be sufficiently large units to replace the parochial administration, but the wealth of unions varied too much. Admittedly, labourers were leaving the depressed areas and emigrating to the towns or overseas, and so the able-bodied pauper was no longer the main problem in the village; but amongst those who remained were some of the least fit, the sick, the old and the handicapped. Institutional care was needed in areas which were reluctant to provide it.

The new administrators

The guardians themselves were changing with the times, although they still exhibited every variety of opinion and differed widely in their enthusiasm for the work. The Webbs, who believed that unions were too small to be efficient, argued that the post of guardian had insufficient prestige to attract able volunteers. This was an exaggeration, for unions still had every variety of government, but corruption and apathy could still be found. The 1870s might have ushered in changes if only because the first generation of administrators were passing away. Rural unions had often been dominated by local magnates or their nominees, an outstanding example being Bromley in Kent, which for nearly 40 years was run by Lord Sydney and by George Warde Norman, a director of the Bank of England. Once this domination was broken, guardians' elections became increasingly political, while the union itself changed from a relatively stable agricultural community into massively expanding commuter suburbs. To meet this challenge, the guardians had to replace the old workhouse with a series of new buildings—an infirmary, children's homes, vagrant wards. Other areas had entirely different experiences, for in many towns the furious political contests of the 1830s and 1840s had virtually disappeared. In London, one of the liveliest centres of local politics, only half the wards were contested in the guardians' elections of 1904, and only 23 per cent of the electorate voted in the contested wards.[50]

Nevertheless, the post of guardian was not popular, and could be most time-consuming. As the administration of the Poor Law became more complex, the weekly or fortnightly meetings of the guardians were supplemented by other committees. A large union usually had a house committee for workhouse management, a series of relief committees to interview applicants, a boarding-out committee in charge of children in foster-homes, a finance committee and a number of *ad hoc* committees. Like most political bodies, the boards were likely to be controlled by cliques of the most active members, and one or two vigorous individuals could dominate the administration.

Guardians became more aware of national developments in the late nineteenth century. In the mid-1860s the Gloucestershire unions had sent representatives to a guardians' conference, and the idea spread. Ten years later there was a regular national conference and 12 district conferences. Vagrancy was the original stimulus, for the Gloucestershire unions wanted to present a united front against tramps, but soon a wider variety of topics was discussed, including workhouse management, the treatment of lunatics, sanitary reform, outdoor relief, and so on: detailed reports were published from 1875. The conferences were well attended by men of social standing, and the Local Government Board sent the district Inspector to present the official view. Indeed, the conferences were probably unrepresentative because they attracted the most active and leisured guardians. Yet the conferences dispel the notion that all guardians were lethargic and indifferent, and some of the papers were very well-informed. Higher standards, however, could not be imposed on all unions: in 1875 the North-Western delegates criticized their absent colleagues in Todmorden, for that most stubborn of unions had only just built a workhouse, and delegates alleged that the Todmorden rates had been kept down by pushing paupers into other unions.[51]

The guardians rarely agreed either on the use of the workhouse test or on workhouse management. Attitudes varied from the south Wales guardian who wished to revive the ancient custom of badging the poor, to the bewildered comment by Major Henry Bethune: 'I know nothing about Poor Laws except from living in a village and seeing poor people that could never save money, having lived for years on nine shillings or ten shillings a week.'[52] Albert Pell, a forceful land-owning MP, was chief organizer, and to him the workhouse pauper was little more than a grim warning to society:

> Paying the penalty of their misfortunes or faults, they serve the useful purpose of warning the young and careless of the need of making provision against the possibilities of ill-health and the certainties of old age.[53]

Chadwick himself came in his old age to defend the principles of the Poor Law: time had not altered his views.[54] Some guardians had difficulty reconciling the workhouse test with their own belief in the virtues of family life: a Macclesfield guardian rejoiced that families had been kept together on outdoor relief during the cotton famine; but a clerical guardian expressed different feelings in a paper entitled 'Christian teaching and the Poor Law':

> It may cause real pain to a Christian-minded guardian to see the angry disappointment of those who have the house instead of a weekly allowance offered them; but the pain cannot be greater than that of the affectionate father who has to use the rod to his child.[55]

Brougham's paternalist justification of the Poor Law lived on: only by such sleights of mind was it possible to reconcile the principle of institutions with the principle of the family, but the argument was not universally acceptable.

Local administration in the 1890s was affected by two further events: the election of female, and of working-class guardians.

No law prevented women from becoming guardians if they owned enough property, but only as women began to assert themselves in public life did they take this opportunity. Few married women had been independent ratepayers, but like the working class, they were enfranchised for local elections by the Local Government Act of 1894. The first women had been elected in 1875, but not until after 1894 did women arrive in strength: there were 1289 women guardians by 1909, distributed in 500 unions.[56] Louisa Twining became a guardian, and helped in 1881 to finance the Association for Promoting the Return of Women as Poor Law Guardians. Some women guardians, like Charlotte Despard in Lambeth, were feminists and later became suffragettes; others had no strong political views, but saw official unpaid work as a more effective social action than the individual charity always considered suitable for ladies. In spite of the growth of educational provision for middle-class women, they had few professional opportunities: debarred from an independent career they took up service in local government, just as the previous generation of active women had turned to personal charity.

Women's work benefited Poor Law administration, though women were largely constrained by their own training and the views of male guardians to work with pauper women and children. Women guardians often worked to remove children from the barrack schools to foster parents or smaller homes. Mrs Jane Elizabeth Senior, the first woman Poor Law Inspector, had in 1873 written an influential report attacking barrack schools because, she maintained, large institutions demoralized children. In spite of an indignant rebuttal from Tufnell, who had always supported barrack schools, Mrs Senior's idea gained currency, and more guardians tried alternative schemes for children, such as fostering, purpose-built 'cottage homes', or 'scattered homes' in ordinary houses. Lady guardians were often asked to oversee the running of these homes and watch over the welfare of boarded-out children. The whole subject sharply revealed the conflict over the virtues of family life versus the large institutions. No single system prevailed, and the barrack schools had important defenders until the twentieth century.[57] In any case, fostering suited only healthy children whose parents no longer had any authority over them, whereas institutions seemed inevitable for ailing and handicapped children, or those whose parents could remove them at any time. Women guardians, however, often encouraged the small institutions as closer to family life.

Since the 1870s voluntary committees of ladies had been allowed to supervise the boarding-out system, and in 1885 the Local Government Board appointed Miss M.H. Mason as a full-time assistant Inspector for these children. Women guardians were also expected to take a special interest in the infirmaries and wards for old people. The first generation of lady guardians, including Louisa Twining, sometimes took a harsh view of 'undeserving' cases, including the unmarried mothers. Miss Twining argued that the lying-in wards should be hygienic, but should be in the workhouse rather than the infirmary, to induce a proper sense of shame in the mothers. Later feminists were more sympathetic, and under Charlotte Despard's guidance the Lambeth guardians deputed their women members to interview the unmarried mothers and find employment for them when they left the workhouse. They also arranged for unwanted children to be adopted. Women guardians initiated no striking new policies, and tended to take a conventional view of women's duties; but they helped to relax workhouse discipline for the helpless inmates.

Working-class guardians were not elected in large numbers at first, but amongst the early ones were men who became famous in the Labour movement, and whose administration of the Poor Law caused a disproportionate stir. In Poplar, Will Crooks and George Lansbury were elected in 1892, Crooks himself having spent some time in the workhouse as a child. Within a few years Crooks was chairman, and the board operated under new principles. 'Poplarism', meaning an open-handed policy of outdoor relief, with little consideration of what the local rates could bear, became a term of admiration and abuse. The Poplar guardians believed that the rich parishes of London, with their high rateable values and low rates, should pay for the poverty of the

East End, not only by subsidising workhouse accommodation through the Common Poor Fund, but by outdoor relief as well.[58] The central authority feared the effects of the wider franchise, and was suspicious of working-class guardians: with the exception of Poplar, however, the new guardians caused little alarm before 1918.

In any case, working-class guardians seem to have been little interested in workhouse reform. British Socialism is a well-known historical chimera, which defies all attempts to impose upon it a philosophical shape. Labour guardians at the end of the nineteenth century were often hostile to the whole concept of the Poor Law, which they rightly regarded as a formidable weapon in the hands of the propertied classes, but they did not agree over reform. Lansbury, to whom Socialism was an extension of Christianity, a man of extraordinary kindness and generosity, signed the Minority Report in spite of its grim intentions towards the 'irreducible minimum' of able-bodied loafers.[59] In 1911 he published a pamphlet entitled *Smash up the Workhouse!* the title of which probably reflected the sentiments of many Labour supporters. It implied that few people, and certainly not the able-bodied, should be in workhouses, but for those who could not avoid them, conditions should be as comfortable as possible. The Poplar guardians reformed their workhouse by gradually replacing the staff, abolishing workhouse uniform, improving the food, and allowing tea and tobacco to the aged. Children of the 'ins and outs' had a special house and went to the local schools: cottage homes were opened for the long-stay children, and later the parish set up a farm colony for able-bodied male paupers.[60] This was financed by Joseph Fels, a wealthy American philanthropist, and was intended not to penalize but to rehabilitate. Yet the Poplar reforms were not exceptional, nor against the dictates of the Local Government Board, unlike the Poplar policies on outdoor relief. The farm colony was a novelty, but the scheme had some vogue at the time, in imitation of a similar experiment by the Salvation Army. The Poplar guardians had inherited a particularly dismal workhouse and hastened to improve it; but they did no more than 'progressive' non-Labour guardians in other unions.

Some Labour guardians concentrated on attacking the workhouse test and ignored the workhouse itself. Many Welsh unions, with their long tradition of hostility to the workhouse system, fell under Labour control, but conditions in Welsh institutions were still poor: impoverished ratepayers could not support expensive workhouses. As late as the 1920s some Welsh guardians were giving outdoor relief as far as possible and neglecting the institutions.[61] The guardians allowed tea, beer and freedom to the inmates, but neglected the buildings and paid staff low wages. Yet the change in composition of boards of guardians could affect workhouse management, if only because promises of kinder treatment were thought likely to attract the working-class voter. The rural unions saw fewer changes, though from 1894 the magistrates were no longer ex-officio guardians. In unions like Bromley the local gentry easily commanded a deferential vote, and continued to sit as elected guardians alongside the new commercial interests.

The role of the central authority may be left to the end, as it was rarely a force for change in the late nineteenth century. The Poor Law Commissioners had been active policy makers, prejudiced in their approach to the problem of poverty, but not inert. The reputation of the Poor Law Board, in contrast, was one of inactivity, and the Local Government Board's little better. The work of charitable reformers stands out in contrast to that of the official bureaucracy. The Webbs saw the Local Government Board as a reactionary body, concerned only to preserve the anachronistic principles of 1834, and they suspected the Board of having engineered the appointment of the 1905 Royal Commission in an attempt to turn back the clock. In Poor Law matters the Board was indeed conservative, tending to concentrate on deterring the able-bodied pauper; and neither its structure nor its finances enabled it to take a firm lead. The very unpopularity of the first Commissioners made succeeding authorities more cautious in their dealings with the localities. They preferred to work through private pressure, steady attrition, unpublicized bargains. The Poor Law Commission had been designed to deter paupers, not to offer them free hospital treatment or specialized care in institutions, and the central authority was slow to shed Chadwick's influence. During the nineteenth century it devised no long-term policy for the large and expensive institutions which were arising, and was reluctant to accept that many workhouses were turning into hospitals. The Local Government Board insisted that official responsibility extended only to the destitute, not the poor, and did not wish to admit to the infirmaries anyone who was capable of paying for medical treatment, even if there were no other local hospitals.

In 1877 Dr J.H. Bridges, one of the two Medical Inspectors, noted that in London the police often sent accident cases straight to the infirmaries, even though no inquiry had been made into their circumstances. The infirmaries did not carry quite the same stigma as the workhouse, and Bridges recommended that the local medical officer should at once refer these cases to the workhouse if they were not serious:

> Evidently...a check must be applied to this abuse, or these Infirmaries will become free State hospitals, resulting in a great increase of pauperism.[62]

Although Bridges disapproved of any approach to free state medicine for all, he did wish to raise the Poor Law infirmaries to the highest standards of the voluntary hospitals. The central authority was handicapped by its lack of medical expertise. Chadwick's well-known distrust of the medical profession may have originated this, for in spite of its responsibility for a greatly expanding hospital system, the Local Government Board never employed more than two medical inspectors for Poor Law purposes. Bridges, an Inspector from 1869 to 1891, wrote of his employers in 1874:

> the atmosphere of a public office, unless when swayed by a very powerful directing hand, guiding it to some public object, is not a healthy atmosphere—its petty intrigues are like those of a little Court, and it needs a distinct struggle to keep clear of them.[63]

But the Board always lacked a guiding hand. Presidents, with junior rank in the Cabinet, came and went rapidly. The more able, like Joseph Chamberlain and Charles Dilke, were in office for too short a time to attempt major policy changes. Professor Macleod argues that the Board also suffered from the consequences of Gladstonian financial methods, in which all expenditure on the civil service was resented, and the number of Inspectors remained impractically low.[64] The Treasury bore the responsibility for the Board's lack of expertise in medicine, architecture, and other professions.

While the Board had very transient Presidents it had a remarkably long-serving permanent staff. Only four men held the post of Secretary in the 40-odd years of the Board's life, and of these, two spent almost their whole careers in Poor Law work. The Inspectors also were long-serving: unlike their predecessors, the Assistant Commissioners, the Inspectors had usually worked their way through the civil service, and had little experience of work outside it. In 1884 Dilke reorganized the Board's staff by opening eight clerkships in the higher division to competitive examination. He intended to attract young men of good education to the Poor Law service, but by the end of the century most of the Inspectors had begun their careers as clerks in the Poor Law department. By 1906 only five of the 13 general Inspectors had not served as assistant Inspectors or clerks, while the chief Inspector, J.S. Davy, was in his 36th year of Poor Law service.[65] Although the change undoubtedly raised the calibre of the Board's staff, a long career narrowly dedicated to one government office encouraged conservatism among the senior officers.

Planning no long-term policies, the Board responded fitfully to pressure from charities, from progressive guardians, and from public opinion. From 1885 workhouse discipline was slowly relaxed. Guardians could buy books and newspapers for the aged (1891), toys for the children (1891), tobacco and snuff for the elderly (1892), dry tea with sugar and milk for deserving inmates to brew at will (1893), and a piano or harmonium for the chapel services and entertainments (1904). The Webbs thought the new electorate had produced this change, for the first general election after the Third Reform Act took place in 1885.[66] Charles Booth's reports and the Parliamentary inquiries also stimulated interest in the aged poor. Yet the Board had long allowed charitable groups to give comforts to workhouse inmates, and acknowledged social change rather than political pressure. One Inspector wrote in 1894: 'The standard of comfort has advanced among all classes and it is not unreasonable that the inmates of workhouses should share in the improvement.'[67] The new regulations were not mandatory: parsimonious or indigent guardians were still refusing to supply even more basic amenities like water closets or hot water in the sick wards. The higher the permissible standard of institutions, the wider the variation between them was likely to be. Nevertheless, an Inspector's description of late nineteenth-century workhouse comforts would have horrified Tufnell:

> From various motives during a number of past years, chiefly from pity for those who are spending their last days in the Poor House,—Workhouse life has been made more and more comfortable and attractive. The work exacted is nothing like as hard as wage-earning work out of doors would be; dietary tables have been rendered more palatable, smoking is permitted; dry tea and tobacco are supplied; passages & c are heated with warm water pipes; large fires are allowed in dayrooms, whether the weather be warm or cold; newspapers and magazines, generally too library books are supplied; spectacles are provided if required; there is a dinner on Xmas day, from which there is often enough to spare for a new years feast as well... There are concerts, magic lantern entertainments

and lectures... There are no importunate creditors, no pecuniary troubles.[68]

That this idyllic picture did not describe all workhouse life will be demonstrated later, but it indicates the difference between the better workhouses of the 1890s and the modest institutions envisaged in 1834.

The composure of the Board was finally shaken by the report of the Royal Commission on the Poor Laws in 1909. This huge report, especially the Minority section, is often represented as a kind of historical time-bomb, which did not detonate until after 1945. The Webbs' suggestions for a Ministry of Labour and a national health service did indeed take years to bear fruit, and even the recommendations on which both reports firmly agreed—that unions be replaced by county administration—was not implemented until 1929. All the recommendations for the unemployed were shelved, but the report did affect institutional treatment more directly. Walter Long, Conservative President of the Board had suggested an inquiry into the Poor Law in 1904, knowing that some action was necessary to deal with rising unemployment, and not wishing the radical wing of the Liberal party to be the only political group with any coherent policies. He considered a plan for transferring workhouses to the county councils, and regrouping them as specialized institutions for the different classes of indoor poor.[69] The permanent officials in the Local Government Board, however, were wedded to traditional solutions to pauperism, and hoped that the Royal Commission would continue to advocate strict policies and a continuation of the workhouse test.

Both sections of the Commission condemned the workhouses and suggested specialized institutions instead. They criticized the debilitating effect of workhouse life on the paupers' character, and deplored the forced mixing of reputable and disreputable poor. The very language of the Minority Report on this subject, as its authors admitted, echoed the words of 1834:

We have ourselves seen, in the larger workhouses, the male and female inmates, not only habitually dining in the same room... but enjoying in the open yards and long corridors innumerable opportunities to make each other's acquaintance. It is...a common occurrence for assignations to be made by the inmates of different sexes, as to spending together the 'day out...' No less distressing has it been to discover a continuous intercourse, which we think must be injurious, between young and old, innocent and hardened.[70]

Although both reports objected to the 'great institutions', they did not attack institutions as such: like their predecessors of 1832 they favoured smaller establishments for economy and segregation.

The Commission stressed the importance of moral segregation, especially for the aged. Charles Booth, who was a member of the Commission, believed that the respectable aged were deterred from entering the workhouse because they might be herded with disreputable characters.[71] In 1908, while the Commission was sitting, the government introduced non-contributory old age pensions. Only old people over 70 on low incomes and of good moral character were to be given pensions; moral character being defined as a previous ability to have stayed out of prison and off poor relief. The moral clauses were unenforceable, and pensions immediately reduced applications for outdoor relief: between 1908 and 1912 the mean number of outdoor paupers fell by nearly 25 per cent.[72] The Commission accurately predicted that pensions would have little effect on indoor relief, for the money was not enough to enable the infirm aged to support themselves outside the workhouse. The Commissioners believed that institutions had two functions for the aged: to take care of the infirm and to remove from society old people of immoral life who were likely to spend pensions or doles on drink. The institution was therefore to be both a refuge and a prison. Yet if the institution were both a place of safety and a place of confinement, the deserving aged would not enter it; hence several small institutions, classified according to the inmates' moral character, would be necessary. The Minority, with characteristic ferocity, advocated compulsory removal of the degenerates to institutions:

> ...not for the sake of punishing these old people, who cannot be reformed, and can hardly be made of any value to the community, but in order to place them where they will be as far as possible prevented from indulging their evil propensities, where they will be put to do such work as they may be capable of, and where they will at any rate, be unable to contaminate the rest of the community.[73]

The deserving should have comforts denied to the undeserving, but problems of classification remained. The Commission hoped to reduce the numbers of people in institutions, but the logic of their argument on the aged poor ran counter to their intention.

The Commission, appointed by a Conservative government, delivered its report to a Liberal one, but Lloyd George and Churchill already had their own plans for social reform. The 1911 National Insurance Act provided both health and unemployment insurance for certain workers, while other legislation for unemployment exchanges and wage arbitration in low-paid occupations also helped to remove the poor a step further from the Poor Law. Neither these nor the old-age pension scheme were comprehensive, and the Poor Law still provided for many of the working population who fell into difficulties. Since the legislation fell far short of the universal provision recommended by the Minority Report, and of the co-ordination of official and voluntary provision recommended by the Majority, the great report appeared to be still-born. The Webbs knew whom to blame: not only the 'devious' Lloyd George, the 'dangerous' Churchill and the apathetic Liberal cabinet; but particularly John Burns, President of the Local Government Board from 1906 to 1914. To many of his radical contemporaries, Burns seemed a traitor to his class, for he had been a commanding figure in the Labour movement, a great agitator, one of the organizers of the 1889 dock strike, and had served a prison sentence after 'Bloody Sunday'. Now, as one of the impeccable Lib-Lab MPs, he was the first working man to achieve cabinet rank. So much was expected of a man with his background that he was inevitably doomed to disappoint; and so he passed into Labour mythology as one who, on first sniffing the air of the Commons, donned a frock coat, betrayed his followers, and began to court the upper classes.[74] The Webbs thought Burns pompous and inept, unable to control the reactionary officials at the Local Government Board.

Yet Burns had not really promised more than he intended to deliver. In his demagogic days he combined denunciations of the employers with exhortations to the working class not to drink, fight, or beat their wives.[75] As President of the Board, Burns wandered London with the police, investigating the condition of the homeless poor, but noting with satisfaction that the habits of the working class were steadily improving. On April bank holiday in 1906 he wrote in his diary, 'I have been out all day and not yet seen a drunken person.'[76] Burns accepted the Poor Law philosophy that personal habits helped to create poverty, and shared with Charles Booth and the Webbs their contempt for the 'residuum.' The poorest section of the unemployed, men who were not trade unionists or politically active, had little sympathy from him, for he saw them as a threat to the industrious classes. He commented on a visit to an experimental farm colony:

... to Ockendon Farm Colony 61 there Tired Tims Weary Willies where young... the others old but thriftless men where skilled did not belong to Trade Unions or Friendly Societies.[77]

In spite of political differences, Burns found in 1906 that he agreed with Mrs Webb on unemployment: 'It is the question of the marginal man.'[78] The 'marginal man', inhabited the section of society least amenable to reform, and was defined by Mrs Webb thus:

... the man not young enough or not skilled enough, or not well conducted enough for employment in normal times. He is no vicious, he is not ill, he wants to work: you cannot reform him, you cannot detain him as a nuisance, he has not sufficient pluck or initiative to wish to emigrate. And yet if you leave him to wander the streets he becomes vicious or ill or hopelessly indolent...[79]

Ironically, Burns was one of the few heads of the central authority to be interested in his work. Undeniably vain, he was soured by his relationships with the permanent officials on one hand and his former Labour colleagues on the other: he saw himself 'wrestling with fossils inside and fools and firebrands outside'.[80] Burns' views on the moral causes of pauperism coincided with Poor Law tradition, and he saw little need for change: poplarism, public works for the unemployed, and farm colonies were anathema to him. He does not seem to have felt the instinctive dread of the workhouse which united many Labour supporters, and, as President, he visited institutions with some complacency.[81]

The Board could not ignore the Royal Commission's report, however, and in the years before the war it made some effort at reforms which should not alter the framework of the Poor Law. The Relief Regulation Order of 1911 tried to consolidate existing regulations on outdoor relief: guardians were urged to give adequate relief instead of exiguous doles, but no standard scales were recommended. The Board was more interested in reforming the workhouses, as this could be done without much administrative change. A series of circulars announced its intentions, which were finally summarized in the Poor Law Institutions Order of 1913, with an accompanying order on workhouse nursing.

The new order accepted the Royal Commission's views on pauper children: as from 1915 guardians were not to keep any children over three years old in workhouses for more than six weeks, and had to provide special institutions or foster homes for them. The Commission had attacked workhouse nurseries as overcrowded, insanitary, and often managed by unsuitable female inmates. The Board pressed for improvements, and in 1913 required the medical officer to examine all infants under 18 months at least once a fortnight. No inmate was to be employed in the sick wards, lunatic wards, or nurseries, without supervision by a paid officer. The order required, for the first time, full documentation of all inmates: in 1911 the guardians were required to start the case paper system for the outdoor poor, and in 1913, proper medical records for the sick, insane, and infants. Although in larger infirmaries this was already being done, many overworked medical officers had neglected it.

The order also allowed guardians more discretion in some areas. They could make their own regulations for searching and classifying inmates, prohibiting certain articles, mealtimes, times of work, rising and sleep, though the Board retained the power of veto. The guardians could relax dietary regulations and pay for a Christmas dinner without asking the Board's permission. All workhouse infirmaries were to have a trained nurse. A House Committee was to replace the old visiting committee, with discretion to spend small sums of money and make alterations without involving the whole board of guardians. The order of 1913 at last abandoned the detailed central regulations which had been so important to Chadwick and his colleagues.

The Local Government Board hoped to improve the care of the sick and the children; in most other matters it finally relinquished the fiction of a unified workhouse system and ratified what was already the case—the diverse habits of the unions. The new regulations might be seen as a final attack on Chadwick's notions of 'discipline'. Seen from another perspective, however, the regulations did little to disturb the monotony of institutional life. By this stage the habits of large institutions were well established, and it would take more than central regulations to alter their everyday patterns. The workhouse staff, rather than the Board, or even the guardians, decided the character of workhouse life. Both conservatives and reformers were committed to the principle of residential institutions, but neither gave much thought to staffing policies, which were crucial to institutional reform.

In 1913 there was also a change in terminology. There were to be no more workhouses: instead there were Poor Law Institutions, with inmates in their wards and patients in their infirmaries, though the term 'pauper' was not officially discouraged until 1931. By such euphemisms Burns and his officials hoped to save the Poor Law: in their private correspondence they continued to use the old words. But the new names reflected a measure of change; workhouses were no longer intended only to deter the able-bodied paupers, but to provide a refuge for the helpless and fulfill a positive social purpose.

4

The Twentieth-Century Workhouse

When the Local Government Board replaced 'workhouses' with 'institutions', they intended to lessen the stigma of indoor relief. Some guardians, anticipating this, were calling their institutions by innocuous or even uplifting titles like 'Hope Hospital' at Salford. Guardians renamed specialized buildings more willingly than the general workhouses, but another view had been heard at the 1904 Poor Law conference:

> ... the time had come when the name 'workhouse' should be done away with and the term 'state home' or 'state infirmary' substituted. The term workhouse was a misnomer. Those institutions were no longer workhouses, and no longer a refuge, or should not be if properly conducted, for able-bodied men and women. They were more and more becoming the home of the aged and deserving poor, and as such should be made as comfortable and be as efficiently conducted as any hospital in the land.[1]

The authorities tried to spare the feelings of the poor in other small ways. In 1904 the Registrar General instructed registrars of births and deaths to safeguard the interests of children born in workhouses by disguising this fact in the birth register. Children could not help being born in workhouses, but adults should make an effort to avoid dying in them; hence the same regulations were not applied to death certificates until 1919. At that date the registrar no longer wrote the letter W in the margin of the entry, and he substituted a fictitious name or non-committal street number for the workhouse address.[2] In the same years a pamphlet popular among guardians affirmed that 'the word "pauper" is out of date; "workhouses" are now "Belle Vue" or "Mount Pleasant": and a distinctive garb is no longer the rule for the inmates.'[3]

The trend for more specialized institutions under the Poor Law continued until 1914. The larger the population of the union, the more likely it was that the guardians would control several residential institutions—a separate infirmary, a children's home, imbecile blocks, or separate cottages for aged paupers. A few unions had able-bodied test workhouses; Manchester pioneered a colony for epileptics, and the unions in the Liverpool district ran a tuberculosis sanatorium. Outside London and the large towns, however, workhouse inmates usually lived in unspecialized buildings, and the workhouse was still the most common type of institution. This may be clearly seen in the proportions of inmates distributed among the various types of institution in the years 1915 and 1929. On 1 January 1915 the Poor Law institutions had not yet been seriously affected by the war: on 1 January 1929 the Poor Law was about to be restructured once again.

Inmates (excluding casuals) in Poor Law institutions on 1 January[4]

	General institutions			Special institutions						
	sick wards		other wards		separate infirmaries		for the insane		for children		total
London	no.	%	no.	%	no.	%	no.	%	no.	%	no.
1915	2817	4.2	28781	42.9	16665	24.8	8073	12.0	10792	16.1	67128
1929	5724	11.8	12760	26.3	16520	34.0	6733	13.9	6778	14.0	48515
England and Wales											
1915	48580	20.0	121417	50.1	29503	12.2	9121	3.8	33687	13.9	242308
1929	61310	29.1	78397	37.3	33454	16.0	9357	4.4	27856	13.2	210374

In 1929, fewer inmates lived in general institutions, and those who remained were far more likely to be in the sick wards; but the proportional decline was greater in London (9 per cent) than in the country as a whole (3.7 per cent). There were also fewer inmates in Poor Law institutions in 1929, partly because other authorities were offering alternative provision, but also because the guardians themselves were more willing to commit certain insane and handicapped inmates to non-Poor Law institutions and pay the cost of their maintenance. In 1915 there were twice as many inmates in Poor Law institutions as a in other homes for paupers: in 1929 their numbers were almost equal. Yet in spite of all pressures towards specialized treatment, in the last year of the system more than 60 per cent of Poor Law inmates were still housed in the sick wards and general wards of unspecialized institutions.[5]

The traditional confusion of Poor Law functions continued, as the cover of most editions of the *Poor Law Officers' Journal* illustrated.

On 25 March 1910 it advertised Elastene hygienic bedding ('the best for large institutions'), steam disinfectors for verminous clothing, dough-kneading machines for workhouse bakeries, cleaning powders, floor polish, loose-leaf ledgers, Dunlop rubber sheets and protective uniforms ('as supplied to hospitals, infirmaries, asylums, all over the United Kingdom'), places in a privately-run tuberculosis sanatorium, insect poison, and blocks of granite for breaking. The *Journal* also carried advertisements for officers' uniforms and cheap clothing for inmates. Institutions provided a splendid market for manufacturers, but few can have had such varied consumer demands as the workhouses.

The trend towards specialization might have proceeded much further had it not been for the war and subsequent depression. Policy towards the unemployed and outdoor poor had become politically contentious, but institutions aroused less controversy. Indeed, they united factions who could agree on little else. Specialized institutions appealed to humanitarians who felt that the helpless would be 'better off' inside them; to eugenists who hoped incarceration would prevent the unfit from breeding; to the medical elite who were themselves becoming more specialized; and to a vague public sense of propriety which disliked mixing the deserving with the disreputable poor.[6] Guardians who established homes for the aged poor or built cottage homes for children received favourable publicity, even if local ratepayers grumbled.

In parts of the country where local government was still relatively uncomplicated, ratepayers were most likely to object to the more elaborate institutions. Hence there were fewer large institutions in Devon, Cornwall and Wales. Guardians argued that the ratepayers could not stand the cost, especially in areas of declining agriculture, but they also appealed to older fears. Since the days when Chadwick and Tufnell had projected barrack schools, critics had said that the poor would suffer if they were sent to distant institutions outside their own unions. In sparsely populated districts, relatives could not afford to make the long journeys to specialized institutions; hence the handicapped and the children would be 'better off' in unspecialized buildings close to home. Economic and social considerations blended in this argument, but administrators resisted it: the central authority favoured specialization, and the Inspectors invariably described unions with general-purpose buildings as 'backward'.

In the cities, public transport made specialization more acceptable, and the ratepayers, though not always relishing the expense, could regard the new institutions with some pride. In 1913 the principle of separation was strongly affirmed in the Mental Deficiency Act and the directive to remove children from workhouses. The Liberal government hoped that legislation on employment exchanges and unemployment insurance would remove the need for labour colonies, but although this notion lapsed, it did not die. The Local Government Board was swept into the current of specialization, though it still described the purposes of Poor Law institutions in a confusing way. The workhouse was now to be of positive benefit to its inmates, while still threatening the improvident. The dilemma appeared most clearly in the case of widows. Guardians usually offered outdoor relief to widows with families, although the central authority continued to argue that widows ought either to support themselves or to enter the house, thus encouraging provident habits amongst living husbands. The Minority Report contended that guardians gave inadequate doles to those women, sometimes as a supplement to low wages: consequently, if a woman worked she had to neglect her family, but if she tried to live on poor relief, the income would not maintain them adequately. In October 1914 the Board drew up a new code: it encouraged more generous outdoor relief to widows, but only to those of good habits who would bring up their families correctly. The workhouse should be used as a threat to 'weaker' women who would have to keep their houses clean and spend the relief thriftily. If a widow proved incorrigibly dirty, drunken or feckless, the family should be removed to the workhouse, where they would be 'better off' materially, and the children saved from their mother's weakness.[7] The workhouse was simultaneously a threat and a place of safety.

Chadwick's tentative ideas of more specialized institutions were thwarted because no authority except the guardians could initiate them. Problems of cost-sharing, location and expense proved too great for guardians to combine to build them, except for the few district schools. By 1914, however, an alternative authority was providing specialized services. The Local Government Act of 1894 established county and borough councils which the 1905 Commission unanimously saw as the natural successors to the guardians. The county councils were larger administrative units than the Poor Law unions, and the Commission expected that larger districts would allow the employment of trained staff and economies of scale of specialized buildings. The councils were also assuming some of the guardians' former duties in registration of births and deaths, sanitation, and hospital provision: they could build hospitals, asylums, and institutions for the handicapped, all of which would encroach on the workhouse population.

The Great War abruptly ended all these developments, for although the impulse to specialize remained strong, economic forces were stronger. Since the 1860s the Poor Law had rarely aroused national controversy: change came less from legislation than from private negotiations between central authority and guardians. The rigid discipline of 1834 gradually relaxed as the country prospered, but after 1914 everything changed, and national problems once again affected the Poor Law. The outbreak of war immediately checked all expenditure on non-essential services, and so halted the building of specialized institutions, either by the unions or the counties. Amongst the first casualties were the new institutions envisaged by the Mental Deficiency Act. The number of paupers, both indoor and outdoor, began to fall. The Liberal welfare reforms had helped to reduce pauperism after 1910, and this decline continued steadily until 1920, with a particularly sharp fall between 1915 and 1917. Between January 1910 and January 1917, outdoor pauperism fell by 40 per cent, indoor pauperism by 25 per cent.[8] Vagrancy almost disappeared as the 'marginal man' found employment—perhaps in the army, more likely in the unskilled jobs which had been vacated by fitter men. Older men still capable of work returned to the labour force, and able-bodied test workhouses and many casual wards closed. Female pauperism also declined: widows and unmarried mothers could find employment in munitions factories or in domestic service where employers could no longer afford to be discriminating. Wars had formerly created pauperism amongst deserted wives and widows of soldiers, but in 1915 public feeling was strongly against these women becoming paupers, and so they were assisted by a separate National Relief Fund.[9]

Yet indoor pauperism did not decline simply because people who were unnecessarily incarcerated took the opportunity to escape. Some did so, no doubt, but in January 1915, before the main exodus began, the Local Government Board estimated that only 11.2 per cent of indoor paupers fell into the 'marginal' category, and this included 'those, who while not suffering from any specific bodily or mental complaint, are weak or feeble from premature senility or . . . are in a greater or less degree inefficient.'[10] Even assuming that all these could now leave the institutions and take their children with them, it would hardly have accounted for the decrease: rather, the guardians were now denying admission to people who would previously have become inmates of institutions.

The infirmaries lost patients because beds had to be distributed between civilians and military casualties. The War Office could requisition Poor Law property and staff, without paying rent to the guardians. By December 1916 the military had taken over 52,000 Poor Law places, 13,000 of them in London.[11] They naturally demanded the better equipped infirmaries, and those close to railways. Apart from wounded and convalescent troops, the Poor Law institutions were also used as barracks for munitions workers, temporary camps for aliens, and hostels for Belgian refugees. These changes affected over 200 unions. The war severely strained the country's hospital resources, and the military took priority. Civilians suffering from long-term illnesses, particularly tuberculosis, could not all have hospital places, even in unspecialized Poor Law infirmaries. This may well explain the paradox that mortality amongst children and adults of working age fell during the war, while that of the elderly rose.[12] Full employment and rising wages may have made the workforce and its children healthier, but did not affect the old, whose incomes were less flexible, and who received less institutional aid and hospital care. Between 1914 and 1916 deaths from tuberculosis rose by 6 per cent, at a time when the mortality rate from non-contagious diseases was falling. As the Poor Law had provided for most of these cases, the diminished service possibly accounted for the increase. People who should have been in hospital were sent home, to the danger of their families.[13]

The remaining indoor poor made involuntary contributions to the war effort. A few old people regained self-respect by becoming paid hospital orderlies—the same work that they had done as workhouse inmates. Many more were shifted to other unions to make way for the casualties; the Local Government Board claimed that they made this sacrifice gladly, but an Inspector commented:

> It was one of the minor tragedies of the war that so many of the sick, old and dying poor had to be provided for not in the institution where they had, as it were, a vested interest, but in some unfamiliar institution many miles away from all their friends.[14]

Inmates suffered from government directives on food economies, which the wealthy could ignore; and the Webbs believed that in some institutions nutrition had been dangerously reduced.[15] Workhouse gardens were turned over to potatoes, and every effort made to economize.

In spite of fewer inmates and greater frugality, the cost of institutions continued to rise. Rising costs before the war, at a time of relatively stable prices, had reflected improved services; but during the war, inflation increased costs while services were cut. Food and officers' salaries took a larger share of the budget. Outdoor relief cost £750,000 less in 1917 than in 1910, but the maintenance of inmates and officers' salaries had increased by nearly £1.5 million in the same period.[16] Institutions had to be maintained, even with fewer inmates, and so the cost per head rose. In Cheshire and the Potteries an inmate's maintenance had cost 8/6 per week in 1914: in 1920 it cost £1/4/9, though the Inspector noted that conditions were worse and the movement towards specialized services had halted.[17] He added, however, that the emergency had encouraged guardians to pool their resources, which was a hopeful pointer towards future rationalization. The cost of buildings and capital loans remained steady between 1913 and 1915, in spite of inflation, and was actually falling between 1915 and 1918, reversing the steady upward trend of the pre-war period. Apart from a few infirmaries which benefited from military investment, the building and maintenance of institutions slumped.

The First World War notoriously generated an enthusiasm for social reform which was largely unrealized after 1918. Reformers took advantage of the apparent growth of government interest in their ideas: and the two factions of the 1905 Poor Law Commission were able to sink many of their differences at this time.[18] Both were represented on the Maclean Committee for reconstruction, which reported in January 1918: the report included recommendations for specialized institutions. But the new Ministry of Health appeared at a time when the sense of national emergency had waned, and it lacked any strong commitment to a particular policy. The Maclean committee had urged that the Ministry have no connection with the Poor Law, but many guardians objected to relinquishing their traditional powers. The Ministry therefore absorbed the old Poor Law administration intact. Although several of the older officials who had postponed retirement during the war now left, the civil servants in charge of the Poor Law department resisted pressure for reform. In the 1920s the older and the younger Inspectors sometimes disagreed, especially (as will be seen) over vagrancy, but generally advocated the deterrent Poor Law. Their views were reinforced by the social unrest which followed the war. The man who replaced Sir James Davy as Chief Inspector in 1913, Sir Arthur Lowry, was a typical Poor Law administrator, who had served the department for over 20 years.

The guardians themselves resented the Maclean proposals that they relinquish their duties to the county councils, for (the guardians contended) a small authority had more personal knowledge of the poor as well as more tenderness towards the ratepayers' pockets. As the depression worsened in 1921, it was even argued that the guardians were saving Britain from revolution through their close contact with local opinion.[19] Paradoxically, the guardians could also be seen as tools of an undisciplined local government democracy, and there was some danger of the Poor Law becoming a test of ideology. It was not the apathetic guardians castigated by the Webbs who obstructed reform, but those who took much pride in their work, especially the urban unions with a heavy investment in infirmaries and specialized institutions. When Dr Addison, the Minister of Health, proposed to hand over the Poor Law infirmaries to the county councils, Poor Law conferences protested loudly. Guardians were proud of the modern hospitals, children's homes, and other institutions which had been built in more expansive days. They resented the slur on their efficiency, and did not wish buildings which had been paid for with local money to be used for wider purposes and unknown patients. Conversely, some of the sleepier rural unions did not object to reform, for guardians had been able to close small workhouses during the war and send the inmates to other unions. In parts of Berkshire and Buckinghamshire it was difficult to find successors to retiring guardians. These rural unions believed themselves under sentence of death, and made few efforts to improve their services after the war.[20] But the impetus for Poor Law reform was allowed to lapse, and the guardians resisted it until they were faced with overwhelming social problems.

Yet the war had more positive effects on the Poor Law, for afterwards no government could commit able-bodied people (except vagrants) to workhouses. This had of course been the logic of pre-war legislation as well, but national insurance was based on actuarial principles: consequently, a man whose insurance ran out would have to rely on poor relief. As unemployment increased after the war, national insurance proved inadequate, but governments knew they could not revive the deterrent workhouse: instead, a vastly complicated system of doles emerged.[21] Even these did not relieve pressure on the Poor Law, for many workers still had no form of insurance, and sickness amongst uninsured members of a family could bring even the insured before the board of guardians. Outdoor relief rates soared, affecting over a million people by July 1921. Even guardians who before 1914 had operated strict policies on outdoor relief knew that the workhouse could not be used against mass unemployment: nor could one send to the workhouse the heroes who had won the war. The numbers of indoor poor began to rise again in 1920, but only slightly compared with outdoor relief.

The war also provoked government intervention in the treatment of certain diseases which had burdened the Poor Law infirmaries, namely tuberculosis and venereal disease. Lloyd George had attempted to encourage treatment of tuberculosis before the war by making treatment free to people insured under the national insurance scheme, and giving counties financial incentives to build sanatoria. The war disrupted these plans, and guardians continued to bear the responsibility. Although the cause of tuberculosis was understood, no remedy existed, but early notification and treatment could prevent the spread of infection. Pulmonary tuberculosis increased during the war, and the Ministry of Health accordingly acted more rapidly on this than on many other problems: under the Public Health (Tuberculosis) Act of 1921 treatment became free, and counties took sole charge of dispensaries and sanatoria. Yet although more sanatoria were built during the 1920s than any other kind of hospital, they were never able to accommodate all cases, and the Poor Law infirmaries continued to take many patients.[22]

A direct concern for the health of troops and workers affected the government's attitude towards venereal disease. Because of its 'moral' character, this illness had always been left to residual authorities like the Poor Law and a few charity hospitals, but punitive conditions in the foul wards did not encourage sufferers to seek treatment. The Venereal Diseases Act of 1917 provided for patients to be treated free and secretly by local authority clinics, while Poor Law medical officers could use public laboratories for diagnosis, and were issued with supplies of salvarsan. The Local Government Board's last report urged guardians to make the foul wards 'suitable and cheerful', though with continuing economies in institutions, the guardians probably did not respond enthusiastically.[23]

The war therefore helped to remove the unemployed and certain types of patient from the workhouse, but had much less effect on the largest groups of inmates—the old, the mentally defective, and the helpless. On 1st January 1920, nearly 30 per cent of all indoor paupers were over 70 years old.[24] During the war they had been forgotten, a non-essential part of the population. Guardians had given up trying to classify them according to their moral character, and staff shortages and worse food in deteriorating buildings affected the helpless most severely. The Maclean committee, which concentrated mainly on the workforce, had little interest in them, nor was there a national policy, except for the vague notion of 1834 that the old should be allowed their indulgences. Geriatric medicine was not a medical specialism of the time, and the level of indulgence still depended on local guardians: in times of severe financial restraint the aged had no high priority.

For the mentally defective, some policy had been formulated under the Mental Deficiency Act, which allowed greater powers of incarceration; but the war ended hopes that these inmates would be separately housed. Guardians could ask the counties to accept certain patients into county asylums, but the Board of Control which supervised the workings of the Act could also approve certain Poor Law institutions to house the mentally defective, usually in 'imbecile blocks' more or less separate from the workhouse. In practice the second expedient was widely used. The Board sanctioned many workhouses for the care of defectives as an emergency measure during the war, even though these buildings were not up to the standard which the Act required. The certificates remained effective throughout the 1920s, defeating the whole purpose of the Act.[25]

Every year more mentally handicapped people required institutional care. This had been noticeable in the late nineteenth century, when the eugenics movement used the statistics as evidence of the 'degeneration' of the British people because of prolific breeding by the feeble-minded. In fact the increase was probably caused by changing definitions of mental disease, combined with growing faith in institutional treatment. The Royal Commission on the Feeble Minded obviously envisaged a much higher rate of incarceration. Handicapped people who might have been unnoticed in the community a few generations earlier, and who might even have been workers in a less complex society, were now seen as needing continuous treatment.[26] By 1927 the Board of Control argued that it expected an annual increase of some 3,000 patients, and that institutional provision could not keep up.[27] The lunacy statistics may also have been affected by the ex-servicemen who returned mentally damaged by their war experiences. In May 1924 the Ministry of Health estimated that the mental hospitals contained 5180 ex-servicemen: others may well have been placed in workhouses, which contained 13,691 ex-servicemen on the same day. Other injured men may have joined the vagrant unemployed on casual relief.[28] The figures did not distinguish First World War veterans from those of the Boer War, but the workhouse was, as ever, the crippled soldier's last resort.

During the 1920s the responsible authorities continually bickered over who should provide the extra accommodation for mental patients. Since there were fewer Poor Law inmates than before the war, the county authorities argued that vacant places should be occupied by the insane, while the Poor Law authorities replied that the facilities were not suitable. In 1925 Sir Frederick Willis, chairman of the Board of Control, convened a conference of the various local authorities. The managers of some county asylums objected to their institutions being clogged by large numbers of congenital defectives, who diverted staff attention from the curable insane. Several psychiatric doctors, however, doubted whether the handicapped could be adequately treated in Poor Law institutions. The medical superintendent of the Wakefield mental hospital said:

> If we could only receive patients at the earlier stage from the workhouses, if we could have patients to treat... with one member of the staff to seven or eight patients, and in the acute wards to two or three, instead of having those same cases treated in workhouses, where there are something like 31 patients to one attendant, I think we should... enable the senile cases to be better treated... and the cases who are curable to be treated and to be cured much more readily.[29]

In December 1924 the Ministry urged guardians to bring their accommodation for mental patients up to the highest standards, and to press other authorities to put the Mental Deficiency Act into full operation: but seven months later the Ministry yielded to requests from the Board of Control, and asked guardians to house more patients in the workhouses, the cost of maintenance to be paid by the counties.[30] H.W.S. Francis, the assistant secretary who negotiated with the Board on the Ministry's behalf, did not like senile and chronic cases to receive expensive asylum treatment, even though he confessed that he had never visited an asylum, and (later) that 'he had no real evidence to go on'.[31] Francis believed that workhouses were quite suitable for defectives, and the Inspectors went to look for vacant places: they did not find many, and several objected to putting mental patients back into old and badly equipped workhouses.[32] A few Inspectors still argued that the patients would do well in general mixed institutions, where they could do the housework, given the shortage of able-bodied inmates.[33] By 1928 the Board of Control was trying to persuade the counties to build new hospitals for specialized treatment, for the economic problems were easing. From the Board, Mrs Pinsent argued:

The main object of the Poor Law Institution is to provide shelter and help for those temporarily in trouble, and for those whose active life is over. It is also difficult, and sometimes impossible, to adapt buildings which have been provided with these ends in view to the needs of young and vigorous defectives who require a full and varied home life in cheerful surroundings...[34]

In times of recession, institutional provision could not keep up with changing medical practices, as the case of epileptics shows. Before the war doctors often classified epileptics with the insane, but in the 1920s the medical profession became more hopeful of curing them, or at least of training them to do useful work under supervision. As usual, this required specialized treatment and extra expense; but the system of residential institutions was not flexible enough to respond quickly, and so many of the mentally handicapped still became paupers.

A similar setback occurred in the treatment of Poor Law children. For this group, unlike most others, the central authority had long advocated separate housing, but even the order of 1913 remained unfulfilled. Guardians were supposed to remove all children from the workhouses by 1915, but the war forced the Local Government Board to rescind its resolution. After the war the Ministry of Health ordered guardians to remove the children, but many rural guardians objected to the cost, while boards who had intended to build separate homes ran into difficulties because of chaos in the building industry. The Ministry was reluctant to enforce the rules; and official reports on the subject were disingenuous. In the 1920s the Ministry claimed annually that over 90 per cent of all Poor Law children in institutions were in special accommodation but in this category it included the children's wards of general institutions. Indeed, some of the 'special' institutions were homes within the workhouse grounds, as in Bromley, where only a wire fence separated children from inmates. Sick children and the children of 'ins and outs' continued to be housed in the general buildings.

It was the administrators, formally committed to the principle of separation, who saw this as a 'failure'. The workhouse children usually had parents who were inmates; and there is no reason to suppose that the poor relished separation in 1920 more than they had in 1834. Rules which sent children to a special institution, possibly several miles from the workhouse, where parents were rarely allowed to visit, were not always agreeable to the poor. The Ministry encouraged fostering by allowing guardians to pay higher sums to foster-parents, but children of inmates still went into institutions. To the public, children in institutions were 'workhouse children', however separate the institution might be, and specialization did not destroy the social isolation of the child.

The able-bodied and the unemployed

Even before the war, few able-bodied people stayed in workhouses, even though the 1905 Commission believed that the shiftless unemployed tended to 'pile up' in the less disciplined institutions. Medical evidence which the Commission itself had collected suggested that only a small proportion of the able-bodied inmates were fit for employment; not necessarily because they were ill (though many had minor handicaps), but because of unavoidable problems like advancing age, lack of height, or deafness.[35] Amongst a sample of able-bodied inmates, a quarter were over 55 years old—an age when they had little hope of finding work as unskilled or casual labourers. Other 'able-bodied' men had hernias or were mentally defective. In 1911 the central authority gave up the futile attempt to classify the able-bodied which had bedevilled Poor Law policy throughout the nineteenth century. On 1 January 1929, 21 per cent of all adults in Poor Law institutions were classified as not suffering from sickness, infirmity, or mental problems, but as usual their age group was not recorded.[36] All contemporary comment suggests that able-bodied people of working age were rarely found in workhouses.

The one exception to this was the unmarried mother, although if she had entered the workhouse only to be confined, she was probably classified as 'sick'. She still suffered from a social stigma so powerful that the offer of outdoor relief could seem an invitation to immorality. Even deserted wives were under suspicion, at least in the first year of desertion: as in 1834 the central authority believed that outdoor relief would encourage collusion between husband and wife to defraud the ratepayers. Treatment of the various classes of unsupported women with children reflected traditional attitudes, as shown in these returns of 1 January 1920.[37]

	on outdoor relief	on indoor relief	% indoors
Widows with children	35,061	892	2.5
Deserted wives	2,356	470	16.6
Other separated wives	1,306	451	25.6
Unmarried mothers	731	2,783	79.2

Although in the 1920s more agencies existed to help unmarried mothers, and guardians sometimes tried to find work for them, the workhouse remained the usual resort of unmarried women of the poorer classes during their confinements. Deserted, divorced and unmarried mothers were a neglected minority group whom even Beveridge felt unable to bring under the umbrella of his national insurance plan in 1942.[38]

Throughout the 1920s, institutional relief was provided by an un-coordinated mass of local authorities and charities, in an unplanned network of specialized and unspecialized buildings. The question of financial support was very confused. The guardians might have to pay the counties to maintain certain handicapped paupers in county institutions; conversely, the counties might be paying the guardians to keep mental defectives in Poor Law buildings. The guardians subsidized private charities which provided homes for unmarried mothers or handicapped children, while other charities paid for extra comforts and entertainments for workhouse inmates. The government paid directly out of national taxes to enable the counties to support clinics and sanatoria for venereal and tubercular patients, while other forms of chronic illness were supported by the poor rates. Fathers of illegitimate children were supposed to pay for their maintenance in the workhouses, as were the families of mentally defective people housed in county or Poor Law institutions. The chances of a distressed persons becoming a pauper were partly a matter of luck—whether he caught tuberculosis or rheumatic fever; whether he lived in a county which provided adequate hospital and asylum care, or whether the county council relied on Poor Law institutions to make up the shortfall; whether private charity was active in his district or not. It perhaps would not have mattered so much if public opinion had not still regarded paupers as inferior to the inmates of other types of institution.

If Chadwick had been able to see the workhouses of the 1920s, he might have thought they had lost much of their deterrent function; yet at this time the central authority made its last attempt to revive the workhouse test. Two factors dominated the last years of the Poor Law: one was mass unemployment, the other the appointment of Neville Chamberlain as Minister of Health in March 1923, and from 1924 to 1929. Mass unemployment, concentrated in the regions of heavy industry, toppled the rickety structure of unemployment insurance and threw ever-increasing numbers of people on to the Poor Law. Outdoor relief had to be given, but the afflicted unions could not

cope administratively or financially. Theoretically the relieving officers should have reported on each case and offered the workhouse or the labour yards as a test of destitution, but this was patently unworkable. Political controversy became more bitter. 'Poplarism' appeared once more, and this time the Poplar borough council refused to pay the contribution to the Common Poor Fund and in 1921 marched to gaol, well-publicized martyrs to their cause. Certain other unions, most notoriously Chester-le-Street and Bedwellty, espoused Poplarism and gave liberal outdoor relief to the unemployed. Previously when unions had borrowed money it had been to finance capital expenditure on institutions; now they raised loans to pay for outdoor relief, with the expectation that the government would have to help if the rates proved unequal to the burden.

Neville Chamberlain entered this arena with that fastidious attention to detail for which he should have become famous, had later events not clouded his reputation. In the 1920s he concentrated on the work which suited him best, seeing Poor Law reform not as a matter of moral principle, but as a complicated readjustment of local government finance and organization. In November 1924 he took the unprecedented step of refusing the Exchequer in order to return to the Ministry of Health. B.B. Gilbert argues that Chamberlain desired reform not as a solution to social problems, but to improve 'functional efficiency'. To Chamberlain, the guardians were an 'administrative excrescence', who, when pressed by an unemployed electorate, would simply offer unrestricted outdoor relief.[39] Nor, according to this argument, was Chamberlain moved by fear of Labour-controlled local government, for heavy debts had been incurred not only by Labour guardians but Conservative ones like Liverpool and Sheffield. Chamberlain saw the unions as Chadwick had seen the parishes: impracticably small and wasteful units with too much power to flout the wishes of central authority. One of his first acts in 1925 was to end the old powers of overseers to collect rates, and replace them with a more unified system of rating authorities.

Gilbert's arguments, though largely just, underrate the political aspect of the reforms of the 1920s, and particularly the role of the permanent officials. Chamberlain's dislike of guardians was indeed not purely political, and the Poor Law itself caused surprisingly little debate during the Labour government of 1924. Chamberlain's diary comments on the waste and muddle in union management, as in this account of a visit to Crediton:

> ... to Crediton Workhouse where received by [the Chairman of the guardians] an old dodderer. At his suggestion attended a meeting of Bd of whom there appeared to be over 40 present. Only four cases were brought up for consid[eratio]n; Of these only one required any decision of the Board... It was a farcical proceeding ... Went round the 'house' only abt 50 inmates though it could accommodate 150. Came back & Chmn made or rather read a speech abt abolition of Gdns all made up of Poor Law Journal stuff.[40]

Yet many interpreted Chamberlain's motives politically. For nearly a century the central authority had complained of guardians who used Poor Law powers in local party interests; and hence the central authority prided itself on its political neutrality. But to Lansbury and his followers the whole Poor Law was a class, and therefore a political, structure. In the past, they argued, the law suited the interests of the rich; when it was used in the interests of the poor, the central authority would condemn this as 'political' and intervene.[41] The civil servants in the Ministry of Health became alarmed that large numbers of unemployed might exert pressure on guardians of their own class, for from 1918 those on outdoor relief were able to vote in guardians' elections.[42] In 1921 the Poplar guardians appeared to triumph; the government passed the Local Authorities (Financial Provisions) bill, which obliged the Metropolitan Common Poor Fund to subsidize outdoor as well as indoor relief. Guardians were also allowed to borrow large sums from the government in order to meet current expenses. Sir Alfred Mond, then Minister of Health, tried to obtain power to suspend defaulting guardians, but in the politically uncertain atmosphere of 1921 the government dared not permit this. Chamberlain, whose party had a large majority in 1924, had fewer difficulties, and in 1926 the General Strike offered him a weapon against Labour guardians.

The strike itself lasted just over a week, hardly time for the Ministry to devise policy, but the miners refused to return to work for the another six months, and this long battle much exercised the Ministry, for guardians were overwhelmed with applications for outdoor relief for strikers' families. Guardians could not legally relieve strikers, but could relieve their families; single men on strike could receive no relief, but medical definitions might be adjusted to classify them as 'non able-bodied' and thus entitle them to relief. In Durham and South

Wales guardians faced riotous demonstrations, sometimes, it was alleged, even provoking them in order to intimidate the relieving and medical officers. A direct attack against outdoor relief for the unemployed would have been difficult; an attack on strikers was not. Chamberlain was able to pass a series of acts which reduced guardians' powers and paved the way for local government reorganization. Two months after the General Strike the Board of Guardians (Default) Act became law, allowing the Minister to assume control from guardians who were unable to discharge their duties, especially those with heavy debts.

The first union affected by the Act was West Ham, which, because technically outside the Metropolis, did not benefit from the redistribution of London income under the Common Poor Fund, and which was close to bankruptcy because of its liberal outdoor relief. A few weeks after the West Ham guardians were replaced by the Ministry's nominees, the mining union of Chester-le-Street met the same fate, and Bedwellty the following year. All these unions were Labour-controlled with high scales of outdoor relief. If Chamberlain did not attack them in openly political terms, it was nevertheless the relief policies rather than indebtedness which provoked Ministerial interference. Sheffield, under Conservative control, would have been bankrupt without government loans, for in August 1926 the outdoor relief bill stood at £10,000 per week. Sheffield's problems were also partly owing to strikes, but since the guardians relieved strikers' families only with loans, kept relief rates to a minimum, and refused relief to single men and families where there was no legal marriage, it retained the Ministry's favour.[43] Chamberlain had no doubt that strikers did well out of the poor rates, and wrote:

> they are not within sight of starvation, hardly of under-nutrition, so well are they looked after by the guardians... they are living not too uncomfortably at the expense of the ratepayers, while the nation is gradually overcome by creeping paralysis.[44]

The General Strike provoked the last attempt to reassert the workhouses as deterrent institutions. The Inspectors also argued that if guardians offered the unemployed the workhouse as a condition of relieving their families outside it, the cost of outdoor relief would be dramatically reduced.[45] The Ministry's power over government loans, originally a concession to Poplarism, could now be used against defaulting unions, for the Ministry could refuse loans, leaving ratepayers to carry the burden until the guardians followed central directives on relief policy. By tough measures, bankrupt unions could be made solvent—but at what social cost?

Like Chadwick, the Ministry sought administrative solutions to structural problems; its report for 1926 attributed the increase of out-relief in Durham entirely to lax outdoor relief policies, ignoring the slum in the mining industry and the disastrous effects of the return to the Gold Standard. Of the General Strike itself, the Ministry noted:

> ... it is a question whether a proper use of the workhouse test would not have been effective in restraining a certain amount of fraud and concealment of resources which undoubtedly took place, and all of which the overworked relief staffs of the Guardians ... could not be expected to detect.[46]

One Inspector approved guardians' policy in Westbury-on-Severn, where strikers' families received orders for the workhouse. The miners' union decided to swamp the workhouse by bringing in busloads of families, but the guardians took in all 868 women and 203 children, most of whom left the next day, and no further relief was demanded.[47] At Cannock:

> A demonstration of 500 which marched to the Institution to demand admission, found the Guardians quite prepared. About 200 elected to go before the Relieving Officers and 172 Orders of Admission were issued, of which 168 were 'honoured'. Within a fortnight all had taken their discharge.[48]

The miners, of course, did not see this as adherence to Poor Law principles, but as a direct attempt to break the strike. A private memorandum in the Ministry commented:

> Probably the segregation of strikers in an institution in large numbers would require police attention at the outset, but arrangements could be made for their distribution in various institutions, and experience suggests that the influx would be either small or of brief duration.[49]

Conservative objections to the extinction of Poor Law unions were diminished by the publicity which renegade guardians attracted. Poplarism was a political movement, associated entirely with the patriarchal figure of George Lansbury, who, more than the leaders of his party, represented the conscience of Labour. Conservative guardians in Sheffield and West Derby might operate deficit financing, but they cut outdoor relief to the bone: when they continued to run into debt, it only showed that the basic problem was economic, not administrative. If Labour guardians had operated the Poor Law according to traditional principles, no doubt the argument for reform would have been lessened, but it was chiefly the Labour guardians (though not all of them) who refused to obey the Ministry's directives. These political problems drove the permanent officials of the Ministry into Chamberlain's hands. Before the war officials had supported the guardians' objections to county control of the Poor Law: in the 1920s they could see no alternative. In November 1925 Francis wrote that the Poor Law was about to be overwhelmed by forces comparable to those during the Napoleonic wars, and that the paupers would take over.[50] The events of 1926 seemed to confirm these fears. The answer was the same as in 1834—to replace the local administration by a larger and more disinterested authority.

The Ministry's internal memoranda described Poplarism as 'a series of offensives directed by a certain political clique against various of the more vulnerable points of the system of local government', and 'the would-be wreckers of the poor law system'. The unions which had given generous relief in the early weeks of the coal strike were 'generally the centres of extreme communist opinion'.[51] The officials were proud of their 'neutrality' during strikes; they pointed out that they had prevented Conservative guardians from refusing all relief to the families of strikers. Yet by the end of the coal strike, about two dozen unions had stopped all relief to strikers' families, by using such devices (recommended by the Ministry) as assessing all family income, including the children's free school meals, and deducting it from relief. In Lewisham, Conservative guardians devised two relief scales and gave the higher to unemployed men who were prepared to do strike-breaking work.[52]

Strikes revealed political and class tensions, but so did the longer battle against Poplarism. The real conflict between the Ministry and the Poplarists was not administrative: they were making different assumptions about a national minimum standard of living. Lansbury and the Poplar guardians argued that the usual rates of outdoor relief were not enough to maintain an unemployed family in health—a point also made by the Webbs. Hence the Poplar scales were based on the guardians' assessment of family need rather than a maximum related to the level of wages or insurance benefits. To the Ministry, 'less eligibility' was still crucial: unemployment should not seem more attractive than work, even for those heads of large families whose wages could never sustain them. But the Ministry's point could only retain moral credibility if harsh outdoor relief policies did not seem to produce physical suffering. This argument the Ministry made again and again:[53] the women and children who left Westbury-on-Severn workhouse after their futile attempt to browbeat the guardians did not 'suffer' as a result; there was no malnutrition in the depressed areas; families of strikers were not unhealthy. It was the argument of 1834: the able-bodied would not suffer if refused outdoor relief, but flourish in new-found independence.

The best that can be said of Chamberlain's Ministry in 1926 was that its views on the health of the unemployed and strikers were based on inadequate information. The medical department did not find epidemic disease amongst strikers, tuberculosis did not increase in the deprived areas, and infant mortality did not rise. The Ministry frequently emphasized that strikers' children received free school meals. In 1928 one of the medical Inspectors, who had been working in South Wales, disrupted this comfortable notion. The people most at risk in the depressed areas, he said, were pre-school children and the mothers, especially nursing mothers, who stinted themselves of food to feed their families. Rickets was increasing in Wales, and Dr Pearse commented:

> The usual diet is markedly lacking in protein, mineral salts and vitamin content. This may perhaps contain a sufficiency of calories, but according to all Canons of diet it is unsuitable for the maintenance of health over any prolonged period and especially for young children and nursing mothers.[54]

Reports of malnutrition embarrased the Ministry, and there is evidence from both the 1920s and the 1930s that such reports were suppressed.[55] Independent surveys, including Rowntree's second study of York in 1936, brought it once more to light. This was not, of course, a new problem. The Poor Law, intended for the bare relief of destitution, had never offered adequate nutrition to outdoor paupers; the new embarrassment in the 1920s was that better medical knowledge of nutrition could be used to condemn both the dole and outdoor relief scales. Yet even this deplorable question showed how the grounds of argument had changed. Social policy had to concern itself with the question of a 'national minimum' of relief, and controversy would focus on what that level should be. The workhouse test, in spite of isolated incidents like those at Cannock or Westbury, was dead.

Nevertheless, for some years the Inspectors demanded a return to strict deterrent principles. In 1928, C.F. Roundell, one of the hard-line Inspectors, reported on relief in London. He lamented the disappearance of the able-bodied test workhouses which had permitted London unions to commit their able-bodied paupers to separate institutions, but admitted that the labour yards formerly attached to workhouses were no longer practicable:

> The old corn mills are now regarded as museum pieces and stone-breaking is, I think, only done in one institution, i.e. Westminster... Discipline in the ordinary workhouse to-day... is not strict.[56]

Like the Webbs, Roundell believed that workhouses were attractive to a type of able-bodied parasite, though he regretfully acknowledged that 'compulsion and compulsory detention are not yet practical politics'. He suggested taking advantage of demands that the unemployed be rehabilitated by setting up an institution for them. 'In order to encourage the more sentimental guardians to send men to such an Institution I should propose to call it a Hostel and to stress the mental training and improvement of morals.' The proposed regime for rehabilitation sounded remarkably like the old test workhouse, with strict discipline, cleanliness, early rising and hard work, rigidly enforced. The 'higher class' of inmates might be given special privileges, and the idle, criminal and vicious should be identified for later incarceration in a labour colony.

The Ministry surveyed London institutions to see if they could be converted to test workhouses: the Fulham guardians agreed to reorganize the institution at Belmont, Surrey, and it was described as a training centre. The men were to be trained in farm work, gardening, engineering and other trades, and were divided into three grades with different standards of accommodation. The better grade of men were paid for their work and the refractory confined to a separate block under severe discipline.[57] The guardians argued that their institution was different from the training centres run by the Ministry of Labour, for, they said, Belmont men were demoralized by pauperism and needed sterner measures to rehabilitate them. This, however, was the last effort under the Poor Law to set up a special institution for able-bodied men, who in a few years became the responsibility of the Ministry of Labour.

By the mid-1920s Chamberlain and his officials had agreed to reorganize local government, but Chamberlain appears to have differed from his officials in that he made no effort to revive the workhouse test. He was pressed by his officials to reverse the Act of 1918 and disfranchise paupers in local government elections; it was calculated that in Poplar and other difficult unions, so many people were on relief that if they were denied the vote Labour would lose control.[58] Chamberlain seems to have at first favoured disenfranchisement, but swung back as other Conservatives feared the unpopularity of this course.[59] Outdoor paupers therefore retained the vote, though they were disqualified from election to local government until 1948. Neither was the Poor Law itself technically abolished until 1948, though Chamberlain's Local Government Act of 1929 began to dismantle the framework of 1834. Although the workhouse test was still legal, it was tacitly dropped. The Poor Law Act of 1930 stated that the workhouse test was not to be the exclusive form of relief to the able-bodied. 'Less eligibility' did not disappear, and during the 1930s governments tried to keep the level of the dole below the lowest independent wages, though as in previous times, large families were hardest hit.

In 1929 the guardians' powers were handed over to the public assistance committees of the county and borough councils. In fact many guardians kept their power over individual cases, for although they lost their powers to raise finance, the new committees were often guardians themselves writ small. Instead of being directly elected, they were nominated by the elected councillors, who naturally tended to select people who already had experience of administering public relief.[60] Inevitably, diverse policies in local relief continued, although this was against the Act's intention. As the Webbs had foreseen, the government had to plug the loopholes, and in 1934 the unemployed became a national rather than a local responsibility, under a new authority, the Unemployment Assistance Board. Only vagrants remained under the Poor Law section of council administration, while the unemployed finally ceased to be the concern of the Poor Law.

For the indoor poor, the 1929 Act should have given new impetus towards specialized institutions, which were now under county control. Against a background of economic dislocation, however, all the Act could do was to reshuffle existing resources rather than encourage innovation. It was possible that buildings could be reclassified to house separate categories of the helpless, but the Ministry did not expect rapid change.[61] The hospital service in particular needed costly reorganization: several boroughs immediately took over the local Poor Law infirmaries, but by early 1934 only one county outside London had converted a general institution into a public hospital.[62] In spite of Chamberlain's new financial incentive—the block grant—in rural areas the mixed institutions continued, a refuge for the old, the handicapped, unmarried mothers, and vagrants. As late as 1939 there were just under 100,000 people (including 5269 children) in general institutions, together with over 10,000 casual poor.[63] The workhouse was a living institution until the end of the Second World War, though its name was an anachronism. Chamberlain had laid the foundations of a more specialized system of residential institutions, but a corresponding social investment was not made until the more prosperous 1950s.

Throughout the life of the New Poor Law, two trends affected the lives of the indoor poor: more specialization and more expense. The report of 1834 had expected that specialization could be achieved by simply rearranging existing buildings, at little cost. Chamberlain's reforms, based on rather similar principles, did accept that some expenditure would be necessary, hence the principle of the block grant. But like the Webbs, Chamberlain believed that a larger unit of administration would also produce economies of scale through specialization. This belief always had been, and remained, entirely fallacious. Specialization was never economical, partly because social expectations of institutions continued to rise with the standard of living. However much the ratepayers grumbled about the cost of institutions, they did not wish to be accused of allowing their sick or elderly poor to be housed in inadequate institutions. In the 1930s many councils commissioned well-posed publicity photographs of their institutions, showing the elderly inmates comfortably seated round the fire, the inevitable piano and wireless in one corner, the pictures of Royalty on the wall, the vase of flowers on the table. The well-scrubbed room was still bare of carpets, and the long dormitories allowed no privacy, but the institution was far removed from the workhouses of the 1840s. Specialization, as will be seen, required professional administrators, and these were more expensive than untrained officers. The day of the specialist had arrived, and the elected councillors, far more than the old guardians, were in the hands of experts.

The inter-war period, in spite of its restrictions on expenditure, was in many ways a climactic period for institutions. Faith in their social importance would never be as strong again. Hospitals and residential homes seemed the obvious places for the sick and the infirm aged, while for the inebriate and the vagrant, institutions not only offered a 'cure', but removed a threat to public decency. These traditional considerations were also affected by new developments, for the structure of the British population was changing. People lived longer: there were more old people and fewer children, and the old were by the 1930s the largest group of people in institutions. It also seemed that the whole tendency of industrial society was to break up family responsibility, and that the elderly would be more in need of indoor maintenance by the state.

In fact, research after 1945 showed that proportionately fewer old people were in institutions than had been in workhouses at the beginning of the twentieth century.[64] The absolute number was higher because of the population increase and shifting age-structure, but by 1951 the trend was against institutions. Old people in homes also tended to be very advanced in age, infirm, or with no immediate family to care for them.[65] Paradoxically, more children went to institutions than in 1911 because the state was more willing to remove them from 'unsuitable' homes. These surveys did not show whether people had become dependent on institutions for longer periods, for greater longevity may have led to longer periods of residence: the same applies to the mentally defective, who after 1913 were more likely to be incarcerated for a lifetime. Chamberlain's ministry, traditionally seen as 'breaking up' the Poor Law, also provided the climax of the institutional idea. Not until after the next war did social critics begin to turn against institutions as such, or at least against the large-scale institutions envisaged by the 1929 Act.[66] In the early years of the Welfare State there was a two-pronged attack on large institutions, by psychiatrists who developed a scientific basis for traditional fears about the effects on institutions on children; and by sociologists who revealed how unwilling comparatively fit elderly people were to be placed in 'homes'. Attacks on institutions were not new; but after 1945 they had wider circulation. It was only as faith in institutions waned that the workhouse system was really weakened.

Chamberlain did not destroy, and had not intended to destroy, the physical fabric of the workhouses. Such a costly investment could not be repudiated. The larger and more expensive a Poor Law building was, the more likely that it would be incorporated into all succeeding schemes of hospital and institutional reform. Thus during the period after 1945, when questions of ideal size were hotly debated, the physical legacy of the Poor Law became oppressive to reformers. Social thinkers who considered institutions to be necessary, usually argued that good institutions should be small enough to keep close links with the outside world and develop a sense of community among the inmates. But the old fabrics resisted this notion. Any existing building was more economical than the purpose-built homes recommended by the experts. Alternatively, if the aged and handicapped were to live in their own homes, the domiciliary services would need drastic reorganization. Domiciliary care might be cheaper than an institution, but it saved time and trouble if an elderly infirm person were placed in a home where all services could be provided under one roof by one staff. In 1960, about 51 per cent of local authority accommodation was still in old workhouse buildings.[67] The principle of 'less eligibility' no longer applied to inmates under the Welfare State, but in the long dormitories and reverberating corridors of the old workhouses, the sense of change was muted. The present continued to inhabit the shell of the past.

5

Officers 1834–1870

To an age which favours the expert, the workhouse officers of the New Poor Law appear disreputable figures. Selected at worst through nepotism, at best because they were honest, they had to serve an institution which was hospital, school and reformatory. Few of the early officers had special qualifications: even if workhouse inmates had been separated as the Royal Commission recommended, and placed under different masters, there would have been no pool of trained men. Amateurism in those years was inevitable, but during the nineteenth century professional skills of all kinds proliferated, and the amateur was at a disadvantage. By 1914 trained people had largely assumed control of the educational and medical services of the Poor Law, even if these officers were often regarded as second-class members of their professions. Nurses replaced pauper attendants in the infirmaries; professional teachers controlled the schoolrooms; but untrained masters still dominated the whole institution. The Minority Report pointed out that the master and matron could not possibly cope with so many different problems:

> ... the men and women whom we harness to the service of the General Mixed Workhouse almost invariably develop an all-embracing indifference—indifference to suffering which they cannot alleviate, to ignorance which they cannot enlighten, to virtue which they cannot encourage, to indolence which they cannot correct, to vice which they cannot punish.[1]

The Webbs, admiring professionalism, wished the different types of pauper to be dealt with by 'experts', but their view ignored nearly 80 years of administrative experience, during which the Poor Law had itself become a profession. Experience alone qualified the officers for their perplexing tasks, but the Webbs' criticism was just: how could officers define their aims in a system with such confused purpose? The

113

basic aim of deterring pauperism was qualified annually by orders from London, counselling kindness to one group of paupers, harshness to another. Upon the shoulders of the workhouse master fell most directly the burden of deciding how far the workhouse should deter the poor. His policy had to conform to the guardians' wishes, but he could easily influence their decisions as he attended the board meetings to give advice. In unions where guardians were not very active, they would see the inmates through his eyes, and he had wide discretion to treat paupers with harshness or sympathy.

Residential institutions impose a routine on staff as well as inmates. Under the pressures of institutional life, the staff run the institution in ways most convenient for themselves, and although they must put up an appropriate front to visitors, they will tend to adjust the rules for their own ends.[2] If the rules are particularly irksome the adjustment will naturally be greater. In the nineteenth century, many institutions, including prisons and asylums, had regulations which demanded much of the staff, but their routine duties were not always directed to any clear purpose. Prison reformers hoped that the massive new prisons wold reform the criminal: the discipline was intended to regenerate; but to the prison officers, untrained and underpaid, this purpose was not clear. They were ordered to impose discipline, and discipline became an end in itself.[3] The workhouses also began to fulfil a different purpose from their designers' intention, but officers were not always responsive to change, and each workhouse was always a world to itself.

The workhouse was almost entirely enclosed, and its contact with the outside world deliberately restricted. Staff as well as inmates suffered from this, and the more subordinate the officer, the more was he imprisoned. He had even less freedom than the inmate, for inmates could discharge themselves at will, whereas the officer could not leave the house without the master's permission. The master himself was expected to be on call in all emergencies. Enforced seclusion, at its worst in the early years, produced tensions among the officers which account for many workhouse scandals. The motives of the Poor Law Commissioners may have been of the purest, but their system set up intolerable strains on human nature, affecting not only the local officers, but the Commissioners' own servants.

The Inspectorate of the 1830s included some remarkable men, but they were expected to achieve an almost superhuman standard. Most of them enthusiastically subscribed to the 'principles of 1834', but there was a barrier between them and the local officers whose work they inspected. Their social status made it difficult for them to understand the problems of workhouse officers, and they had little to do with the outdoor officers. The austere standards of Chadwick demanded enormous efforts of the Inspectorate: in spite of their small numbers they were supposed to visit each union twice annually, and the peripatetic life could be exhausting. 'I have no station, no habitation fixed anywhere,' wrote Tufnell, 'but migrate from Inn to Inn.'[4] The first Inspectors were threatened with physical violence by local crowds, or widely insulted, as Charles Mott reported in London:

> I have received... many of the most filthy and disgusting anonymous letters some of them even threatening my life, and I have occasionally been saluted in the streets, by perhaps a cabman or hackney coachman as 'pauper starver...'[5]

Inspectors had no superannuation until 1859, and many continued to work beyond the age when they could adequately perform their exacting duties.[6] Like the workhouse master, the Inspector had to learn his trade by experience, but he had greater compensations: an interesting and adventurous life, a salary which maintained the rank of a gentleman, a month's holiday every year, and considerable freedom. The local officers also had heavy responsibilities, but few of the compensations. In 1841 the Poor Law Commissioners devised standards for them which enjoined total steadiness of character under conditions designed to try it excessively:

> The discipline of a workhouse is to be maintained by an undeviating adherence to rules, and a steadiness which defies provocation, while it deliberately enforces obedience to orders by legal and authorized means... The habits of many of the inmates of a workhouse will often be coarse and depraved, but the conduct of every officer... should correspond with what those habits ought to be, rather than with what they actually are.[7]

Before 1834 small parishes had rarely employed more indoor officers than a master and matron, who were sometimes paupers themselves. In Wallingford, for example, the impoverished parish beadle and his wife were paid 12 shillings a week to 'set things straight and keep all quiet'.[8] Manchester workhouse, on the other hand, with over 600 inmates in the early 1830s, had a full-time governor and matron, lunatic keeper, weaving master, lodgekeeper, schoolmaster, apothecary, and chaplain.[9] The practice of 'farming' the workhouse, especially in large parishes, had already created a group of entrepreneurs who would take the duties of administration out of the vestry's hands. Some parishes regarded salaried officers as essential to keep the workhouse running smoothly; others objected to paying any officers apart from the master and matron, and expected the paupers to do all necessary work.

From 1834 the master and matron carried heavier responsibilities. The medical officers at first occupied an inferior position, but their profession was to enjoy a rise in status so remarkable, and so fundamental to the later development of the system, that it must be considered separately. In addition there were the workhouse chaplain, who was usually a non-resident officer with other clerical duties outside; and the schoolteacher and porter, who were subordinate to the master. All unions were supposed to employ these officers as a minimum workhouse staff, but many small unions still fell short. The Commissioners expected that former non-commissioned officers from the army and retired members of the police would be the best type of men to act as masters. Unions were discouraged from retaining former parish servants unless they were of proved efficiency, but many local studies indicate that guardians preferred to retain officers from the past, or, not surprisingly, to use the newly created posts as an opportunity for nepotism.

The Commissioners' first instructions emphasized the disciplinary duties of the master: he was to 'enforce industry, order, punctuality and cleanliness', to see that the able-bodied were put to work, to call the medical officer in case of illness, and to keep accounts of workhouse stores and property.[10] He had no further concern for the welfare of the inmates except to read prayers morning and evening, and to see that grace was said before meals. His difficult charges made-self-control vital, as Sir Francis Head explained to Kentish guardians:

> ...he should be a person accustomed to the habits of your peasantry, acquainted with their character, of irreproachable moral conduct, with great firmness and mild temper.[11]

The Commissioners did not rule that the matron must be the master's wife, but propriety and economy alike dictated that a married couple would be most suited to these duties. Although there are instances of these officers not being married couples, this was very unusual: the Webbs later argued that an inferior matron might be employed because her husband was a good master, or vice-versa.[12] The Commissioners required only moral qualifications of the matron:

she was to be comparable to a 'trustworthy female servant', and be paid at the same rate. It was her duty to take charge of the female paupers and to manage the domestic work of the house. She also had considerable discretion in the nursing of the sick, a duty which became more significant during the nineteenth century, and gradually transformed the matron's work from that of housekeeper to professional nurse.

Poor Law regulations governed the domestic life of the master and matron. If the master became a widower (or the matron a widow), his own career would end unless he could provide an acceptable substitute, such as a daughter or female relative. An ambitious labour master, or master's clerk who wanted a master's post would have to find a suitable wife, often from amongst the nurses or teachers in his institution. An unmarried master was appointed by the Bromley guardians in 1888, for they wished to retain their recently widowed matron, but the new master realized he would be unable to find a better post without a wife, and so laid his private circumstances before the board:

> Gentlemen,
> Being very anxious to obtain a joint appointment as Master & matron of a union workhouse and my greatest disadvantage being single, may I solicit the sanction of the Guardians to marry, my wife being outside the workhouse buildings.[13]

The guardians did not object.

Masters and matrons were usually required to be without dependent children, for guardians did not wish the couple to be distracted by domestic cares, and all their energies were to be kept for the Poor Law service. Until the last years of the nineteenth century, advertisements for masters and matrons usually stated baldly that couples must not have dependent children, though guardians might accept children who were sent to live elsewhere, or who went away to school. Since the master was paid partly in kind, ratepayers might grumble if his family claimed a share of workhouse rations. By the end of the century he might be permitted to keep his family in the house and pay for their maintenance, but this was more common in large institutions where the master had his own separate house.

The Minority Report deplored these rules because they were thought to reduce the number of eligible candidates for Poor Law positions, but other problems also arose from them. In the early years the master's position was insecure: he had no regular holidays unless the guardians were indulgent, and no guaranteed pension; he was denied the ordinary comforts of family life; held to account (in theory at any rate) for every drop and every crumb consumed in the workhouse; made responsible for much of the statistical data demanded by the central authority; and given great power over the other workhouse staff and the inmates. He had to keep nine different account books, including minute details of food wasted in cooking. Many masters needed a clerk or assistant master to keep the books, but only in the large institutions did the Commissioners encourage this, and even in an institution of nearly a thousand inhabitants, only one clerk might be permitted.[14] Under such conditions, workhouse scandals were almost inevitable.

Most local studies have found deficiencies in the first officers of the New Poor Law. The more flagrant abuses were eagerly seized on by the anti-Poor Law campaigners, and have provided colourful material for historians,[15] but these were only the detected offences. Excessive acts of violence or deprivation were against the rules; a master risked his job if he indulged in them. Also against the rules were any misappropriation of food or property, or undue familiarity with female paupers, but the master had a large area of discretion where he could tyrannize over inmates and look to his own interests without committing a technical offence. His greatest power was his control over the minutiae of the house; his greatest temptation his relations with local tradesmen. He had much discretion in day-to-day purchases, and an unfavourable report from him could end a lucrative contract for food or clothing. In 1841 the Commissioners forbade workhouse officers to profit from inmates' work or the sale of workhouse refuse, but such perquisites were hard to prevent.

Although the rules forbade the master to alter the diet or discipline of the house without the guardians' consent, many guardians did not wish to spend time debating the details of workhouse management, and if the master maintained discipline and economy, guardians were disinclined to interfere. Successive central authorities complained that guardians took their duties of workhouse visitation lightly; and visits were usually made with the master's prior knowledge. Sporadic visits from the Inspectors could hardly check all abuses, for the Inspectors had to be more concerned with the large evils of dirt and overcrowding rather than the minor tyrannies of the master. Guardians could not be compelled to visit the workhouse regularly: at Andover, for example, the guardians had been almost entirely apathetic, and the master had virtually unfettered authority. The chairman of the board, the

Reverend Christopher Dodson, had not visited the workhouse for five years before the scandal broke, nor had he read any of the Commissioners' regulations for three years.[16]

The Commissioners' regulations were also an obstacle to independent workhouse visitors; and the master could refuse entry to anyone who came without warning, including the guardians themselves. Until the later years of the century, many guardians refused to allow press or public to attend their meetings; this varied with local custom, but the Commissioners favoured secrecy.[17] Hence the workhouse could be closed to public scrutiny, and if the guardians were indifferent, the master was almost unsupervised. Only the work of active reformers like Louisa Twining could break down these barriers, for to the central authority the desire to enforce discipline overrode the claims of public scrutiny.

Consequently, workhouse masters who were overworked, uneducated and often unsupervised, were often tempted to abuse their authority, as is shown by the numbers of them who were dismissed. From the late 1860s the central authority published annually the numbers of officers dismissed, but these accounts did not always include London, nor did they always include 'voluntary' resignations which in fact had been enforced. From the rough list of officers which was kept at the central office between the late 1840s and the 1920s it is possible to trace the causes of masters leaving their employment. The figures here are taken from 147 provincial workhouses, and give some indication of the reasons why 882 masters had left their posts between about 1860 and 1920.[18]

	no. of masters	%
Left for another Poor Law appointment	209	23.7
Died	146	16.6
Retired, or ill	103	11.7
Left 'voluntarily' (no explanation)	103	11.7
Resigned under pressure to do so	86	9.7
Reasons not given	74	8.4
Wife died, or ill	63	7.1
Left 'to a better appointment'	63	7.1
Dismissed	27	3.1
Temporary appointment, or union altered	5	0.6
Matron dismissed	3	0.3
Total	882	100

Although only 3.1 per cent of masters were actually dismissed, another 9.7 per cent left under pressure, usually after complaints serious enough to be investigated by the central authority. The category of those who left 'voluntarily' or without explanation may also include a number of masters who left under pressure from the guardians, but whose faults were not brought before the central authority. A breakdown by decades of the dismissals and forced resignations shows a slight decline until 1900, then a more rapid drop:

Forced resignations and dismissals by decade (% in brackets)

	1860–9	1870–9	1880–9	1890–9	1900–9	1910–20
Resignations	11 (12.9)	22 (12.5)	22 (9.6)	15 (7.8)	11 (7.6)	5 (3.7)
dismissals	2 (2.3)	8 (4.5)	6 (3.8)	8 (4.2)	3 (2.0)	—

No master could be dismissed without the central authority's consent, and the central register was kept in an attempt to prevent a dismissed master taking a Poor Law post elsewhere, for the central authority could also refuse to accept his appointment. But many such masters did find work in other unions, as the career of George Catch illustrated. In any case, only the most venal or careless officers were caught. Auditors might detect peculation, but masters could easily conceal petty (or even serious) tyranny.

Official procedures inhibited the Commissioners from detecting misdoings. Complaints against an officer would usually come from paupers, and allegations from this source were always distrusted. If the central authority received a complaint from a pauper, it returned a printed answer stating that it was 'forbidden by law' to intervene in individual cases; the complaint would be forwarded to the guardians, who would usually refer it back to the master. The Commissioners usually ignored anonymous letters, though paupers naturally appreciated the benefits of anonymity. The situation was very difficult: masters could be unjustly accused, for the nature of workhouse discipline made this inevitable, but the Commissioners made little allowance for the weakness of the inmates in relation to the master. The master himself had to register any complaint by an inmate in a special book: examples of these books which survive have very few entries.

The central authority sometimes received complaints against a master for a long time before taking any action. Written complaints from inmates could be inhibited by illiteracy, lack of writting materials, or the cost of postage, but in London letters could be delivered by hand. Hence notes like the following frequently arrived at Somerset House:

Gentlemen, Do for Gods sake take into consideration the sufferings of the *poor of Lambeth Work-house* ill used and half starved—the Master a *perfect brute* swearing at sick and aged driving them to Work when scarce able to stand—some of you I know to be men of feeling—my information I know is correct.

Yours respectfully
A Parishioner[19]

P.S. The food scarce fit for Hogs.

Here the Commissioners accepted the Inspector's comment that the charge was groundless—but they later had considerable trouble over both the master and the dietary. Two successive masters of Lambeth provoked numerous complaints from paupers over a number of years:[20] the guardians persuaded the Commissioners to ignore the complaints, until pressure from ratepayers, the press, and other workhouse officers forced an inquiry. Both masters hastily resigned, but not before they had mistreated inmates for several years without hindrance. Lambeth was not unique. Many local studies show that guardians tended to stand by the master in spite of all evidence of misbehaviour towards paupers, and often against the wishes of the central authority.

P.J. Dunkley, observing Poor Law administration in county Durham, argues that parsimony encouraged guardians to retain inferior officers.[21] If a master would accept the low salary which was offered, then guardians would not wish to dismiss him whatever his deficiencies. In times of economic distress, guardians were likely to react by attacking their officers' salaries, as happened in Durham during the 1840s. The central authority tried to prevent salaries from being pushed below a reasonable point, for they knew that officers would then be tempted to look for illegal perquisites.[22] The guardians might have been attached to their officers for other reasons: sometimes relatives or connections of the guardians were appointed to union posts, but, more simply, guardians approved of the officers' efforts to make the workhouse deterrent. The notorious Catch, whose harshness the guardians repeatedly defended, was not an underpaid master by Poor Law standards, and the guardians defended him to the Poor Law Board in these terms:

He has introduced into the workhouse better discipline and order than have prevailed there for many years past. He is economical in management and has been highly successful in enforcing industry among the numerous able-bodied paupers with which Lambeth is burdened.[23]

Catch was finally found guilty of cruelty to the able-bodied women, many of whom were said to be prostitutes. As in the Bath case cited in Chapter 2, the central authority was not disposed to be very critical of this type of discipline, but Catch had overreached himself by attracting too much publicity over several years in different unions, and had also become bankrupt just before taking the Lambeth post. His last offence had been to terrify one of the disreputable young women so much that she fled: thinking she had hidden up a chimney, Catch and the medical officer tried to smoke her down with a burning mixture of chloride of lime and sulphuric acid. Since she was not there, the mixture fortunately did no more than choke nurses and other paupers in the room. H. Fleming, the Inspector, noted uneasily, 'If Mr Catch had been an old & faithful Officer, with an excellent general character, I think this act of his might have been passed over with a severe reprimand. But considering his previous history, the odium which his apt has brought upon the P.L.B...' there was no course but dismissal.[24]

Guardians and central authority both tended to dismiss offences perpetrated in the pursuit of 'discipline', whereas neither would condone peculation. Compare the generous attitude towards Catch with the attempt by the Poor Law Board to have a Lambeth medical officer removed in 1869 for a trifling use of workhouse medical supplies for his own family. He had served the union relatively blamelessly for many years. Here the guardians (whose families he also treated from workhouse stores) successfully defended him. Since 'discipline' was the whole purpose of the house at that time, the central authority understood the masters' problems. Even the most tender apologist for the poor could not deny that the habits and behaviour of some paupers made the officers' lives difficult. London and many provincial unions were on the travelling routes of immigrants and vagrants. A master might have to maintain discipline in a ward full of abusive or intoxicated casuals: in London he often had help from an attendant or the police, but in small unions he had to cope on his own. The master of East Retford (Notts), employed by excessively economical guardians in an old workhouse where rain continually poured through the roof, reported in 1842 a minor insurrection amongst the able-bodied men:

> Robt Mowthorp [?] whose leave was with holden on Saturday last—made his escape over the wall of the Buildings—and went to Carlton and brought his daughter back with him with an Order of Admittance from the Relieving Officer... and on his return objected to work, and said that he would break no moore stons, his objection caused the other Able bodied paupers to Revolt—but when informed that they would be dieted—they repented and went to work as useal.[25]

The threat of a bread-and-water diet worked in this case, but in larger workhouses the master could face a full-scale riot if he tried to alter the diet or work of the able-bodied paupers. The divided nature of his responsibilities caused problems: in a union with many casuals the guardians would want a disciplinarian master, but the kind of Tartar favoured for this work would probably not be suitable for managing children, the aged and the sick. The Inspectors were still commenting on the conflicting claims of discipline and kindliness in 1895.[26]

Recent writers like Dunkley have usually blamed inadequate salaries on the guardians rather than the central authority, and certainly in the 1840s the Commissioners often tried to prevent the guardians from reducing officers' salaries below the point where honest men would apply for the post. Nevertheless, the Commissioners had their own faults. From the earliest days they hoped to establish wage scales for officers according to the size of the workhouse. Salaries had to be approved by Somerset House before district auditors could pass them, but the usual problem of Poor Law administration then arose. The Commissioners could refuse to allow an excessively high salary, but could not increase an excessively low one. Any letter from a union requesting some change in salaries provoked a bureaucratic bustle. The Inspector would comment on the calibre of the officers and the propriety of the request; then one of the clerks wrote a memorandum on the level of wages in unions of comparable size, or with comparable problems. The central authority would quote precedents from other unions, while the guardians would argue that their own case was unique.

In Kent, the Assistant Commissioners had tried to unify officers' salaries, just as they tried to impose uniform diets and out relief payments. Tufnell was particularly devoted to the idea of the lowest acceptable wages, and tried to stop unions paying better than their neighbours, though without success. Tufnell thought £80 per year with board ample for any master—apparently he did not allow for the different sizes of workhouses, and grumbled because unions outside Kent paid better.[27] The Commissioners, however, tried to calculate the master's responsibilities: he might find his salary adjusted according to the number of his assistants, and be faced with the prospect of a lower salary if a master's clerk were appointed. The central authority took little account of human limitations, and did not prevent a master undertaking too much work in order to keep his salary up. After the disaster of Catch, the Lambeth guardians decided to attract a superior type of master by offering £200 instead of £150 a year, but the Poor Law Board were unwilling to sanction this because the City of London workhouse had a master with £175 and only one clerk, whereas the Lambeth master had both a clerk and an assistant master. The Board's secretary recommended that the increase be sanctioned only if one of the subordinate officers were dismissed— which suggests that the thought the master could do two men's work for an extra £50 a year.[28] In this case the guardians had their way, but the argument was typical of the central authority. It is not surprising that masters tried to manage without salaried assistants; instead they surreptitiously employed literate paupers to keep accounts or check stores, in return for pocket money or extra rations, though the central authority strongly disapproved of this.

Different levels of salary inevitably created a ladder of preferment in the Poor Law service. In Wales the impoverished farmers on the boards of guardians were jealous of officers whose incomes might be as high as their own, and did their best to keep salaries low, whereas in cities like Manchester and Liverpool, which had long been employing professional managers for their institutions, high salaries were paid. The tiny workhouse at Aberayon brought its master only £30 a year from 1860 to 1914. By contrast, in 1869 Liverpool paid the master £350 for managing up to 3,500 inmates; Birmingham (1994 inmates) paid £250 without rations; and Manchester (1894 inmates) £240.[29] With the matron's salary usually about a third of the master's in large unions, and with servants and lodging provided free, the master and matron of a large institution could live very comfortably. The larger the workhouse, the better their own apartments were likely to be.

Masters and matrons thus varied considerably in status and remuneration, and although Louisa Twining dismissed them all as people of the 'low and uneducated middle-class,' they were constantly jockeying for the best posts. As nepotism and jobbery became less common, a career structure opened for masters. By the 1870s large unions rarely appointed a master who had not considerable experience in the Poor Law service; advertisements specifically required it. A matron, too, would stand a better chance if she were a trained nurse. A small rural union with a low salary was likely to accept masters of little education, or, if it attracted better men, to be unable to keep them. The little union of Cleobury Mortimer, which paid only £30 a year between 1854 and 1918, had 17 masters in that time, whereas the average turnover of masters in the 147 provincial unions mentioned above was about seven per union in the same period.

Nevertheless, Louisa Twining's comment had some force; a master's post was at best comparable to a modest tradesman's in social status, at worst, inferior to a skilled artisan's. The master had one of the necessary attributes of middle-class status in abundance—domestic servants—but the use of paupers for this work carried little prestige. The nervous desire of the lower-middle class for social mobility and security was shared by workhouse masters, but with important qualifications. Most of them seem to have regarded the Poor Law service as an end in itself, not as a road to something better. As previously shown, 28.3 per cent of a sample of masters died in office or retired from it: a further 23.7 per cent took up other appointments under the Poor Law: only 7.1 per cent specifically left to 'better' themselves. For most masters, their post was as high up the social ladder as they were likely to go. For the retired military or police officer it probably offered sufficient security and social advancement; nor was there any obvious path to other types of institution. Workhouse managers had low status compared with the governors of charitable institutions like the voluntary hospitals. A hospital secretary or steward in the first half of the nineteenth century could command from £100 to £300 a year, considerably more than all but the best paid masters.[30] Hospital posts therefore went to more educated men.

Few institutions compared in career structure to the workhouses. Other public institutions such as gaols and county asylums were fewer in number. Charitable institutions of all kinds proliferated during the nineteenth century, but although trained nurses or teachers could move from Poor Law to other types of institution, it was harder for the untrained workhouse master, with his low social reputation, to do so. It is not possible to demonstrate on a wide statistical basis whether the pattern of recruitment of masters changed during the nineteenth century; but local records may be consulted. The workhouses in Bromley and Lambeth show a change in recruitment which would reinforce the argument that the Poor Law provided an enclosed career structure. Not only the enormous workhouse in Lambeth, but the much more modest one in Bromley, were requiring Poor Law experience of new masters; they recruited not only from masters of smaller institutions, but assistant masters, clerks, and 'labour masters' (the men responsible for supervising inmate labour). In the later years of the century, the Bromley guardians even sent a selection committee to see whether applicants for the post of master were doing efficient work in the institutions from which they applied.

A further breakdown by decade of the movements of the 882 masters who had left their employment, indicates that Poor Law promotions were becoming more frequent:

% of all withdrawals per decade[31]

Reasons for leaving	1860–9	1870–9	1880–9	1890–9	1900–9	1910–20
Another Poor Law post	11.7	14.2	18.7	31.0	34.2	27.6
'To better themselves'	11.7	14.8	7.0	3.6	2.7	3.7
Dying, or retiring	32.9	29.1	27.0	27.3	22.3	32.8

Since Poor Law officers did not have pensions, masters frequently remained at their posts well into old age. Inspectors complained that this impeded efficiency, but guardians would not turn away an old servant who had no other income. This, of course, was common in many occupations, but Poor Law officers had fewer advantages than civil servants or officers of county institutions. Inspectors and clerks at the Poor Law Board received pensions from 1859; officers of asylums for pauper lunatics could be pensioned at their employers' discretion after 1845, whereas guardians could not pay pensions from the rates. Workhouse officers made their own arrangements by paying into one of the small friendly societies which served them. In 1850 they objected to proposed legislation to attach part of their salaries to pay for superannuation; they earned little in cash, and relied on the free accommodation to make low salaries acceptable. Masters and relieving officers also had to pay for insurance as surety in case they defaulted. In 1864 legislation allowed, but did not compel, guardians to superannuate officers at their own discretion, but did not stipulate the level of pensions.

The Poor Law Commissioners originally planned a minimum of five officers for each workhouse, apart from the master and matron, but even this was too much for some guardians. Early Poor Law records do not always distinguish workhouse officers from outdoor staff, but a return of 1849 reveals the following:

Numbers of staff in 591 unions, including district schools[32]

	numbers	total wage	average wage p.a.
Masters & matrons	1,238	£44,369	£35 (or £71 per couple)
Chaplains	415	19,140	46
Schoolmasters	284	7,423	26
Schoolmistresses	423	7,009	16
Porters	347	6,340	18
Nurses	171	2,161	12
Labour masters (usually non-resident)	20	936	46

These figures do not distinguish workhouse medical officers from district medical officers; in many workhouses the medical officer also had outdoor duties. Nor do the returns mention staff such as paid cooks, seamstresses or bakers, whom some large unions employed; but unspecified staff of this kind, both indoor and outdoor, numbered only 264. All officers except the medical officer, chaplain and (usually) labour master, received board as well as the money wage.

The 'average' workhouse, holding about 225 inmates in 1849, had a staff of six officers, of whom the medical officer and chaplain were part-time. The average, of course, conceals wide extremes. The 707 schoolteachers in 591 unions were not distributed evenly. The smallest unions employed no teachers, while larger urban unions might have a separate school with a sizeable teaching staff. In parts of the country where no local schools for the poor existed, the children might be educated by a literate pauper, who, unpaid, does not appear as an 'officer' in the returns. The unions who employed no paid porters or nurses inevitably used paupers for this work. The Commissioners objected more to the use of inmates as porters than as nurses; presumably the porter's position required greater fidelity.

The only two officers with comparable standing to the master were the chaplain and the medical officer. For much of the nineteenth century the master and the doctor disputed control of the infirmary, and the doctor finally won a qualified victory. In the early years, however, the doctor's position was less secure than other officers' because of his annual contract. The chaplain was differently placed. Unlike the medical officer, he was a professional man of standing.

While in the 1830s the doctor was still struggling for social recognition, the clergyman was assured of gentility: even the lower echelons of the Church of England commanded respect by virtue of their calling. Neither the guardians nor the central authority controlled the chaplain's appointment completely, for the bishop of the diocese had to ratify it. Since a chaplaincy was part-time work, the bishop wished to see that it did not conflict with the clergyman's usual offices: on one occasion a bishop refused to approve an appointment because he considered the salary too low (but this was unusual).[33] The chaplain's status ensured that he would receive a salary which compared favourably even to the master's. Much depended on local custom. Basford, a Nottinghamshire textile union with 200–300 paupers in the workhouse during the winters, paid the chaplain an unusually low salary of £24 a year, while the master and matron together received £100. Bridge, a small rural union in Kent, with an average of 183 inmates in bad years, and only 100 in good ones, paid its chaplain £50, while the master and matron earned only £70. Yet the chaplain's duties were far less exacting than the master's; he had to read prayers and preach on Sundays, catechize the children once a month, visit the sick if the master requested it, and minister to the dying.

Chaplains were therefore expensive compared with the inferior workhouse officers. The Commissioners accepted the expense less for religious than for disciplinary reasons; the chaplain was the spiritual ancillary of the master. Public opinion would not allow paupers to be denied the consolation of religion, but the Commissioners argued that if paupers went out on Sunday to attend church, all manner of evils would result. Therefore a chaplain, as a kind of Sunday gaoler, could not be avoided. Hoping that one chaplain would suffice for all religious denominations, the Commissioners reported in 1836:

> ... the rule prohibiting paupers from quitting the workhouse on a Sunday must apply to all classes of adults alike ... if the rule should be relaxed in favour of any particular sect, the other inmates of the house would undergo a nominal conversion.[34]

In their rather simple disciplinary view of the chaplain's function, the Commissioner underestimated the religious temper of the day. The 1830s, following the repeal of the Test and Corporation Acts, witnessed some of the most intemperate conflicts between the Church and the Dissenters. The Commissioners assumed that guardians would appoint a Church of England chaplain, and did not expect the strong resistance to this in unions where most of the guardians were

Dissenters. Some unions objected to appointing a chaplain, not only because they resented the Church's monopoly, but because they did not want such an expensive officer when the inmates could easily attend the local church at no cost. Kent, an Anglican stronghold, soon appointed chaplains, but in the few unions without them, Tufnell demanded that the paupers be allowed to attend church only under strict supervision and in workhouse uniform, ('they hate this public exhibition, and the marching prevents their making disorders'.)[35] Resistance was much stronger in the north, where the Commissioners' views were interpreted both as an attempt to proselytize Dissenting inmates and to provide more jobs for the clergy. Each pauper had to state his religious affiliation when he entered the workhouse, and in unions where Dissent was strong, it seemed pointless to appoint a Church of England chaplain. The Commissioners soon realized that they had put their hands in a wasps' nest, but, unpopular as they were, they could not afford to offend the Church as well. The bishops had supported the Poor Law Amendment Act through the Lords, and clerical magistrates were *ex-officio* guardians. The Commissioners therefore tried to prevent Dissenting ministers from conducting services in the workhouse, but also accepted that no religious ceremony should be forced on paupers of other persuasions.[36] Consequently, non-Anglican paupers had to be allowed out on Sunday, though the Commissioners warned guardians that supervision, or at least a certificate of chapel attendance from the minister, would be necessary.

In 1844, the Commissioners reported that 144 unions were still refusing to appoint a chaplain. The areas with most deficiencies were Lancashire (10 unions), the West Riding (13), Durham (12) and Cornwall (7)—all places where Dissent was strong.[37] Even in the 1860s, religious disagreements among the Sheffield guardians prevented the appointment of a chaplain—the inmates went to their respective churches, and the clergy signed attendance certificates. The guardians liked the arrangement, for Wesleyan ministers held services in the workhouse, and the Church of England clergy visited the inmates for no charge.[38] Amongst the unions in north-east Lancashire, only three appointed chaplains, while the rest used the free services of Methodist ministers.

Church and chapel-going guardians could at least agree to keep catholic priests out of the workhouse, and the central authority received many complaints from the Catholic community. Some workhouses, like Liverpool, had a high proportion of Irish inmates, and Catholics argued for the appointment of a Catholic chaplain. A similar dispute long vexed the prison service, but with anti-Catholic feeling still high, some guardians would not even permit priests to enter their workhouse, far less appoint one as chaplain. The Commissioners counselled tolerance, but not Catholic appointments. The churches seem to have played little part in workhouse life in these early years. Chaplaincies were not as prestigious here as unpaid chaplaincies in an orphan asylum or charity school, where the governors might include people of wealth and quality. Paid attendance at the workhouse, for services rarely attractive to guardians, had little appeal. Usually the chaplain was a local curate, who had an interest in supplementing his stipend, for the incumbent would have other work on a Sunday. If the incumbent were interested in Poor Law matters, he was more likely to be found on the board of guardians. In spite of active voluntary work by some individual clergy, chaplains did not usually appear in the workhouse except for their regulation duties. Such an intermittent visitor was not expected to take a strong interest in workhouse administration.

As with the other officers, the guardians tried to extract the maximum work from the chaplain for the least possible pay, and, like the other officers, the chaplains were not always the best representatives of their class. Bromley union, which tried in the 1860s to employ a full-time chaplain for £100 or less, actually had seven of them between 1864 and 1876, most of whom were unsatisfactory. One was given to vulgar language and misusing the sacramental wine—it was said that two guardians offered him £70 to resign. Another was dismissed after becoming indebted to local tradesmen, guardians, and other officers. He begged the Local Government Board for sympathy for his 13 children, and added:

> Altho I do not say that the souls of the inmates of a union workhouse are less valuable than those of other people, still the circumstances complained of cannot affect them, as they might a city or country congregation.[39]

The master dominated all other officers, and any complaint from him could cost them their jobs. Tied to the workhouse at all times except when the master gave leave; without holidays, pensions or family life, and on wages which were usually little more than a domestic servant's, these officers had an unenviable life. The school-teachers were particularly dispirited, for their duties were really those of full-time attendants, and in most unions they had to supervise the children constantly. Schoolmistresses often had to bathe the children, mend their clothes, and act as general nurses. The first teachers were often unqualified, and any literate person could apply for the post. An advertisement for a schoolmaster in Blean (Kent) in 1840 brought replies from some of the indigent lower-middle classes. Only one, a publican's son, offered any teaching experience—six years of Sunday school teaching.[40] The teachers also resented their imprisonment with the pauper children, and their enforced association with other workhouse officers. Guardians inflicted petty humiliations on them; in several Kent unions the schoolteachers' rations were fixed at twice the amount of the paupers'. The guardians interpreted this literally, and because the usual diet of Kentish paupers was bread and cheese, the unfortunate teachers received large and inedible portions of these. The schoolmaster of Blean pleaded for £10 a year in lieu of rations so that he could buy his own food, but it was some years before the guardians consented.[41] Other unions provided a diet for officers which was carefully graded according to rank; hence in Eastry the master received exactly twice as much bread, butter, tea, potatoes, milk and porter as the inferior officers.[42] As usual, the central authority objected to 'extravagant' salaries, and in 1836 tried to prevent St Olave's (London) from paying its schoolmistress £50 a year, when there were 'only' 48 girls in the workhouse.[43]

Conditions for teachers became a little more favourable after 1848, when the Treasury began to make direct grants to unions to subsidize teachers' pay. The grants were on a scale related to the teacher's qualifications and competence, and by these means the central authority hoped to encourage guardians to employ qualified teachers. But this did not make teachers independent of the master. Like the masters, the teachers tried to move from union to union, either to seek better conditions or to avoid dismissal. The records of dismissals reflect only the cases who caused scandal, and in less glaring instances guardians might rid themselves of an undesirable officer by passing him on to another union. In 1862 the Bromley guardians pressed their schoolmistress to resign after she had fought with other officers, and when the children were found to have verminous heads. In their reference for her, the guardians ambiguously wrote that 'It [would] give them much satisfaction to hear that Miss Smith has obtained the situation of Schoolmistress in the Rochford Union.'[44] The central authority was slow to weed out unsatisfactory teachers, especially if they were trained. In 1871 the Poor Law Board at last refused to sanction the appointment of W. Robinson as schoolmaster, since he had worked in five unions in five years, and left all of them under a cloud. It seems that an erring officer was given more than one chance to redeem himself; the second-rate man had to be accepted because few trained people were willing to work for Poor Law salaries.[45]

The porter's was the humblest of the officially recognized posts, although his duties were onerous; he was not supposed to be an inmate or ex-pauper, but a responsible officer who could command the inmates' respect. Someone had to man the workhouse gate at all times, and an inmate would usually relieve the paid porter at night. The porter had to prevent all unauthorised entry to the workhouse, to admit all who applied for relief, and to search for forbidden commodities such as tobacco or alcohol. Even the porter, therefore, had power over the inmates which perhaps compensated for his low pay and lack of family life. Whereas the master usually had to be a married man, most other officers were expected to be single. Sometimes a schoolmaster and mistress might be a married couple, and porters in larger workhouses might be allowed a wife who could be made wardress of the female probationary ward, or act as seamstress. One porter at Lambeth managed to keep a wife and eight children outside the workhouse, but resigned hastily when the guardians discovered it.

Few workhouses had any facilities for the staff; they had few hours of leisure and so only in the larger institutions was a special room allotted to them. The master and matron might have their own apartments, and be waited on by pauper servants. Under these monotonous conditions, surrounded by inmates whom it was their duty to discipline rather than to aid, the workhouse staff existed in a manner which awaits the pen of a Chekhov to describe. Union records are full of the petty squabbles of workhouse officers, for if incompatible people found themselves in such a group, their lives were bound to be hateful. This was a feature of many residential institutions, especially where the staff were allowed little liberty.[46] The following is an example of the type of case which frequently arose. In Blean, the master and matron had to eat with the other officers, and their rations were all taken from the common stock. The portions were unequal, as described above, and jealousy inevitable. The master and matron, as befitted their station, bought themselves coffee, green tea, extra sugar, butter, eggs and bacon, which they consumed under the anguished eyes of the less affluent officers. The master wrote to the guardians:

I do not wish to disparage the porter—but I do distinctly say, if we have the porter forced upon us to take his meals, it will (in the eyes of the inmates) very much lessen the position we have held, as master and matron of this union.[47]

The porter had been a pauper himself, but was jealous of his dignity and refused to cut the inmates' hair in case he lost caste. When the master and matron were allowed to withdraw for meals, it left the schoolmistress with the schoolmaster and porter; she objected to the habits of both of them. The workhouse was isolated, which affected the nerves of the staff; in 1854 the porter resigned 'being unable to give satisfaction, and quite tired of this secluded way of living'.[48]

Similar hostilities occurred in urban workhouses, though a larger staff was at least spared the tedium of the same small company. The central authority throughout this period discountenanced 'unnecessary' expense designed to make staff conditions more tolerable. When the Manchester guardians bought some books for the workhouse officers, they were surcharged by the auditor, although the chairman argued that the institution was some miles from town, and the officers were caring for 1900 inmates: 'their duties require them to be almost permanently in the house, and they are almost prisoners there'. The books considered suitable, incidentally, were 48 volumes of the Waverley Novels, Macaulay's *History*, Blackwood's *Tales*, some illustrated books of travel, and, inevitably, *Self-Help*.[49]

In the conditions under which they worked, the officers had little incentive to be kind to workhouse inmates. Their own lives offered little except the chance of power over these relatively helpless subjects. The institution took its toll of staff as well as inmates, and the stress which both the central authority and the guardians laid on the enclosed nature of the institution made it difficult to avoid the very evils which the authorities condemned. Bullying and favouritism are possible in any institution, but the peculiar circumstances of the workhouse further encouraged them. The master had much discretion over the quality, if not the quantity, of meals, and over privileges and punishments for the inmates. His discretion exceeded that of a prison governor, for he could grant temporary freedom. By allowing an inmate to run errands or drive a union cart, the master gave him both liberty and the chance to earn small sums of money, and this power was exerted over the subordinate officers also.

It is not easy to tell whether the workhouse officers were better or worse than officers of other institutions in fulfilling their duties. Cases of cruelty occurred in institutions of all kinds, even for the children of the respectable classes. The staff at Cowan Bridge, where Charlotte Brönte went to school, inflicted both physical and mental torments on their charges, again because of the poverty of the institution. The Inspectors knew the problems which the officers faced, but absolved the central authority from blame; historians have accepted their word rather uncritically. Guardians, argued the Inspectors, could prevent abuses if they carried out regulations to the letter. Even in the case of Catch, the Inspector blamed the guardians for not providing special accommodation for the turbulent able-bodied paupers in Lambeth workhouse. Without sufficient staff or separate accommodation, the master and his subordinates were driven to use force, and the Inspector commented:

> the constant exercise of such force must inevitably tend to demoralise the officers themselves, and on this head I think it only fair to the officers to point out the difficult position in which they are placed in dealing with these inmates. I consider that the guardians are themselves to blame in not making... provision for dealing with them...[50]

The historian need not concur with this convenient analysis. While the guardians often treated their officers shabbily, the central authority rarely defended the officers' real interests: although it tried to prevent unrealistically low wages, it also discouraged guardians from offering the higher salaries which might have attracted a better type of officer. In the absence of any clear Poor Law policy the officers could hardly understand their own duties. Since the central authority apparently put 'discipline' first, the officers naturally saw discipline as their main function. Hence the early officers acted as warders, rather than healers or attendants, in this multi-purpose institution.

6

Officers 1870–1929. A Second-Class Service?

Nothing reveals the changing function of the workhouse more clearly than the growth of a professional staff within it. Once staff labour had begun to replace inmate labour, the institutions could be seen as offering a social service rather than acting only as a deterrent. In the early days, a very small staff seemed adequate to supervise inmate labour, but by the late nineteenth century this simple formula was out-of-date. Yet the combination of service with deterrence was bound to affect the quality and morale of the staff, and although the earlier stereotype of the vicious workhouse officer faded, the reputation for harshness and incompetence remained. The Minority Report implied that the workhouses were run by unskilled, second-rate officers, expert at nothing except a mechanical maintenance of discipline: guardians expected no more of their officers than that they keep the institution clean, 'the steps pipeclayed, and the regiments of books of entry in order for the inspector'.[1]

Officers' salaries absorbed an increasing proportion of the national expenditure on poor relief (See Figure 2), rising from about 12 per cent in the 1870s to 17–18 per cent in the first decade of the twentieth century. In the early 1920s the wages bill accounted for nearly a quarter of all expenditure. In cash terms, the amount spent on Poor Law officers trebled between 1870 and 1905.[2] Yet rising costs did not reflect rising wages. In small unions money wages for most officers rose little, if at all, during the nineteenth century. In large unions the guardians gave staff periodic increases, but new officers started at a low salary and worked their way up. During the last decades of the century, as food prices fell, guardians could save money on officers' rations. The cost of officers rose after 1896 when they finally won the right to pensions, but the increasing cost was mainly due to a proliferation of officers.

The central authority kept records of only the more important Poor

Law officers, and did not always distinguish between indoor and outdoor staff, but even these limited records show certain changes:

Numbers of principal workhouse officers[4]

	1849	1872	(% change)	1906	(%)	1920	(%)
Masters, stewards, superintendents	1238	716	(+17)	812	(+13)	816	(0)
Matrons		734		835	(+13)	916	(+9)
Medical officers, indoor	2680	741	(+56)	1010	(+36)	1021	(+1)
Medical officers, district		3458		3718	(+ 7)	3554	(−4)
Chaplains	415	544	(+31)	599	(+10)	546	(−8)
Schoolteachers	707	924	(+30)	448	(−51)		?(very few)
Nurses	171	1406	(+722)	6094	(+333)	8980	(+47)

Outdoor staff also increased, but not as significantly as the indoor officers: relieving officers, the most important of them, increased from 1257 in 1849 to 1892 in 1906.

Plainly, the new nursing staff alone must have increased the cost of salaries, and even when most other posts were affected by wartime labour shortages, the nursing staff still expanded. Although figures of nursing staff indicate the gradual change from workhouse to hospital, other changes were also significant. The central authority kept no record of ancillary staff except in its correspondence with individual unions. Hence the numbers of indoor and outdoor staff cannot be compared effectively. Junior clerical staff proliferated as the business of unions became more complex, and larger unions also appointed outdoor officers such as dispensers, assistant relieving officers, and ambulance drivers. Guardians had other legal functions than Poor Law administration, and outdoor officers sometimes combined several duties: after 1873 relieving officers worked as 'inquiry' officers to see whether children of outdoor paupers were attending school, while district medical officers were often public vaccinators. Paid rate-collectors replaced the unpaid overseers. Guardians also paid part-time staff, such as the policemen who helped to control the more turbulent workhouses, and a few unions shared with local charities the cost of district nurses.

Nevertheless, in all but the smallest workhouses the indoor officers increased far more than the outdoor officers. Schoolteachers alone decreased: from 1861 guardians could send workhouse children to local schools, and the 1870 Education Act made such education widely available. By the end of the century even the great barrack schools employed fewer teachers and relied more on local schools. But guardians had to replace the teachers with children's attendants and 'industrial trainers' who were less expensive than qualified teachers. The new specialized institutions inevitably required more domestic staff, for in schools, infirmaries, convalescent homes and homes for the aged, little work could be demanded of the inmates.

For example, the small Kentish union of Bridge actually went against the national trend, for its indoor officers decreased during the nineteenth century, as did its inmates. By 1900 the house rarely held more than 100 paupers, less than half the average of the 1840s when there had been six indoor officers. The union employed no nurse until 1876, and never employed more than one at a time. There had been two schoolteachers, but the last left in 1886, when the children went out to the local school. No paid porter ever seems to have been employed. Nor did the outdoor staff increase much, though a second clerk was appointed from 1896, and a rate collector from 1880. By contrast, Burnley, a medium-sized urban union in Lancashire, shows clearly the change from workhouse to hospital. Bridge's population was growing very slowly, Burnley's very rapidly. The guardians never employed a chaplain, and the first nurse was not appointed until 1876, but after that the staff expanded steadily. By 1901 there were four qualified nurses and two probationers; by 1916, six qualified nurses and 32 probationers. A dispenser was resident from 1899, and the medical officer became resident from 1902. A dentist began to visit in 1896 and a surgeon in 1919. Burnley never made much effort at education: the porter doubled as schoolmaster between 1861 and 1865, after which the children went out to school. The outdoor staff increased also, though not as rapidly.[5] The histories of the two workhouses are encapsulated in the statistics of their employees. Bridge had the kind of stagnant rural workhouse which distressed the Royal Commission of 1905; with such a small number of officers and inmates it could provide few special services. The best that could be hoped for in this union was that if any serious illness occurred, the guardians would send the patient to the nearest voluntary hospital. Burnley, on the other hand, moved within 20 years from an extremely ill-equipped workhouse, much abhorred by the Poor Law Commissioners, to a modest general hospital.

Central records, however, do not show whether the basic work was being done by paupers or paid servants. The humbler workers, paid by the day or even by the hour, signified as great a change in the workhouse as did the salaried officers. In 1881 the two large workhouses in Lambeth employed about 103 people, and another 46 worked in the schools: 20 years later there were another 82 indoor staff, the largest increase being in nurses, cleaners, laundresses and maintenance workers.[6] Able-bodied people in the institutions still had to do housework, but since most workhouse inmates were now elderly or handicapped, smaller unions felt the lack of able-bodied pauper servants. The Minority Report claimed that unions sometimes kept able-bodied imbeciles as servants rather than sending them to an asylum.[7] In spite of the remarkable increase of Poor Law officers, critics of the system continued to argue that institutions were understaffed. Social standards rose, and the Commission of 1905 naturally compared the workhouses with the larger staffs of voluntary hospitals.

Much of the expansion in officers' employment occurred at the bottom of the hierarchy, especially in work done by women: this trend affected the officers' bargaining power. More doctors and nurses represented an increase in professional expertise, but untrained officers still had considerable authority, and both factions of the 1905 Commission deplored it. The Local Government Board did not attempt to assess staff-inmate ratios, even when the numbers of able-bodied inmates had greatly decreased. The Local Government Act of 1888 made a slight gesture towards encouraging guardians to employ more officers by paying their salaries out of county rates rather than poor rates, but this was a fixed grant based on the number of officers who had been employed by the union at the time of the Act, and it did not achieve its aim. Some of the small unions who reduced their staff actually received a larger grant than their salaries bill warranted, while unions which were rapidly expanding received a totally inadequate contribution towards salaries. Unions had no incentive to employ more than the minimum of officers, and parsimonious guardians were constantly tempted to leave the institutions understaffed.[8]

The Local Government Board negotiated separately with each union over the number of officers, accepting the Inspectors' view of whether a workhouse was adequately staffed. In 1881 it was still possible for the master of the Bishop Auckland union to argue at a Poor Law Conference that a workhouse with 300 inmates and 20 casual paupers needed only six indoor officers.[9] This provoked the inevitable response from a guardian that if only six officers were needed for 320 people, then in smaller workhouses six were too many. The master felt that cooking, cleaning and all other work could be left to the more 'efficient' inmates. The Local Government Board was slow to give up this attitude, perhaps because its own officials were overworked and badly paid. Only in medical questions did the Board begin to intervene: an order of 1913 required that an institution with more than 100 beds for the sick must have an appropriately qualified superintendent nurse.

Such dynamism as the Board was able to generate came mainly from its two medical Inspectors, as will be seen in the following chapter, for they were supported by the BMA and other public bodies in their desire for more nursing staff. Concern at the shortage of trained nurses also forced the Board to advocate more paid servants and cleaners in the infirmaries. A departmental committee in 1902 argued that nurses would leave if their duties involved too much scrubbing and laundry work—if there were no female inmates to do these chores, outside labour must be employed.[10] The war exposed staff shortages once again, and the Ministry of Health did suggest an appropriate ratio of one nurse to every six helpless patients, or to every nine infirm patients (the voluntary hospitals had a ratio of one nurse to every three helpless patients). The Inspectors encouraged this policy but could not enforce it, and the Ministry did not try to regulate the numbers of other workhouse staff.[11]

A.H. Downes, the medical Inspector, also affected staffing policy in his report on workhouse dietaries. Downes wanted to improve the nutritional quality of the diets, especially for long-term inmates; he also argued that children, especially, should not have their appetites jaded by monotonous food.[12] The regulations stated that inmates should be given strictly weighed portions regardless of their appetites; Downes believed that if more varied food were given in quantities according to individual demand, there would be no more waste and no need to fatten the workhouse pigs on leftovers. Hence professional rather than pauper cooks should be employed to minimise waste.[13] Only the larger unions followed the Board's advice to employ professional cooks, kitchen staff and storekeepers, believing (probably rightly) that the extra salaries would outweigh other possible savings.

When they became employers of labour on a large scale, the guardians subtly changed the nature of the Poor Law. Not only were workhouses beginning to offer services instead of merely discouraging pauperism, but sometimes the guardians used their power as employers to keep people off the rates. In the past, guardians had often employed officers who might otherwise be paupers themselves, but by the end of the nineteenth century salaried officers were rarely selected in this manner. But the unskilled work of the house could be done by the local poor, especially widows. Local records indicate that guardians offered work as charwomen, kitchen helpers, and so forth, to women who applied for outdoor relief. Widows always made up a large proportion of the outdoor poor, and this was one way of using them in the Poor Law service. Widows with small children were perennially exploited on the labour market as 'sweated' domestic labour, and the guardians' own wage rates hardly improved the situation. Guardians could threaten a woman and her family with the workhouse if she refused to work at the guardians' rates—and it is likely that many women undertook the dreary labour of the house in order to avoid residence in it. During the 1870s the Inspectors had addressed themselves to the question of able-bodied widows, and Henry Longley argued that they ought to be relieved in the workhouse—but that if public opinion would not stand for this, then an effort ought to be made to employ them as workhouse servants.[14] In the 1880s, whenever Merthyr Tydfil union had no able-bodied labour in the workhouse, it compelled women on out relief to come in as servants at six pence per day and rations. Lambeth sometimes employed women in the institutions, allowing them to live outside, but placing some of their children in the schools without requiring the mother to pay for their maintenance. Some women possibly found this arrangement convenient, but it broke up families, and the mixture of relief and employment suited the ratepayers' pockets.

Transfer of certain workhouse infirmaries to the armed forces during the war revealed the deficient staffing ratios compared with the voluntary hospitals, and so more nurses were to be found in workhouses by the end of the war. At this time the central authority abandoned its old practice of scrutinizing the terms of appointment of each officer. From 1921 the guardians no longer had to report each new appointment to the Ministry of Health; but each union submitted its numbers of employees and cost of salaries for checking once a year.[15] The guardians no longer had to apply to the Ministry for permission to pay doctors' fees for operations, nor for anaesthetists' fees, and they could make their own arrangements for officers' families to live in the institution. The Ministry retained the right to sanction an officer's dismissal, for this was considered an essential protection against capricious guardians. The bureaucratic checks had been designed by the Poor Law Commissioners to prevent unnecessary local expenditure, but the problem was now one of encouraging guardians to employ an adequate staff. In the economic conditions after 1921, neither the Ministry nor many guardians were pressing for more expense of this kind: the problem of financing outdoor relief for the unemployed overwhelmed them.

Why then, did the Poor Law officers continue to bear the reputation of a second-class service? Overwork and long hours were a feature of many types of employment. The Webbs would have replied that unspecialized officers were not capable of managing the transference of the workhouse from a mixed institution to a specialized one. For older officers, brought up to think mainly of discipline, the changeover must have been awkward. In 1881 the master of Bishop Auckland had taken a wide view of his responsibilities, which were:

> ... to evolve order, to arrange and classify [the paupers,] to listen to their various wants, troubles, complaints and wishes; to care for the suffering ones tenderly; and to rigidly exact from the able-bodied shirk his quota of labour, to help to support the house that shelters him; to keep and preserve provisions, clothing and stock; to prevent waste; ... to keep his books and accounts; to exercise a gentle sway and controlling influence in harmonising any little differences that may ... arise between the other indoor officers.[16]

Poor pay, lack of training, and the unspecialized nature of the workhouses were all offered by the 1905 Commission as reasons why the Poor Law officers did not give satisfactory service. Above all, the dreary life of the institution, and their own virtual incarceration within it, continued to sap the officers' spirits. The ideals of the Bishop Auckland master were impossible to realize.

In spite of these indisputable problems, by 1909 the Poor Law officers were making some attempt to turn themselves into a professional service, and hoped to achieve a higher status by raising their standards. The medical staff achieved a limited success, but the rest were fighting heavy odds. The central authority never tried to raise the quality of Poor Law staff, with the important exception of the nurses. If the service remained second-class, it was because guardians kept it so, and the central authority did not direct otherwise.

When at the end of the nineteenth century the Poor Law officers began to combine to defend their interests, they were inhibited by their ambivalent social position and the administrative separation of unions. They were in a weak position to attempt trade union tactics. Each board of guardians had its own pay scales and conditions of service, while the staff were organized in such strict hierarchies that combination was difficult. They found it easier to negotiate directly with the Local Government Board, in hopes that it would introduce favourable legislation or put pressure on the guardians. Officers feared a penurious old age, and the question of superannuation united them more than any other, leading to the formation of the National Poor Law Officers' Association (NPLOA) in December 1884. After ten years of lobbying, backed by several boards of guardians, the officers finally achieved legislation compelling guardians to contribute to superannuation payments based on the officer's length of service, and to levy a contribution from the officers.[17]

The Association did not wish to be a trade union but a professional body, reflecting the social aspirations of its members. The most active group within it were the clerks, for chief clerks usually had a legal training and were the most educated and highly paid officers. Masters, matrons, relieving officers and some of the other principal officers also took an interest in the NPLOA, which aimed at the salaried officers rather than the humbler staff like porters and storekeepers. Strikes were discountenanced; gentlemanly negotiation was the favoured method. The medical officers, with their own association formed nearly 20 years before, and with the backing of the BMA, did not need the new Association, but some did join. By 1892, however, the Association was said to include less than one tenth of Poor Law officers, and by 1898 less than one third. In 1893, the occupations of 4,344 of the 6,180 members were stated:[18]

	numbers	%
Clerks and assistant clerks	213	4.9
District and indoor medical officers	510	11.7
Masters and matrons	473	10.9
Schoolteachers	125	2.9
Chaplains	40	0.9
Other workhouse officers	1071	24.7
Relieving officers	653	15.0
Assistant relieving officers, overseers, collectors	756	17.4
Other outdoor officers	262	6.0
Other officers	241	5.6

Indoor officers thus made up a large proportion of the membership, in accordance with their strength in the whole profession. Membership tended to fluctuate because officers regarded the NPLOA as an *ad hoc* body. As soon as superannuation became compulsory, more than 2,000 officers left the Association, though by 1906 membership had climbed back to 9,847.[19] In 1929, when the NPLOA agreed to merge with the National Association of Local Government Officers (NALGO), it claimed a membership of some 13,000, but half of these had not paid their subscriptions.[20]

The NPLOA wanted a progressive scale of salaries which should be proportional to the amount of responsibility in each union, and also to improve conditions of service. Guardians differed greatly in such matters: some automatically gave paid leave, others never did. In the 1890s officers still had to pay a substitute if they took a holiday. Long hours, poor food and accommodation, and discrimination against officers with families were also matters for complaint. After the Superannuation Act had been passed, officers found that it affected their mobility, for superannuation payments were not transferable, and guardians might be deterred from hiring an older, experienced officer if they would have to pay his full superannuation.[21] The officers did not object to the rule that master and matron be a married couple, for this maintained the family income, but they objected to a long-serving officer being dismissed on the death of a spouse, especially as some guardians used this power to evade their responsibilities over superannuation. The NPLOA gave legal advice to officers who were in dispute with their employers.

Like other associations of the lower-middle class, the NPLOA was successful less because of its trade union activities than because of the benefits it began to offer its members. It had a benevolent fund and approved society in which members could insure themselves. In 1890 the Poor Law and Local Government Officers Mutual Insurance Association (LOGOMIA) was set up to help officers with the guarantee bonds which guardians required of those in positions of trust. Clerks, masters and relieving officers had previously paid heavy premiums to commercial insurance companies for this purpose, but the new company was able to cut the premiums and offer other insurance services. By 1929, when the company was taken over by NALGO, it was a successful enterprise.[22]

Other organizations reflected both the officers' concern with their status, and their inability to combine. The humbler officers tended to join the Poor Law Officers' Union rather than the NPLOA, and most of the salaried officers had their own societies, including the Association of Workhouse Masters and Matrons, the Clerks' Association, and the Relieving Officers' Association, all of which represented the interests of their group to the Local Government Board. These organizations held national meetings, and also brought together officers from neighbouring unions. The Metropolitan Relieving Officers' Association often met to hear lectures and discuss Poor Law topics, but indoor officers were less active, possibly because they could not easily leave the institution. The central authority sometimes consulted these organizations, and many of them gave evidence to the 1905 Commission, but none had much influence over their employers, the guardians.

In 1892 the weekly *Poor Law Officers' Journal* began publication in Rochdale, and continued until 1929. It tried to keep officers informed of changes in the law and of administrative decisions which affected the service. It carried advertisements for staff, together with news from the unions. It approved the actions of 'progressive' guardians, and exposed those who were nepotistic or who paid unreasonably low wages. In other matters the *Journal* was conventional: it commended unions who were generous to the sick and aged, reported enthusiastically on the opening of children's homes, and advocated severe treatment of vagrants and the able-bodied unemployed. Like the Poor Law conferences, it attacked the reports of the 1905 Commission, and particularly the 'socialist' intentions of the Minority Report.[23] It welcomed Labour-controlled guardians, however, as it hoped these would be more generous towards employees. The *Journal*, like the guardians' associations, did not support county control of Poor Law administration, for the officers feared heavier responsibilities and staff cutting in the name of rationalization. The officers thus paradoxically viewed guardians both as their enemies and their chief support.

The *Journal* campaigned for better conditions for indoor officers, and supported more variety and entertainment in the workhouse as an encouragement to both officers and inmates. The old-fashioned officer was tempted into relieving his boredom by drinking and tyrannizing over the paupers, but if the workhouse were more pleasant, the officers would benefit also. The *Journal* applauded guardians who provided well-furnished staff apartments and common rooms, and derided the Inspector who in 1910 objected to officers holding their annual dance in the institution:

> ... indoor officers already suffer many unnecessary social deprivations, and ... it ought to be a pleasure... for those in high places to discover how the conditions of the indoor officer can be made to approximate as nearly as possible to the home life of the average person outside the institution walls.[24]

Just as advertisements in the *Journal* show that workhouse provision had become a minor industry, so they also reveal the growth of professionalism amongst the officers. Firms specialized in officers' uniforms and furniture; printers offered literature for their instruction. Officers had to keep up with changes in the law and administration, for they were legally obliged to resist guardians who evaded the law. Masters and medical officers were supposed to report any erratic action by the guardians in workhouse administration. Several annual publications, as well as the regular *Local Government Gazette* offered to keep staff abreast of the times. Numerous handbooks advised officers of their responsibilities, and the clerks in particular had many books to guide them in the complexities of Poor Law administration. *The Law of Settlement and Removal of Union Poor*, by J.F. Symonds, went into several editions, and had to be revised whenever that intolerably complicated law changed. Merely keeping up with the regulations, the Minority Report argued, took up far too much of an officer's time.

The Poor Law officers aimed at professional status, using the same methods which had proved successful with doctors, architects, and other aspiring professions. Professional training, judged by competitive examination and a certificate of competence, were seen as the necessary means; and the executive committee of the NPLOA put forward their own claims to control the system:

> Medical colleges and schools grant medical diplomas that no one would ever seek to question. The Incorporated Law Society conduct examinations for enrolment as solicitors—the value of their examinations is never questioned . . . Two things alone give value to any certificates of competency granted—(1) A board of examination constituted of capable members. (2) Thorough examinations.[25]

But the NPLOA finally decided not to set up its own examining board because its competence *would* be questioned: the Majority Report noted the officers' efforts at improved status, and recommended that the Local Government Board set up an examination system.[26]

In 1903 the Metropolitan Relieving Officers' Association decided that training and certification of officers was essential, and a course of instruction was begun at the London School of Sociology and Social Economics. The school, a new venture under the wing of the Charity Organization Society, offered lectures and examinations, first to relieving officers and later to clerks and indoor officers. The first examination in March 1906 produced 28 passes and ten failures.[27] The

COS had pioneered the 'case paper' method in social work, with detailed investigations of each applicant for help. The Poor Law, by comparison, usually operated erratically; few detailed records were kept, and much still depended on a guardian happening to know the applicant. The COS hoped that relieving officers and others would be trained in the new system, which would have produced a more individualistic approach to the poor. Some 'advanced' guardians such as Lambeth had adopted the system and needed efficient officers to implement it.[28] The training course was adopted in Liverpool University, and by 1909 was being extended to other centres. The London School of Sociology, insufficiently financed, did not survive, and in 1912 became a department of the Webbs' new institution, the London School of Economics. The training course continued under a joint committee of the old School and the NPLOA.[29] Thus, into this first experiment in the training of social workers, was injected a strong dose of the characteristic COS attitudes to poverty, later criticized because they encouraged social workers to relate social problems to individual rather than to social failings.[30] This was a debate for the future, because the scheme did not affect Poor Law officers as much as had been hoped.

The Majority vainly hoped that in time guardians would appoint only trained officers. The examinations continued under the auspices of the unofficial Poor Law Examinations Board, one member of which was nominated by the central authority. The NPLOA and the Association of Poor Law Unions (which represented many boards of guardians) both supported it, but the venture was not successful. A curriculum on the theory and practice of Poor Law Administration was open to officers in many parts of the country; in 1925 the *Poor Law Officers' Journal* claimed that guardians often required such qualifications,[31] but local records and advertisements for officers in the *Journal* do not support this. Examinations might help to improve the status of new officers, but long-serving officers were not enthusiastic. In 1927 the National Association of Relieving Officers suggested that certificates be made compulsory for all relieving officers except those who had been in the service more than five years, but the value of the certificates was dubious.[32] It was easier to demand qualifications of nurses, for the standards had already been set by the voluntary hospitals, and there was a large annual intake of new nurses. In the end, training for officers was never widely accepted under the Poor Law, although the examinations were an early example of an attempt to encourage qualified social workers rather than amateur administrators.

Officers improved their conditions less by their own efforts than through the fortunes of war. During the war years, officers were even more stinted of rations because guardians took seriously the government's plea for economy, but national wage levels were rising, and the officers benefited. Even wartime rations compared favourably with those of the 1840s. In 1917 the Basford officers had ample quantities of fruit, vegetables, puddings, pickles, tinned fruit and sardines—and eight pints of ale a week, though they agreed to reductions in eggs and milk, and to accept rabbit in lieu of more favoured meats.[33] Many officers joined the forces, leaving the institutions short of staff, and it was discovered that matrons and the wives of the relieving officers often carried out their husbands' duties with equal efficiency. In 1916 the Whitley Committee was appointed to consider ways of reducing labour unrest, and it recommended voluntary councils of employers and employees to settle disputes. In 1919 some effort was made to apply this to the Poor Law service; the Association of Poor Law Unions set up both a national committee and local ones, with a membership half of guardians, half of officers. The Paddington guardians, for example, set up a joint conciliation committee to discuss working hours, salaries and conditions of employment. It required a two-thirds majority to pass any resolution. At this time the Civil Service received a large war bonus, and some guardians did the same for their officers. Salaries went up by about 20 per cent, but there were still wide variations from union to union.[34]

At the central Poor Law conference in 1920, several officers spoke at length on their conditions of service, an unusual topic for these assemblies. The clerk of Rochdale union argued that guardians were always torn between the interests of paupers and of ratepayers, and that the officers were generally forgotten. He said of the indoor staff, 'the officer's position spells "servitude"; and the ratepayers are allowed to be scandalous profiteers'.[35] Another officer supported him:

> They knew what it was to be an officer in a small institution, when they considered that almost the whole difference between an inmate and an officer was that there was just a little higher scale of diet... The atmosphere itself was so depressing to a lover of liberty that only those who had imposed upon themselves a vow of self-sacrifice could endure it.

The officers were still disgruntled with their lives. Fittings of more easily cleaned materials began to replace the lead and brass of the nineteenth century; modern cooking ranges were installed; the officers had pianos, radio sets, neat uniforms paid for by the guardians, and more jam. Nevertheless, they compared their lot unfavourably with workers in other institutions. The medical staff naturally looked to the example of the voluntary hospitals, with their higher staffing ratios and shorter working hours. It is instructive to see the comparisons chosen by the other officers. In 1909 the two representatives of the Workhouse Masters and Matrons Association described their position to the Royal Commission; automatically, they compared themselves with governors of prisons. The Governor of Usk prison, with 137 prisoners, could expect £700 a year and a house—more than double the pay of a master of a similarly-sized workhouse.[36] The clerks compared themselves with civil servants. In 1920 the Rochdale clerk compared the pay of relieving officers unfavourably with that of police inspectors.

It was perhaps fortuitous that the penal service came most readily to mind when the Poor Law officers were contemplating their lot; but it is also an example of the tradition of social discipline associated with the Poor Law. Yet in comparison with other lower-middle class groups, the Poor Law officers had achieved a fair measure of security, if not a high degree of professional respect. Officers employed by other local government authorities were much slower to win pension rights, and their pay was often inferior to that of Poor Law officers. When the NPLOA was absorbed by NALGO, the historian of the latter union comments:

> Difficulties were inevitable, especially for the more senior officers moved from the exclusive, sometimes lush, and often easy-going pastures of the paternalistic guardians into the impersonal and harsher fields of a local authority public assistance department.[37]

If the officers did not see Poor Law service in this mellow light, it was possibly because of the social distaste which their work still aroused. One factor which caused the officers to resist control by the county councils was fear of 'impersonal' employment. Under the Poor Law, guardians and senior officers came to know each other well, and while this could produce tension, it could also encourage guardians to protect the interests of their staff. Their relative readiness to accept superannuation schemes contrasts with the indifference of other local authorities, and so the officers not unreasonably feared that the destruction of the guardians would affect their own security.[38]

The indoor officers were not entirely able to shed the brutal nineteenth century image. The masters, as previously suggested, were more likely to have worked their way up the Poor Law hierarchy than to have been appointed from outside, but the regulations requiring a trained nurse in the workhouse meant that matrons with nursing qualifications were much in demand. The Webb's comment that masters were sometimes appointed on their wives' merits is borne out by the reminiscences of one former officer: he remembers his last master in the 1920s as an imposing figure with a military moustache, but his wife, a trained nurse, really ran the institution.[39] Needless to say, although the matron's work was far more difficult and responsible than in the past, her pay was not on a level with the master's, though as a proportion of his salary it crept up from about one-third to a half or more. In large institutions, the master had more servants to manage and less personal contact with the inmates. He still had power over able-bodied paupers and vagrants, but in many other cases his authority was passing into the hands of the medical officer. After the order of 1913 which emphasized the responsibilities of the medical staff, a master would have been foolish to countermand the doctor's wishes, for the doctor had to supervise not only the sick, but the elderly, children, and pregnant women. Better conditions encouraged masters to be more honest, temperate and kindly than their predecessors, but the relatively low pay did not attract very educated men.

In other respects the master had more autonomy. In the earlier years of the New Poor Law, guardians had to interview all candidates for workhouse appointments, including cleaners and laundrymaids. By the end of the nineteenth century, guardians usually left this to the master, who merely reported to them when he appointed new staff, although the guardians still appointed the salaried officers. Matrons and guardians tussled over who should appoint nurses: after 1913 this was usually left to the matron, if she were a nurse, or to the superintendent of the infirmary. By the 1920s much of the master's time in a large workhouse was taken up with hiring and supervising domestic staff; he reported regularly to the guardians on such details as repairs to the boiler, or the need for extra laundrywomen, with virtually no comment on the inmates. The house committee took over the work of hearing inmates' grievances and recommending action in individual cases. But the master still decided which part of the workhouse an inmate should be sent to (except the medical cases), and what work he should do. In a large institution he might now be more influenced by his subordinates' reports than by his own knowledge.

As the inmates' lives became more comfortable, the officers became more powerful. The most effective means of discipline was to withdraw privileges, and by the end of the century there were more privileges to withdraw. The master could no longer decide how much leave an inmate should have, for most guardians now had set rules, but by classifying him as disreputable or badly behaved, the master could prevent him having any leave at all. In Southwell, the workhouse punishment book shows that stopping the tobacco allowance was a favoured means of discipline, though the diet could still be reduced to bread and water for 24 hours for 'serious' offenders.[40] By the early twentieth century guardians were allowing head of families to leave the workhouse and look for work; and it was the master's word which decided who should have this privilege. Inmates could complain to the guardians, but the arguments against this were as strong as ever; masters could easily retaliate, and if guardians contradicted the master it would upset 'discipline'.

When the Local Government Board insisted the paupers be classified according to their moral condition, the difficulty was whether to classify according to past life or present behaviour. The Poor Law Commissioners had believed that only present behaviour was relevant, but in 1895 an Inspector argued that this placed temptation in the master's way:

> Whatever precautions are taken to make the guardians or the house committee responsible, they must necessarily proceed on the report of the master, whose powers (already too despotic) will thus be increased to an undue extent, with the result that the inmates will be even more subservient & more anxious to curry favour than they are at present.[41]

The workhouse was at least a more open institution, and the paupers more protected from the worst excesses of the old type of officer, but by 1918 the problems of workhouses were those of many institutions. The inmates had to contend less with conscious cruelty than with indifference and traditional attitudes. If a master had spent many years in the Poor Law service, he could be slow to change his habits, even in such simple matters as asking for armchairs for elderly inmates rather than wooden forms without backs. Masters had a greater chance of influencing their employers before 1929 than afterwards, for they had more personal communication; but, weighed down by administrative detail, handicapped by their own lack of training, and in a social position where deference to the guardians was natural, the masters were not likely to initiate change.

Other officers also suffered the reputation of a second-class service. Schoolteachers were fewer in number, but those who remained still felt inferior to the members of their profession outside the Poor Law. Witnesses to the 1905 Commission argued that Poor Law teachers had less control over the children than ordinary schoolteachers, and that the governors of Poor Law schools still took children out of the classroom to do household work. Nor did the pay or holidays of these teachers compare with those in the elementary schools, and they were still expected to work long hours as the children's attendants.[42] Classrooms in district schools were overcrowded, for there was no fixed maximum of seats, unlike the public elementary schools. By 1908 the proportion of trained teachers to pupils was as high in the Poor Law service as in other schools, but they had different types of certificates, which were not highly esteemed. It was therefore argued that only teachers unable to get work elsewhere would apply for a Poor Law post. The Board of Education reported that:

> ... some of the teachers had stuck fast in the old grooves, and are unable to adapt themselves to the freer and more intelligent methods of teaching to which they were first introduced when the new system of inspection was established in Poor Law Schools and individual examination of scholars abolished in 1905.[43]

The officers who began to replace teachers in caring for the children also suffered from isolation. Guardians could not appoint untrained schoolteachers, but the matrons of children's homes needed no qualifications. Officers in the smaller homes were often untrained and poorly paid. Although an institution for 30 children was not a real substitute for family life, the officers were at least able to escape some of the monotony of a large district school, and had more freedom of action. By the 1920s, Romford union (Essex) paid the superintendents of its homes only £60 per year with board; there was a rapid turnover of staff and few applicants for the posts. One critic amongst the guardians commented: 'The "Scattered Homes" system combines all that is poverty stricken and depressing about a poor dwelling with all that is stunting in the institutional life.'[44]

Like the medical staff, the workhouse chaplains actually gained in prestige. A slight cooling in sectarian controversy aided this, but because the churches were putting greater effort into work among the poor by the later nineteenth century, the post of workhouse chaplain received more social respect. Larger workhouses were employing two or more chaplains to attend to the various denominations, and tension had relaxed far enough to allow Roman Catholic chaplains in some workhouses. New workhouse buildings from the 1870s usually included a chapel, furnished partly by the guardians and partly by local charities. The chaplain could make his own arrangements here, instead of conducting the services in a hastily-rearranged dining hall. The Local Government Board allowed the guardians to buy an organ or harmonium, and even to employ an organist. Religious quarrels continued, however, and the Romford guardians became seriously agitated in the 1920s about how much to spend on improving the Anglican and Nonconformist chapels in the workhouse. When the Church of England chaplain took the children for confession, the guardians were horrified, and sent the children to the local church to avoid his influence.[45]

Charitable workers in the institutions could strengthen the chaplain's position, assisting him in visiting the helpless, and providing extra comforts. Local records, on the whole, show that the chaplains attended zealously to their work in spite of poor pay, for chaplains' salaries did not rise although the chaplains devoted more time to their duties. A few unions employed full-time chaplains, but usually the work was still part-time, and the salary regarded more as an honorarium. In 1927 the guardians of Chippenham union reviewed their chaplain's salary, which had been raised from £50 to £60 during the war. They found that the chaplain paid 104 calls a year, and debated whether it would be right to lower the salary to £50 again:

> ... one member said: 'if those visits aren't worth at least half-a-guinea a time for a professional gentleman like a clergyman, in all weathers, finding his own transport, then they are worth nothing. Why should we "sweat" our parsons?'[46]

The board finally compromised at £55. In the early years of the New Poor Law the guardians seem to have paid their chaplains relatively well and demanded little of them: by the twentieth century the position was reversed. Nor did the chaplains concentrate only on religious ministrations; they could frequently be found arranging entertainments for the inmates and co-operating with local charities to provide social events in the workhouse. In Lambeth in 1906 the Catholic chaplain and his friends amused the infirmary patients with songs and violin playing on New Year's Day: hardly the religious discipline envisaged by the Poor Law Commissioners.

In larger workhouses, relations between the staff became more formal and hierarchical. Different grades of staff, like servants in a great house, had their own codes of behaviour toward each other. The ancillary staff were in an inferior position, and did not usually eat with the established staff. Large numbers of young nurses also created problems, and they were forbidden to speak to the male staff unless it were strictly necessary. While not as claustrophobic as in the early days, the institution continued to strain the personal relationships between staff, and between staff and inmates. Deadening routine, in an institution always subject to strict economies, affected staff in different ways. The 1905 Commission took evidence from workhouse officers, and descriptions of their attitudes to their work ranged from cheerful optimism to almost total indifference. The master of Bethnal Green classified the men rigidly under a system of his own, and was hopeful of forcing out the 'loafer' while keeping the rest comfortable and active. The matron of Lambeth able-bodied women's wards, which also housed elderly and imbecile women, could think of nothing to stimulate them except further deprivation of privileges, and had no hope of achieving anything with them.[47] As in modern institutions, work with the incurably sick or severely handicapped affected the morale of the staff.

In spite of the recommendations of the Royal Commission, neither the central authority nor the guardians really tried to improve the calibre of the staff, and this doomed the officers' own efforts to failure. It is easy to criticize the staff as petty tyrants, hidebound by regulations, unable to relax their disciplinarian attitudes. But they were what the institutions made them, and it is more surprising to find that some of them surmounted their harsh environment and were able to make life more tolerable for inmates within the limits imposed by the regulations. Problems of staffing did not end with the Poor Law, but continue still. When the workhouses began their slow transformation into county hospitals in the 1930s, there was no great change in the staff. A few older masters whom the Inspectors felt to be less competent were pensioned off, while others took the post which is now that of hospital secretary. The relieving officers continued as public assistance officers, the ancestors of today's social workers. Other institutional staff continued as before, and some are still to be found, nearing retirement, in National Health hospitals. There was, after all, nobody to replace them.

The county councils were not necessarily more generous towards their officers than the guardians had been, and the Ministry of Health took little initiative until the creation of the National Health Service. Modern institutions employ a very large staff compared with the old workhouses, but still do not satisfy those who believe that institutions are useless if they do not provide a personal service to each inmate. Professor Tizard and others have examined the debate on the role of staff in institutions: while rejecting Goffman's argument that institutions necessarily make discipline their chief aim, they reveal the division amongst sociologists as to the optimum size and staffing ratios of residential institutions.[48] One side contends that institutions with too few staff will inevitably lean towards discipline and strict routine as a way of relieving the staff of their burdens: another viewpoint is that the size of staff is less important than the nature of authority among them, and the kind of training they have received. Hence, one solution offered is to have a very high proportion of staff to inmates; another is to make the relations between staff less hierarchical, for staff with some autonomy of action will be more committed to their task than those who have no freedom of action, irrespective of their numbers. There is no disagreement over the size of institutions for the handicapped and for children: modern observers agree with those nineteenth-century critics who believed that large institutions destroyed family life, and wished to foster more personal relations between staff and inmates. Where medical treatment is concerned, however, the same problems occur as in the case of workhouses: a very small institution, unless handsomely financed, will not be able to provide a range of specialized services. The continuing debate shows how far we still are from solving the problems of institutional life, in spite of decades of specialized training for staff, and the development of academic disciplines which have brought all the armoury of research to bear on the problem.

The continuance of the large Poor Law buildings is itself an obstacle to change. These represent too large an investment to be swept away overnight; and yet they are not amenable to modern ideas about institutional care. The buildings inherited from the Poor Law were both relatively understaffed and extremely hierarchical in their administration, and their traditions persisted under the National Health service. Although Goffman's cynical comments on the actions of staff may not be accurate for all modern institutions, they may with propriety be used to illuminate the behaviour of workhouse staff. The relationship between officer and inmate was that of patron and client:

staff did not necessarily abuse their power, but they could force inmates to conform to the institution's private code. Conditions of work, pay, and their secluded lives, continued to encourage petty tyrannies amongst the staff well into the twentieth century.

At late as 1960 Professor Townsend commented on institutions for the aged in terms which reveal the bridge between old and new. At that time the old workhouse buildings were still a major part of local residential services for the aged and handicapped. Townsend investigated 39 Poor Law institutions still in use, and noted the low pay and poor staffing ratios compared with other types of institutions. His impression of the staff sums up the last years of the Poor Law officers, for many of them were still in their posts:

> Some were dedicated to their work and many others acted with sympathy and good-humour in a depressing environment. But it would be idle to pretend that many of them were imbued with the more progressive standards of personal care encouraged by the Ministry of Health, geriatricians, social workers and others since the war. Their horizons were limited by their experience and by the lack of opportunities afforded for further training. A few among them were unsuitable, by any standards, for the tasks they performed, men or women with authoritarian attitudes inherited from Poor Law days who provoked resentment and even terror among infirm people. And although there may have been only one such person for every ten or 20 who acted with at least a reasonable measure of humanity, he or she could do untold harm.[49]

7

The Medical Staff and the Infirmaries

1834–1867

Like the lay officers, the doctors and nurses in the workhouse system
suffered from the reputation of a second-class service.* Even in the
1920s a professional meeting of doctors could describe the Poor Law
infirmaries as 'little better than the rubbish heaps of practice'.[1] Yet
during the nineteenth century the medical staff emerged from a
subordinate role to become the most important of the indoor officers,
and provided the vital link between the workhouse and the public
hospitals which replaced it. The Poor Law Commissioners regarded
the medical officers as a necessary nuisance, but the doctors gradually
came to influence the treatment of all inmates. The nurses, whose
existence was not recognized in 1834, became the most numerous class
of workhouse officers. By 1929 the infirmaries ranged from fully-
equipped modern hospitals to the small sick wards of certain rural
unions, where no full-time nurse was employed and the sick inmates
barely separated from the rest.

The Webbs were convinced that until the state medical services were
freed from the crippling restrictions of the Poor Law, the medical staff
would remain a second-class service,[2] for the professionalism of the
medical staff suffered from the limitations imposed by confusing the
treatment of the sick with the discouraging of pauperism. Yet not all
the problems of the infirmaries can be attributed to the Poor Law. As
growing numbers of helpless people were committed to institutions,
the infirmaries had to accept larger numbers of the chronically ill, the
incurable, and the dying, whom no other institution would take. The
nature of the medical service reflected the type of case it had to treat,
and growing specialization in the profession tended to exacerbate the
difficulties.

---

*For the sake of brevity I use the anachronistic word 'doctor,' though the term
was not widely used until the late nineteenth century.

The obvious difference between the doctor and the other officers was that he belonged to a profession which was rapidly gaining in social esteem. By the mid-nineteenth century, the profession had established much stricter control over medical qualifications. In 1842 the Poor Law Commissioners anticipated the Medical Act of 1858 when they decreed that no medical man could be employed by guardians unless he were qualified in both medicine and surgery and had at least two of the formal qualifications then available. As soon as the Medical Act was passed, Poor Law doctors had to be registered under it.[3] Formerly the guardians had been able to employ even the most flagrant quacks if they pleased, and although unqualified men were not immediately purged from the service, the foundations were laid for a professional body.

The workhouse doctor could compare his institution with the voluntary hospitals in which he had trained, and he would remember the great prestige of the senior staff in those hospitals. The provincial doctor was becoming less isolated from the medical world; he could, if he chose, subscribe to the new medical journals such as *The Lancet*, or later to more specialized ones such as *The Hospital*. Begun in 1886, *The Hospital* carried news of the Poor Law infirmaries as well as other types of hospital, and criticized those which fell short of the current ideal. The career of the medical officers must be seen in relation to the development of the medical profession as a whole, but their Poor Law employment placed them under different obligations from the ordinary general practitioner. They were men with divided loyalties, to the ethics of their profession and to Poor Law conventions. This dualism was reinforced by the nature of their employment, for nearly all of them combined workhouse duties with private practice. In the voluntary hospitals, consultants were unpaid, but undertook the work for its prestige, its contact with wealthy patrons, and the fees from teaching. The workhouse doctor had to accept an underpaid Poor Law post because his private practice did not support him adequately, or because he wished to keep other doctors out of his territory. A workhouse doctor did not expect his work to increase his prestige, rather the reverse.

There seem to be no reliable figures for the numbers of full-time workhouse doctors. Under the Old Poor Law a few of the larger unions had employed a resident dispenser or apothecary. As the town infirmaries grew, the guardians had to employ full-time doctors, but in 1900 only 44 unions had resident medical officers, and there was no indication of how many had full-time but non-resident doctors.[4] By

1920 about 26 unions in London and 54 in the provinces had resident doctors, while in 24 more the doctor was full-time; but private practice was still the mainstay of the profession.[5] Some combined the posts not only with private practice but with the post of district medical officer and public vaccinator against smallpox as well.

The doctors had their own organizations much earlier than the other Poor Law officers. From 1854 a series of associations protested against the doctors' conditions of service, and in 1868 Dr Joseph Rogers founded the Poor Law Medical Officers' Association. The British Medical Association, whose roots went back to 1832, also spoke up for the Poor Law doctor. At first these doctors seemed in need of special protection: until 1854 their contracts were annual only, and the guardians could dismiss them at will. Even after 1854 the guardians could still manipulate the doctor's contract: if he lived outside the district they did not have to offer him a permanent contract. By 1862, 711 out of the 3552 doctors were employed on this basis.[6]

Although after 1842 medical appointments were no longer offered for tender, guardians could exploit the weaknesses of local doctors. The medical profession was highly competitive, and guardians knew that weak or possessive local practitioners would often accept Poor Law work at uneconomic salaries. At a time when patronage was still important in building up a practice, the doctor may also have hoped that his contacts with the guardians would bring him private practice—though it was also argued that the gentry would not wish to employ the 'parish doctor'.[7] Poor Law practice was a sign of weakness because of the many unattractive conditions of service. A notorious relic of the Old Poor Law was the requirement that the doctor provide all drugs and medical appliances out of his salary. Guardians were sometimes more prepared to buy drugs for the infirmary than for outdoor patients, but the size of the infirmary was important: in smaller unions the doctor was his own dispenser. In a hierarchical profession, the Poor Law doctor's prestige suffered because he was subservient to laymen, the guardians. Only doctors who had failed to establish a sufficient practice would seek employment from a corporate employer such as the guardians, the armed forces, or the prison service.

Critics of the service always argued that its professionalism was hampered by corrupt or ignorant amateurs, including the other workhouse officers, the guardians and the central authority. Joseph Rogers saw his career as a struggle against obscurantism, as his brother wrote:

He had to reckon with sordid London vestrymen, perhaps the worst class of men with whom honest people have to deal, and with the officials of the Poor Law Board, who were determined, as far as possible... to shirk all responsibility.[8]

In 1909 the Minority Report made similar criticisms of an amateur administration. In the nineteenth century it had seemed more reasonable for laymen to control medical employees: the 1832 Commission had included no medical men, and had virtually ignored them in its report. It assumed that medical assistance to the poor would continue, but made no specific recommendations. This vagueness gave full scope to Chadwick's distrust of doctors, for he believed that sanitary reform rather than medicine was the effective answer to disease. Hence the Poor Law kept doctors on a tight rein: the tender system and lump sum payments were supposed to prevent medical profiteering. Tufnell wrote of the medical officers with contempt:

... like all men with a little smattering of learning, they are exceedingly fond of using the hardest names the dictionary can supply. [They deceive the guardians into ordering] enormous quantities of mutton, wine, arrowroot, etc.—an evil which is now daily increasing, and... is adding to the amount of pauperism and the poor rates.[9]

The Commissioners even intended to give the guardians powers to reject the doctor's recommendations on food for the sick, but had second thoughts on this.[10] Yet many guardians still ignored the doctor's advice: in Basford, for example, they forbade him to order more than tea and gruel as 'extras' for the sick until a board meeting had sanctioned further extravagance.[11]

Erroneous though the views of Chadwick and Tufnell may now seem, they hit the medical profession on its weak spot. The therapeutics of the time had severe limitations, and sanitary engineering was indeed a more effective measure against infection. Nosology was still in its infancy, and not until eight years after the passing of the New Poor Law did William Farr in the newly created Registrar General's office lay the foundations for a standard definition of the causes of death.[12] From the 1840s the guardians could pay the district medical officers an extra fee for three types of treatment: smallpox vaccination, midwifery, and certain surgical operations. These were areas where the benefits of medical skill were reasonably well attested.

The workhouse doctor was not paid extra for operations, for the Commissioners argued that he ought to send surgical cases to a voluntary hospital if possible. Chadwick's scepticism may perhaps have been productive at this time. If the doctor were allowed to order extra food, for which the guardians paid, and discouraged from ordering drugs of dubious value, he might unwittingly be employing the best means of cure for an undernourished population. As medical knowledge advanced, however, the regulations became a severe handicap.

In the 1830s, when there was little professional discipline in the medical profession, the guardians assumed that they could reasonably control their medical officer. By the mid-nineteenth century the profession had its own effective code of discipline, more effective than the erratic views of guardians. The Poor Law doctor had constantly to refer to the workhouse master, who was in charge of the routine administration of the infirmary. In badly run unions like Andover, the 'extras' rarely reached the patients, but were appropriated by the officers, and the doctor had no means of ensuring that his orders were carried out. In denying the doctor control over the infirmary, the Commissioners also denied him power in areas where he could have done good, especially the sanitary condition of the institution. From 1842 he had to report on possible health hazards in the workhouse, but was powerless to institute reform. As late as 1891 the medical officer of St Olave's infirmary (Bermondsey) was complaining that the relieving officers sent patients to the infirmary without consulting him: 'Today I am obliged to put them in a ward and leave them to nurse themselves.'[13]

In the mid-nineteenth century there were innumerable stories of the atrocious conditions in many workhouse infirmaries, always overstrained in times of epidemic when they became fever hospitals. In Blean in 1856 the doctor wrote that 60 patients were in an infirmary designed for 30, and that the sick were bedded throughout the workhouse, lacking proper care, and spreading infection.[14] In Lambeth in 1846 the assistant medical officer was dismissed for writing anonymous complaints about the matron and an illiterate night nurse, who had not called him when a patient was dying.[15] In Andover the doctor had known about the brutal treatment of indoor paupers, but had not complained to the guardians because he feared it would cost him his job. There were several famous indictments of the infirmaries, including those of Frances Power Cobbe and of Florence Nightingale, who declared Liverpool workhouse to be 'worse than Scutari'.[16] *The*

Lancet sent a commission to investigate the London infirmaries in 1865, and the medical critics did not mince their words:

> At St Martin-in-the-Fields the... ground floor rooms look like basement cellars, and this is due to the fact that the site is an ancient and well-stocked *churchyard*; and these rooms, with this offensive abutment of churchyard earth blocking up the windows on one side, have been converted into surgical wards.
> ... At Greenwich the site is below water-mark, and the foundations are liable to be flooded... Several of the wards (e.g. the laying-in ward) have no water-service at all...[17]

The Poor Law Board knew of these circumstances, not only from reformist officers like Joseph Rogers, but from the reports of their own Inspectors. Like many doctors, the Inspectors believed that disease could be spontaneously generated by the stench arising from decaying matter; hence they took note of workhouses which were in damp areas or subject to noisome odours. One Inspector, Basil Cane, described Lambeth's foul wards in 1854:

> As showing the necessity for a vigilant supervision of these Wards, it may be mentioned that on observing a jug of salt under a Wardsman's bed, and enquiring for what purpose it was kept there he told me that he could not do without it, for he used it to destroy the lice which he sometimes found in the beds.[18]

In Rogers' autobiography Cane appears as a typical representative of the apathetic Poor Law Board, for Cane had defended the terms of medical officers' appointments. Yet in those times Cane's opinions on the cause of disease were at least as sound as Rogers'. They disagreed over the solution, for Cane felt that disease could be effectively prevented without improving the lot of medical officers; Rogers did not.

The Board had been forced to hold inquiries into individual workhouses, revealing deplorable health conditions, but had done little about them.[19] The Board lacked leadership, and its political position was weak. The health of workhouses could not be improved without coercing guardians into spending large sums of money. The middle-class public who deplored the horrors revealed by *The Lancet's* widely publicized report, also objected to all efforts to increase the powers of the central authority. It required steady pressure from critics in the 1860s to produce legislation. *The Lancet's* attack led directly to the formation of the Association for Improving Workhouse

Infirmaries, in which Rogers was a leading figure. Rogers attracted many famous supporters, including Dickens and J.S. Mill, and the public was for once persuaded to sacrifice economy to reform. The Metropolitan Poor Act of 1867 not only spread the cost of the indoor poor amongst all the London parishes, but provided for infirmaries with an administration separate from the workhouse. Lunatics, fever and smallpox cases were removed from the management of guardians altogether, and a new authority, the Metropolitan Asylums Board, was to provide hospitals for them. Nineteen London parishes, some of them with the most notorious infirmaries, were required to build new separate infirmaries.[20] Unlike workhouse infirmaries, these new hospitals were controlled by the medical staff, and so the Act assisted the rise of the medical expert.

Rogers always linked the appalling conditions in many infirmaries with the weakness of the medical officers: poorly paid doctors had insufficient authority and had to concentrate on their private practice. Neither the public nor the central authority, however, would readily accept the connection between hospital conditions and the financial problems of the doctors. Demands for reform could be interpreted as medical self-interest; higher salaries would cause higher rates. Rogers came from a struggling family—he was the 13th of the 16 children of a country doctor—but believed that his profession conferred a certain social status. He despised the 'low' tradesmen with whom he had to deal on London vestries. Yet in many country practices the doctor was regarded as little more than a tradesman himself, and certainly much inferior to the *ex-officio* guardians. In spite of their efforts to combine, the medical officers had little success in improving their conditions of service before the Great War, for the central authority believed that it could improve the infirmaries without any major change in the status of the medical staff.

An ancient fear was reflected in another restriction on the medical officers. The infirmaries could not be used for medical education or research. To the doctors, this was the ultimate proof of inferior status, since much of the prestige of the voluntary hospitals came from their work in these fields. Medical students were admitted into the infirmaries in 1867, but banished again in 1869. Here the Board simply bowed to public fears. The peculiar dependency of sick paupers would make them vulnerable to medical experiments if they were not protected. The pauper was thus free from becoming a subject for clinical investigation, while the patient in the voluntary hospital had to submit as part of his free treatment. A regulation which the doctors saw as an insult seemed to laymen a necessary safeguard.

The policy of the same voluntary hospitals added to the Poor Law doctor's burdens, for most voluntary hospitals excluded chronic cases, and also infectious and venereal cases.[21] Hence the doctor in even the best workhouse infirmary would feel aggrieved, for not only was he subject to the dictates of laymen, but he received the least amenable patients, who could not be denied admission to the workhouse. In fact, his complaints about the shortage of drugs were probably of little relevance, given that so many of his patients were elderly, tubercular, or with other chronic ailments which the therapeutics of the day could not relieve. Nevertheless, the doctor was understandably at logger-heads with guardians who refused to pay for drugs, and who might even define cod-liver oil as a 'drug' and refuse to supply it. Nor could the doctor depend on the supply of other basic requirements. Most guardians subscribed to one of the truss societies which provided charitable help to sufferers from hernia—a common condition produced by heavy labour. In 1855 the Blean guardians decided to buy trusses in bulk, although the doctor objected that they were unsuitable and did not fit.[22] The great truss factory in Trafalgar Square, to which Arnold took exception in *Culture and Anarchy,* symbolized more than the philistinism of the Victorian age.

It has been argued that the quality of Poor Law doctors had much improved by 1870, because fewer of them were being dismissed from their posts.[23] Yet this is an inadequate guide to their calibre. If guardians were lax, the doctor had every temptation to shirk his duties. Grosser offences like drunkenness apparently diminished, but perfunctory attention to the patients was a failing harder to control. Better medical education and tighter professional control were bound to improve the service in the long run; but the sheer lack of incentive must have affected the Poor Law doctor burdened with routine administration, not required to keep medical histories of the patients, but to account in detail for any 'extras' which were ordered. The doctor also had to spend time classifying all paupers, not merely the sick, to assist the master in determining their work and diet. The doctor also had to estimate a pauper's fitness to withstand punishment if he had committed a workhouse offence, and so the medical routine was also part of discipline.

It is difficult to see how the workhouse doctor could fulfil the various responsibilities laid upon him, and maintain his private practice as well. He had to be sanitarian, surgeon, psychiatrist, midwife, and disciplinarian, as well as physician. In the unspecialized days of the medical profession this was acceptable; but medicine was rapidly becoming more specialized, and nowhere more than in the hospitals. The case of the insane inmates illustrates this awkward position. The workhouse doctor was obliged to commit to an asylum any insane pauper who appeared dangerous, but with harmless cases he could use his own judgement or bow to the wishes of guardians who objected to the high cost of asylum treatment. 'Acute' cases, regarded as curable, would be accepted into county asylums, leaving the 'chronic,' or congenital cases in the workhouses. Hardly anyone argued that these inmates ought to be disciplined in the same way as the able-bodied paupers, but were they medical cases or not? Doctors followed their own opinions, and so many of these inmates were classified as 'able-bodied' and therefore given an inferior diet. Medical officers who considered them a non-medical problem were likely to leave them in the dubious care of pauper nurses, in conditions which were vehemently criticized by the Commissioners in Lunacy.[24] The Commissioners argued that no considerations of economy should deter the doctor from taking proper care of these inmates, yet in Leicester workhouse he visited the insane only once a quarter, and elsewhere the doctors attended the insane only if they became physically ill. Both overwork and the confused state of medical thinking on the question prevented the workhouse doctor from taking this responsibility more seriously.

Doctors also had to decide how to classify inmates who were ambulatory but not physically fit, including epileptics, the partially deaf, etc. The medical decisions produced the erratic statistics of the 'able-bodied' which were always so politically sensitive. Some medical officers classified all the aged or handicapped as non-able bodied in order to obtain special privileges for them; others did the reverse. The description 'able-bodied' of course carried implications of moral culpability which the workhouse discipline was designed to correct; and it was the doctor who actually made the moral judgement.[25]

In the early years of the new Poor Law the growing discipline of the medical profession was not enough to protect doctors from ignorant guardians or from their own temptations. Dr Henry Rumsey, one of the first advocates of a national health service, was able to speak well of the 'hard-worked and well-informed medical practitioner, toiling in a populous district, [thinking] with vexation of time and labour now wasted in mere pencraft, upon bundles of ruled paper, which serve no higher purpose than that of economic checks upon poor-rate expenditure'.[26] Dr Francis Anstie, one of the *Lancet* commissioners, had a closer experience of the temptations of an urban workhouse doctor:

> He has 250 acutely sick, besides a great many infirm, under his care in the workhouse, and he has also to dispense all the necessary medicines; for these duties he is paid at the rate of 2s 5d per diem! With a blunt and startling frankness he confessed that the whole business was a ghastly joke; that to save himself from the pecuniary ruin which the neglect of his private practice would have involved, he was obliged to make his attendance on the sick paupers a merely perfunctory business: that he never used the stethoscope in cases of chest-disease, because it would take up too much time; and . . . the medicine which he prescribed . . . was regulated chiefly with a view to facility of dispensing it, rather than to curing the patients.[27]

If the doctors were victims of the system, the same is true of the first workhouse nurses. Most nursing was done by the paupers themselves, and even the small band of professional nurses were, of course, untrained. The profession of nursing hardly existed, and commanded little social respect before the days of Florence Nightingale. The voluntary hospitals had similar problems, but some of them did at least employ literate and reasonably orderly women.[28] The Poor Law Commissioners had not stipulated the duties of a workhouse nurse; she had the same status as other pauper servants, and like them, could be rewarded with extra rations. The Commissioners forbade guardians to reward pauper nurses with alcohol, but in practice they often received it. The Commissioners disapproved of any attempt to pay pauper nurses for their services, and even in the 1850s the central authority resisted the employment of professional nurses for work which they regarded as part of the inmates' duties.[29] The master retained control over all supplies to the infirmary, while the matron was usually in charge of the nurses, the food, cleaning and laundry. The relation of matron to nurses was of housekeeper to servants, rather than the professional one established by Miss Nightingale.

The results of this system are well-known. The records of almost any union will produce a dreary tale of nursing inefficiency, neglect, and cruelty. Paid and pauper nurses alike had heavy labour and long hours; often they had no separate quarters, but ate and slept in the ward with the patients. Like other workhouse officers, they were on call night and day: few unions made separate arrangements for night nursing. Bound to the workhouse routine, without family life, without status, in buildings which demanded the utmost labour if cleanliness were to be maintained, the nurses exacted what pleasure they could from their environment. The workhouse reformers of the 1860s unanimously condemned the nursing service: drunkenness, indifference and incapacity were common enough. Paupers also knew that it was in their interests to bribe the nurses to secure the minimum of attention.[30]

The Poor Law Commissioners had not foreseen the great expansion of hospitals, and had recommended that the sick poor be given outdoor relief as far as possible. All they required of workhouse nurses was sobriety, and, on afterthought, enough literacy to read the doctor's instructions. The rapid developments in the voluntary hospitals brought workhouse nursing into disrepute, particularly in the 1860s, when professional nursing began to expand. Florence Nightingale took an interest in workhouse reform, and with her supreme ability for backstairs intrigue, pressed for professional nursing of the sick poor. The forces ranged against the old system were thus a combination of upper-class charity and nascent professionalism, as embodied by Louisa Twining, *The Lancet*, Rogers and Miss Nightingale. It was useless to argue, as the Manchester guardians did, that the standards of care were better than the poor could afford in their own homes,[31] for the standards had to follow the voluntary hospitals.

Historians have always accepted the reformers' view of pre-Nightingale workhouse nursing; indeed there is no evidence to contradict them. Most of the nurses, being paupers, could not defend themselves. The system was designed to ensure that it was the poor who oppressed the poor. Pauper nurses were often elderly women who had no hope of employment outside the workhouse, but were condemned to endless toil within it. Yet until the end of the century they remained the core of the nursing service. One of Louisa Twining's anecdotes arouses unintentional sympathy for them:

> The lying-in ward... which was only a general ward without even screens, had an old inmate in it who we discovered to have an ulcerated leg and cancer of the breast; yet she did nearly everything for the women and babies, and often delivered them too. The women's hair was not combed, it was 'not lucky' to do so, and washing was at a discount. The doctor and myself could not imagine at first why the temperatures went up, and the babies nearly always got bad eyes and did badly.[32]

The combination here of kindness, squalor and superstition sheds a less hostile light on pauper nursing, but the possibilities for abuse were very great. The reformers wanted not only administrative change, but to import a middle-class element into the workhouse, as Dr Anstie explained:

> The nursing must be performed by a numerous staff of trained and paid officials, including special night nurses, under the superintendence of a person not only specially experienced, but of good education and general social culture, for by such a chief only can proper discipline be maintained.[33]

This ideal was much more difficult to achieve than in the voluntary hospitals.

1867–1914

From the late 1860s it appeared that everything was ready for the rise of the medical expert in Poor Law administration, but this happened so slowly that the period between 1867 and 1914 must again be seen in terms of the forces inhibiting the medical staff. The gap between the physical conditions in infirmaries and the homes of the poor widened rapidly, especially in towns, but the gap between the infirmaries and the voluntary hospitals widened yet more. This must be set against a background of rapid expansion in hospital provision. In 1861, voluntary hospitals had provided only 18.51 per cent of the hospital beds in England and Wales: but by 1911 they provided 21.89 per cent, while local authorities independent of the Poor Law provided another 16.7 per cent. Although the responsibility of the Poor Law authorities was therefore declining proportionately, in numerical terms it continued to expand. In 1861 workhouses provided about 50,000 beds for the sick; in 1911, 121,161.[34]

At the same time there was both an administrative and a medical revolution in the voluntary hospitals. The advent of trained nurses encouraged order and hygiene. The gradual diffusion of antiseptic techniques made safer the operations which anaesthetics had previously made painless. Finally, from the 1880s onwards, bacteriology conquered the medical profession, and precipitated a rush to discover the micro-organisms of specific diseases. All this added to the prestige of a profession which was already claiming respect on account of its superior education and ethical standards. The Poor Law doctors shared in the new esteem for their profession, but remained at the bottom of its hierarchy.

In 1865 the able Dr Edward Smith was appointed to the Inspectorate: he had no power to decide medical policy, but dealt with medical matters in individual unions. Under the Local Government Board, two such medical Inspectors were appointed. In 1867 the President of the Poor Law Board, Gathorne Hardy, made a famous statement to the Commons:

> There is one thing that we must preemptorily insist on, namely, the treatment of the sick in the Workhouses being conducted on an entirely different system; because the evils complained of have mainly arisen from the workhouse management, which must, to a great extent, be of a deterrent character, having been applied to the sick, who are not proper objects for such a system.[35]

By 1870 there were three conditions which had been lacking in Chadwick's time: the central authority was willing to discriminate in favour of the sick poor; the Inspectorate had some medical expertise; and the doctors themselves were organized from 1868.

The Local Government Board, however, failed to press for reform. Its medical department, which dealt with public health and sanitation, was separate from the Poor Law Inspectorate, and there was friction between them. The medical Inspectors could not supervise all the infirmaries, and in any case, both the Board and the guardians could ignore their suggestions. The Board had no more power to coerce parsimonious guardians than had the Poor Law Commissioners: the Metropolitan Poor Act allowed it some control in London, but the threat of *mandamus* remained ineffective elsewhere. Gathorne Hardy had wisely provided a carrot to London guardians in the Common Poor Fund, part of which could be withheld if guardians overcrowded their accommodation, but neither Hardy nor his successors could wield a stick.[36]

The Poor Law doctors also strangely failed to become an effective pressure group. Repeatedly they approached the Board for changes in their conditions of service, but their grievances were never entirely redressed. Improvements came piecemeal in the unions. The guardians were not compelled to pay an economic salary, nor to provide dispensaries. From the mid-1860s the central authority recommended that guardians pay for cod-liver oil and quinine, but in 1877, 182 unions still paid for neither, and 521 unions paid for no other 'drugs' except those two.[37] The Poor Law Medical Officers' Association wanted more state regulation of their conditions of service, as they knew their own weakness in negotiating with guardians. The Board replied that the employment of doctors was entirely a local affair.[38] By 1900 the doctors had won no significant victory except the right to superannuation (1896), and although the Board usually encouraged guardians to improve the infirmaries, it took less interest in the staff.

Hence the Poor Law Commission of 1905 criticized the service severely. Physical standards in the infirmaries had improved since the 1860s, and even the small rural wards were (on the whole) clean and orderly, though poorly equipped, The Webbs commented that the 300 small country workhouses neither had nor needed a resident doctor, but that conditions of service still tempted the doctors to shirk their duties, sometimes attending the workhouse only two or three times a week.[39] They revived the old accusation that the doctor, deprived of drugs and appliances, would prescribe food and alcohol instead. In these infirmaries all types of cases would be placed in one ward. In the large towns, the guardians had to appoint full-time doctors because the size of the institutions required it, but Dr John McVail, who had conducted an intensive survey of infirmaries, noted that even in these large, modern establishments the doctors were overworked in comparison with doctors in voluntary hospitals. Camberwell, for example, had six doctors to 819 patients, and three of the doctors had duties at other institutions. McVail concluded that 'even where Guardians provide excellent, or perhaps extravagant, modern buildings... yet... they are likely to adopt unknowingly a policy of sweating, both as to the amount of work required and as to the payment made for it.'[40] Representatives from the BMA and the Poor Law Medical Officers' Association urged that infirmaries be brought up to the standards of the voluntary hospitals, and be opened for medical education.[41]

The workhouse doctor was still hampered, not only by the apathetic central authority and economical guardians, but by his own professional views, and particularly the conflict of interest between his private practice and his workhouse duties. As general practitioners, the medical officers often resented their patients being removed to hospitals, with a consequent loss of fees, and this extended to workhouse hospitals as well. Even in the 1920s the Poor Law Medical Officers' Association was objecting to patients being removed from the care of the district medical officers to the full-time infirmary doctors. Like many general practitioners, they resented the growing specialization in their profession.[42] The Association itself remained essentially a general practitioners' union in spite of the importance of the workhouse infirmaries. Although within a few weeks of its inception it had 600 members, it seems never to have attracted much active support from Poor Law doctors. The annual meeting after the 1870s were small affairs, usually held in London and attracting few doctors from elsewhere.[43] Unlike the NPLOA the role of the Association was almost entirely defensive, and it served mainly to assist individual doctors who were in dispute with the guardians. Even here, pressure of a more forceful kind could only be marshalled by calling on the BMA, for the more powerful union was by the early twentieth century having some success in forcing guardians to pay better salaries. In areas where it was strong, the BMA could ensure that no doctor applied for a vacant Poor Law post if the salary was considered too low, and it would prevent advertisements from being placed in the medical journals.[44]

Poor Law doctors relied on the *British Medical Journal* for information about their association, but in 1911 *The Poor Law Medical Officer* appeared as a short monthly supplement to the successful weekly *Medical Officer*. The supplement disappeared soon after the war, and its contents were mainly complaints about guardians, both in particular and in general, in contrast to the strong professional content of the parent journal, which was aimed at the medical officers of health, with stirring articles on sanitation. The Poor Law doctors had no professional interest to bind them together except a sense of grievance. Their Association therefore had to compete for membership with the BMA and other medical groups, as well as the NPLOA. The London infirmary doctors also had their own association. The BMA, which included about two-thirds of the profession in 1900, was undoubtedly the most attractive. Yet although the BMA sometimes fought effectively for individual workhouse doctors, it was strongly committed to private practice and hostile to the idea of a state medical service. Salaries did not greatly interest the BMA, which concentrated on the fee per case, whereas workhouse doctors were becoming salary earners in the large infirmaries. Consequently, many of the full-time medical officers became rather isolated from the rest of the profession. In 1913 the Bethnal Green medical officers horrified the Poor Law Medical Officers' Association by accepting the guardians' request that they treat the Poor Law staff, for no extra fee.[45]

Nor did the Poor Law doctors all wish to become full-time public employees. The young and the poor were always tempted by the lure of a regular salary and a pension, but established members of the profession often rejected this. As state service in the past had meant employment by guardians, many doctors assumed from past experience that they would be exploited. Guardians were still prepared to use the forces of the marketplace even more shamelessly than doctors: one Ipswich guardian rejoiced at a conference in 1901 that doctors were ready to accept inadequate salaries in order to keep others out of their district, 'And many of them had ripe experience, and as a rule they did their work well.'[46]

Dr Fuller, the medical Inspector, did not share this comfortable impression. He stated that rural guardians usually had to recruit from the lower ranks of the profession, and that the doctors were slack in their duties.[47] He wished the state to take over some of the responsibility for the doctors' salaries, both to ensure the quality of the service and to prevent exploitaton. His ideas were shared by the Medical Officers' Association, who, while resisting the idea of a state-run service, nevertheless believed that their conditions would improve under a large employer than the guardians. This contrasted with the ideas of the other officers, who still supported the guardians and feared county control. After 1909 the NPLOA could not effectively represent both doctors and the other staff. Fuller argued that low salaries were partly the doctors' fault, for they lacked cohesion as a 'working body of men', and were too ready to undercut each other.[48] In spite of the efforts of their professional organizations, medical blacklegs remained a problem.

The battle for salaries did not really become joined until after the National Insurance Act of 1911, when many more doctors took up contract practice. Meanwhile, the Poor Law doctors were largely committed to piecework rates. In some unions the workhouse doctor could earn more from extra fees for extra services such as midwifery, and certifying lunatics, than from his basic salary. In 1872 the workhouse doctor at St George's-in-the-East earned £100 basic salary, together with £35 for district medical work and another £123 in fees.[49] This was an exceptionally high rate for fees, but many workhouse doctors in London earned as much as one third of their total pay in this manner. When resident doctors were appointed they usually accepted a single salary with board and lodging, but provincial doctors continued to receive a fluctuating income based on several different calculations. Piecework confused the problem of doctors' salaries, and provided the guardians with a weapon. They could not dismiss the doctor without the central authority's consent, but they could refuse to renew his contract for vaccination, or they could refuse to call him to certify lunatics. If they had a grudge against him, they could summon one of his competitors for these services.

Poor Law doctors often shared the general hostility of their profession to the encroachments of state medicine on private practice. From the 1880s the Local Government Board began to sanction medical treatment for people who were not technically destitute, but who could not afford private medical care. To many doctors, private insurance which guaranteed the patient's personal choice of doctor, seemed superior to the expansion of the Poor Law system. The ineffectual Poor Law doctors are in contrast to their successful colleagues, the medical officers of health, who were far more committed to a state-run medical service. The BMA encouraged these officers, who concentrated on sanitation and social statistics: they successfully demanded full-time, adequately paid posts to prevent any conflict of interest between public duties and private patients.[50] The Poor Law doctors had no such clear vision: as Poor Law doctors they wished to be free of lay interference, but as private practitioners they were members of a social world in which the guardians might be important contacts. Professional independence was not safeguarded in the desperate search for private custom.

Apart from conflicting interests in their divided employment, the workhouse doctors often fell into Poor Law assumptions when treating their patients. The problem of defining the 'able-bodied' was compounded by the desire of guardians to classify paupers according to their moral character. Unlike their predecessors in 1832, the Royal Commission of 1905 valued medical expertise, and would have given to the doctor the task of sifting out all those who were incapable of looking after themselves because of moral weakness. Although the history of the public health movement was studded with the names of illustrious social investigators who had laboured to prove that much pauperism was due to disease (including Chadwick himself), there remained an uneasy suspicion that a certain amount of disease was due to drunkenness and immoral habits. Chadwick argued in his sanitary report that filth caused bad habits amongst the poor, which in turn caused disease; but the Webbs, more influenced by eugenic ideas, believed that the bad habits of the 'residuum' were hereditary, and that their illnesses were often the end product of genetic deficiencies.[51]

Hence the doctor should have power to commit such people compulsorily to various types of institutions.

The doctors in turn were often tempted to make moral assumptions on the nature of pauperism. A BMA questionnaire, answered by 1900 Poor Law doctors, had revealed them as strongly committed to the principle of institutions: workhouse inmates should be classified according to moral character, and feeble-minded unmarried mothers should be incarcerated. Children of vicious parents should be taken away from them; able-bodied inmates should have extra work and less food; incorrigible vagrants should be sent to labour colonies.[52] Beatrice Webb invited the medical witnesses to the Royal Commission to admit that sickness could be the result of bad habits: several of them obliged. Hence the Minority Report demanded public education in hygiene, combined with coercive measures for those who would not conform. Under the conflicting claims of professionalism and the Poor Law tradition, several of the medical witnesses argued that infirmaries should be removed from the 'Poor Law taint', while advocating severity towards the able-bodied.

Although the doctors failed to achieve their main aims in this period, they were not entirely thwarted. Guardians could virtually ignore their workhouse doctor in 1870, but in 1914 they would have hesitated. Few laymen could challenge the value of medical expertise in nutrition, sanitation and therapeutics. A determined doctor, now a man with some status, could intimidate guardians, as in Chelmsford, where in 1903 the workhouse doctor challenged the guardians over their refusal to replace a nurse who had left. The doctor had power to replace a nurse temporarily until the next board meeting; he threatened to continue doing this until they appointed a permanent officer.[53] Guardians were most likely to ignore a doctor's recommendations if large expenditure were involved. The doctors often longed for the latest equipment in the infirmaries—Röntgen ray machinery, septic facilities, and the most modern hospital paraphenalia—but few guardians were prepared to keep up with the rapid advances in medical techniques. If the standards of the infirmaries were usually inferior to the voluntary hospitals, they were also better than some of the private hospitals which catered for the middle classes.[54] Middle-class guardians sometimes felt that they were providing a better service for paupers than they could afford for themselves, and this thought did not encourage them to spend.

The calibre of workhouse doctors before 1914 is no easier to judge than those of their predecessors. The chairman of the infirmary committee of the Birmingham guardians, himself a doctor, described them thus:

> the ranks are filled chiefly from two classes: first, the young and needy practitioner, who is glad of the stipend until he has established himself in practice, when he promptly ceases to hold the appointment; the other, the middle-aged or old man who has never been able to make an income sufficiently large to enable him to do so... [55].

Sneers about the youthfulness of resident medical officers were common: a lady guardian claimed to have mistaken the medical officer for the messenger boy.[56] In fact the medical superintendent of the large infirmaries was usually an experienced man: of the 24 London superintendents listed in the *Medical Directory* for 1905, only two had been qualified less than 10 years, and only three for more than 30. The 30 assistant medical officers whose qualifications were listed were indeed young men: 20 of them had been qualified less than five years. This was of course similar to the practice in the voluntary hospitals, where the residents were usually young men waiting for promotion. The young residents in Poor Law hospitals, however, did not benefit from the regular visits of consultants, and their responsibilities were correspondingly heavy.

The ages of provincial doctors are not known, but the main handicap to efficiency was not age but the general conditions of service. In the rural infirmaries they must often have treated cases which were beyond their competence,[57] though this was a problem shared by country practitioners who were distant from specialists' advice. Conditions in the Poor Law service still tried the quality of workhouse doctors to the utmost, and sometimes they were unequal to the strain. Very few medical officers were dismissed from the service after the 1860s,[58] but records of individual unions show that a dangerous amount of inefficiency could produce an official caution rather than dismissal. In Bromley, for example, a child died in 1911 because the overworked infirmary doctor had forgotten that it needed an operation.[59] The guardians accused him of incompetence, but they expected him to run a large infirmary single-handed, with a grossly inadequate team of nurses, and their own regulations required him to keep detailed records of the 'extras' he ordered, not case-papers of his patients. The doctor was in charge of an infirmary with 300 infirm and chronic patients in residence every week. In a six-month period before the war he assisted at 22 operations, delivered 21 babies, officiated at 49 deaths, and had to supervise 37 lunatics and 31 imbeciles. He had little time for paperwork, nor was it surprising that he took little interest in therapeutic occupations for the aged and infirm.

The workhouse doctors lacked supervision, unlike the residents in the voluntary hospitals. Neither the guardians nor the lay Inspectors could judge their medical competence, and the central authority could not intervene unless guardians complained. Dr Fuller felt that the state had not enough power to be rid of inefficient officers.[60] Hence the possibility for abuse remained, not subject to precise analysis, but with disastrous effects on the reputation of the service.

In the nursing service, relations between laymen and professionals were even more strained. Guardians accepted the need for trained doctors, but were less convinced of the need for trained nurses. Nursing was a new profession: it had been proved on the battlefields and in the voluntary hospitals, but guardians often argued that the type of patient usually found in workhouses did not need specialized attention. As a Norwich guardian put it:

> Personally he did not think that they required such a large staff of highly trained nurses in Poor Law institutions. A large number of the cases were chronic cases of old age or sickness, and what they really required was a person of motherly and kindly disposition, who would look after the old people and administer to their comfort. (Applause).[61]

Many rural guardians hired only one trained nurse and left the rest of the work to untrained women or female inmates. Even in the large infirmaries, there was a gross deficiency of nurses in comparison with the voluntary hospitals. McVail saw this as the single greatest problem, and compared staff numbers in eight teaching hospitals with nine local authority hospitals and nine large Poor Law infirmaries:[62]

	Teaching hospitals	General hospitals	Poor Law infirmaries
Average no. of beds	502	170	387
Ratio of beds to nurses	2.70 : 1	3.83 : 1	10.60 : 1

McVail added that even in hospitals with identical numbers of beds and nurses, Poor Law nurses might be more seriously overworked because they had to cope with infectious diseases, venereal cases and the 'foul wards', when no local hospitals would accept these patients.

Even if guardians were willing to hire trained nurses, the work was unattractive. Trained nurses were in short supply even in the voluntary hospitals. One of the secrets of Miss Nightingale's success was that she had created a profession for 'ladies'. She did not intentionally restrict her training to middle-class women, but the Nightingale legend, coupled with Miss Nightingale's own strict standards, attracted women from comfortable backgrounds. They did not work for the salary, but in a spirit of service. Florence Nightingale also demanded higher standards of accommodation for them than the old-style nurses had expected. The matron, although responsible to the doctors, had autocratic control over the management of the wards, and the system produced formidable professional women who expected, and generally got, respect from both the doctors and the patients.

The Poor Law infirmaries offered fewer attractions. The guardians not only refused to pay the same rates as the voluntary hospitals, but rarely offered the nurses decent living quarters. The master's wife usually managed the infirmary, and many guardians persisted in seeing it as a housekeeper's job. In 1865 the Poor Law Board ineffectually protested against pauper nurses, and the Local Government Board later urged guardians to employ only paid nurses, but it did not insist that these nurses be trained. Dr Edward Smith, although appreciating the value of trained nurses, knew they were hard to find, and suggested that pauper women of good character be paid a salary for nursing and be removed from the pauper lists.[63] As no supply of trained nurses was forthcoming, the central authority from the 1870s encouraged the larger infirmaries to train nurses internally by taking on probationers who would receive a year's instruction from the medical officer and head nurse. The shortage continued, however, and spurred Louisa Twining in 1879 to found the 'Association for Promoting Trained Nursing in Workhouse Infirmaries'. The Association did useful work in financing the training of nurses, but it could never meet the demand.[64] According to Miss Twining, the grosser evils of the previous decades had been replaced by 'passive cruelty'. The paid nurses did not abuse their patients, but were forced by overwork to neglect them:

> The old and infirm were put to bed and kept there, for there was no one to dress them, and the passive cruelty was general; the bed

sores were frequent, though called 'eczema', and yet what could one nurse, much less an untrained girl, do with 80 or 90 cases under her care?[65]

Workhouse nursing did not attract ladies, still less nurses who had been trained in the voluntary hospitals, but the full training seems to have attracted girls of the lower-middle classes, daughters of professional men, farmers and shopkeepers.[66] They needed some education in order to take the written examinations, and they were usually in their twenties, as the Local Government Board believed that nursing was too heavy a labour for adolescent girls. The minimum age for candidates was fixed at 25 in 1873 and 21 in 1900. The training in the infirmaries was not as thorough as in the voluntary hospitals, and the girls often regarded it as a path to more lucrative private nursing. The untrained nurses had fewer expectations, and were more likely to be working-class girls who took the post in preference to domestic service. Nurses' training was not at this time subject to regulations, but higher prestige attached to nurses from the teaching hospitals, who had usually undergone at least three years' training. As the profession depended mainly on young women who were not permitted to continue their work when they married, it was necessary to provide a large and regular supply of probationers for all the hospitals.

By the time that Arthur Downes (1889) and Andrew Fuller (1893) became medical Inspectors, the central authority was less committed to a policy of deterrence, and workhouse discipline was relaxing. Downes was to spend 30 years in his post, and was to take part in many important inquiries. In 1891 he wrote a memorandum on workhouse nursing, arguing that the use of paupers as nurses was uneconomical as well as inefficient, for these women were likely to misappropriate food and destroy expensive equipment: only trained nurses should be employed, they should be decently housed, and the ratio of nurses to beds should be no more than one to 15. Downes stressed that the sick poor should receive nursing as efficient as in the general hospitals, and that the 'sick poor of the better class' should not be made to feel repugnance on entering the workhouse to receive treatment.[67] No official action was taken, however, until the *British Medical Journal* launched another vigorous attack on workhouse nursing in 1895.

Typically, the Board would not act until it had some public support. In 1897 it finally passed an order forbidding the employment of pauper nurses, though they were still allowed to work in the infirmaries under the supervision of a trained nurse. The Board also tried to classify workhouse nurses according to the amount of training they had received. All infirmaries with a staff of three or more nurses had to employ a superintendent nurse of at least three years' training. 'Assistant' nurses needed only one year's training, but the term was still used for women without any training at all. Consequently, the order created two classes of nurses in the Poor Law service: only infirmaries with a resident doctor could train the superintendent nurses, while the smaller infirmaries with 'minor' schools could train only assistant nurses. As infirmaries with less than three nurses were not required to abide by these rules, in 1901 only 63 (of about 300) rural infirmaries had superintendent nurses.[68]

In 1902 a departmental committee on workhouse nursing reported that probationer nurses had increased from 936 in 1896 to 2,100 in 1901, but recognized that most of them would not stay in the service.[69] The committee believed, rather complacently, that there were enough workhouse nurses, but warned that Poor Law nursing was becoming less and less attractive; daughters of the wealthier classes would not enter a service where professional opportunities were limited. In the same year the nursing profession itself began a steady campaign for the registration of nurses, and the Midwives' Act of 1902 was the first to demand certain qualifications for an important section of the profession. The Act also affected infirmaries, for workhouse nurses now needed a midwifery certificate in order to take charge of confinements. The committee recommended also that the head nurse, not the workhouse matron, manage the infirmary.

The Poor Law conferences discussed the report at length; many guardians did not wish to reduce the powers of the matron, and joked about the inability of two women to run a household harmoniously. Some of the leading Poor Law nurses also gave papers: they were the matrons (in the modern sense) of the separate infirmaries. They resented the inferior qualifications of workhouse nurses, and did not wish to be seen as Poor Law officers, but as part of the nursing profession. Downes, who had been a leading member of the committee, was attacked by the matron of Birmingham infirmary for retaining the dual qualification of workhouse nurses: he had to fall back on the old argument that workhouses did not need expensively trained nurses for the typical infirm patient. The small country infirmaries, with little variety of patient, and their dull routines, would never attract highly qualified women. Downes added that 'he could not see a way of giving everybody silver spoons; some must be content with electro-plated'.[70]

As the nurses became more professional, they shared in the disciplinary tasks of the workhouse staff, for they had to be more than the ministering angels of Nightingale myth. Guardians in the larger unions were anxious lest discipline break down in the infirmaries, where inmates had to be treated according to their illness rather than their deserts. The Bath guardians, who in the late nineteenth century carefully placed all inmates in moral categories, tried to extend this to the infirmary, but the medical staff insisted that food and medical treatment could not be prescribed according to the pauper's morals. Guardians who supported better training for nurses argued that only women of this kind would be able to maintain effective discipline.[71] In 1909 the visiting medical superintendent of Liverpool infirmary argued that 'a sick person should be on quite a different footing to a vicious one', but some guardians did not believe that a pauper ceased to be vicious because he was sick.[72] As full-time attendants, the nurses were in the front line of discipline, as the regulations for Lambeth nurses indicate:

> To preserve order and decorum amongst the patients, to see that the rules are duly observed, to prevent loud talking, improper conduct or conversation, or smoking in the wards.[73]

It would be unwise to press this point too far. Nurses in all hospitals were supposed to control their patients, and Miss Nightingale had encouraged habits of military discipline in the profession. All hospital nurses were themselves subject to a variety of petty regulations, and their own behaviour had to be above reproach. In the Poor Law service, understaffing reinforced the impersonal treatment of patients which the idea of hospital discipline had begun. Like other workhouse officers, the nurses had little time for diversions: in 1906 the Lambeth nurses worked from 7.30 a.m. until 8 p.m., and went to bed at 11. They had one half day off per week, and alternate Sundays from 2–11 p.m. They were discouraged from intruding too much domesticity into their quarters, which a sympathetic guardian described as 'hutches'.

> Bedrooms are to be kept tidy, and the occupants are requested to avoid having too many knick-knacks, as they give extra work to the servants.

By 1913, although the head nurse had more control over the

infirmary, relations between medical staff and other officers were still strained. The nursing order of 1913 did not compel small institutions to employ full-time qualified nurses. By that time, women from the training schools required a salary of £35–45 per year, with board, but country guardians often refused to pay as much, for they could obtain a less trained woman for £20–25. Remote unions had difficulty in attracting nurses at all, and one Inspector reported from the South Midlands in 1913 that there was such a shortage of trained nurses that the guardians employed partly trained girls who had been sent away from the schools because they were unfit. At Banbury the superintendent nurse had only £35 per year, for which it was impossible to attract a capable trained woman, and so:

> ... she was hardly fitted to hold the post of a parlour maid and like all her class she was not strictly truthful so that when inquiries were made it was difficult to fix the blame, and there was always friction.[74]

The only defence offered of the inferior type of nurses frequently found in small workhouses was that their work was so repulsive that intelligent women were repelled. The same Inspector added:

> The ordinary small country WH with perhaps 15 to 30 inmates of the sick wards—mostly 'bad legs' or ordinary senility cases—does not provide work enough either to attract or to keep out of mischief a trained nurse on night duty.

One rational suggestion, rarely adopted, was that these nurses combine their infirmary work with district nursing. Even in the large infirmaries, the central authority continued to argue that the higher proportion of chronic cases was sufficient justification for the high ratio of beds to nurses. The medical profession itself fostered this belief, for the prestige of the medical elite was inexorably entwined with the treatment of the acutely ill in the voluntary hospitals. Some eminent doctors were not unwilling to perpetuate the division between hospitals for acute and for chronic illnesses, and so to relegate the infirmaries to a perpetual second-class status. Lauriston Shaw, physician at Guy's Hospital, recommended to the 1905 Royal Commission that the more interesting cases be removed from the infirmaries, and that the voluntary hospitals be allowed to dispose of their chronic cases to the Poor Law with less difficulty.[75] The infirmaries would not then need to offer specialized treatment or surgery (thus making them even less attractive to the best doctors and nurses).

There were two replies to this common argument. The first, made by the Webbs and McVail, was that although chronic cases did dominate the infirmaries, there were always enough acute cases to make it necessary for skilled assistance to be available. The large infirmaries were taking more acutely ill patients every year because the voluntary hospitals had not enough beds. Street accident cases often came to the infirmaries, especially in London, where the voluntary hospitals were nearly all too far from the suburbs. The larger infirmaries performed more operations every year, also. Voluntary hospitals could refuse to admit more patients if they were becoming overcrowded, the infirmaries could not; and the infirmaries continued to take infectious cases, including tuberculosis, which the voluntary hospitals could refuse.[76]

The Poor Law nurses offered a second argument. They knew that even if infirmaries contained mainly chronic and senile cases, these often required as much skilled and careful nursing as the acutely sick. 'Infirm' patients who were of little interest to a doctor could be difficult and time-consuming for nurses.[77] Some of the 'chronic' cases were also victims of medical definitions, for chronic cases who were not interesting to doctors before 1914 were more interesting after the war as new treatments were discovered. Workhouses also had to admit the dying, and the shortage of nurses doubtless made an institutional death the more lonely.

From 1867 to 1914 the Poor Law medical service still suffered a second-class reputation, in spite of the improvements to the physical state of many infirmaries. This classification was partly owing to the diverse conditions in the service, from the full-time doctors and well-qualified nurses in London to the perfunctory part-time doctors and untrained nurses in the small workhouses. But the poor reputation was due as much to medical as to social definitions. While both doctors and nurses gave the highest respect to the teaching hospitals and took less interest in 'routine' patients, the ablest members of these professions inevitably found the Poor Law service repellent. Fear of lay domination, poor pay and overwork played a part, but the staff also suffered because they felt isolated from the mainstream of their profession.

The Medical Staff and the Infirmaries

1914–29

From 1914 the workhouse medical service was influenced by the growing debate on the possibility of a comprehensive state health service. The war affected hospitals very markedly, precipitating changes which were not reversed as effectively as other aspects of wartime government control. The workhouse infirmaries and their staff were an essential part of the wartime medical services; and Poor Law doctors and nurses left for the front or stayed to work in infirmaries which had been converted to military hospitals. Even the poorly trained workhouse nurses became a valuable asset, for the medical service relied increasingly on hastily trained volunteer auxiliaries. Surgeons, specialists and equipment had to be shared between the hospitals, exposing most plainly the deficiencies of the Poor Law infirmaries. Staff in war hospitals received military pay, bringing the salaries of Poor Law nurses up by around 30 per cent.[78] The War Office naturally selected the best-equipped of the infirmaries, throwing a heavier burden on the rest, who had to take in patients from the appropriated hospitals.

In some infirmaries the war removed old staff and encouraged new ideas. The locum who replaced the Bromley workhouse doctor was horrified to find that the old women in the infirmary spent their time sewing shrouds, an ancient practice which the previous doctor had not thought to question.[79] The doctors themselves hoped that after the war the infirmaries might retain their new status and new staffing ratios be maintained, they still did not contemplate a full-time profession, but demanded higher rates for piecework and extra responsibilities.[80] By 1917 the future of the service seemed in the balance; the Maclean committee adopted the argument of the 1905 Commission that the Poor Law infirmaries should be transferred to county authorities. At the same time, the Labour Party was advocating an amalgamation of the voluntary and the Poor Law hospitals. In 1920 a Ministry of Health committee under Sir Bernard Dawson again recommended that preventive and curative medical services should be combined under non-Poor Law authorities. The Dawson committee would have continued the divided nature of practice between public and private patients, but even this moderate suggestion alarmed the BMA, who objected to the encroachments of the state. Although for the first time a doctor was at the head of the central authority, Dr Addison's bill was defeated: it would have allowed local authorities to take over the infirmaries, and was strongly opposed by both guardians and the medical profession. In any case, it was a half-hearted measure which would probably have encouraged the more active local authorities to take over the best infirmaries, while leaving the guardians with the care of the elderly sick in the smaller institutions.

After 1918 there was probably a growing division of interest between the workhouse doctors and the district medical officers. Salaries and conditions of service under the Poor Law could be safeguarded only by state intervention, yet the BMA was hostile to this as a matter of principle. The workhouse doctors favoured amalgamation of rural infirmaries as the only way to bring them up to the best hospital standards. More full-time infirmary doctors were being employed: the Ministry did not keep accurate records of them, but in London alone their numbers had increased from 77 to 117 between 1905 and 1923.[81] In the same period the number of beds under their charge rose from 15,845 to 21,668 and 28 consultants from the voluntary hospitals were also regularly employed as visitors. In the larger infirmaries the doctors rarely had any private practice, and in London there was also a tentative movement to employ the district medical officers full-time.

Nor were the large infirmaries merely receptacles for the chronically ill. The West Middlesex Hospital (Brentford) performed 30 operations in 1876–7, but in 1929 there were 452 operations. The very change of title in the large unions from 'union infirmary' to 'hospital' after the war was revealing. In 1905 all the London institutions had called themselves 'infirmaries' or 'sick asylums', and 15 of them had added the tell-tale adjectives 'parish', 'union', or 'workhouse'. In 1925 only three of them did so, and most of the others disguised themselves under oubriquets such as 'St Andrew's Hospital, Bow'.

In the 1920s more doctors came to favour state medicine. The sanitarians had originally believed that much disease could be prevented by public hygiene, but by the 1920s the limitations of this approach were becoming more obvious, and there was more interest in personal hygiene and clinical medicine. Public sanitation was not enough to guarantee the health of the population. The work of Sir Arthur Newsholme, chief Medical Officer of Health 1908–1919, pointed towards a combination of the preventive and curative branches of public health under one authority. Although he was dismissed by Addison when the Ministry of Health was established, Newsholme actively publicized the employment of doctors in the state service, and tactfully criticized the objections of the BMA. Newsholme, like many doctors, had begun by thinking that only infectious disease should be the concern of the state, but later took a much more comprehensive view. Just as doctors had previously confused the symptoms with the disease itself, he said, so they had confused the causes and effects of poverty. Chadwick had argued that removing disease would reduce poverty; Newsholme reversed the argument:

> Poverty and disease are allied by the closest bonds, and nothing can be simpler and more certain than the statement that the removal of poverty would effect an enormous reduction of disease.[82]

In 1922 Newsholme was elected President of the Poor Law Medical Officers' Association, a post with little responsibility, but his election symbolized the possibilities which some doctors could now see in state medicine as a noble ideal rather than a supplement to private employment.

Newsholme desired a system of public hospitals in which the infirmaries should be equal to the voluntary hospitals, for the voluntary hospitals could never meet the whole demand for hospital beds, and it was impossible to restrict the infirmaries to the chronically sick.[83] The distinction between patients and paupers in the two types of hospital was rapidly disintegrating, and it had always been based on the fiction that the charity patient was more 'deserving' than the pauper. After the war many voluntary hospitals had serious money troubles, and began to charge their patients and to pay their consulting staff. By this time it was apparent that the section of society most lacking for hospital care was, in Lord Dawson's words, 'the large class which includes the highest type of artisan and a large proportion of the middle class', who could afford a general practitioner but not hospital treatment.[84] Guardians had always been permitted to recover the cost of infirmary treatment from paupers or their relatives; now Lord Dawson was suggesting that the infirmaries accept paying patients without turning them into paupers.

In the early 1920s several unions had done this, often without permission from the Ministry.[85] Bolton had accepted private patients and allowed their own doctors to visit them. Unions tried to attract private patients by letting them wear their own clothes instead of infirmary garments. Ironically, since most of the Ministry's powers still operated through the district auditor, the Ministry could not prevent guardians from *making* money out of patients, although it tried to prevent them charging more than the cost of treatment. In some unions the guardians accepted paying patients at the request of the local voluntary hospital when the latter was overcrowded, or because there was an unmet need for certain types of treatment. The Edmonton guardians were permitted to take maternity cases from the local authority hospital at a charge of 28 shillings a week, as there was no other accommodation for them. Lord Dawson wished to give the paying patients better standards of comfort than the paupers, but the Poor Law representatives on his committee argued that this would disrupt the whole framework of the Poor Law and cause trouble in the institutions.[86] But in 1920 another old barrier fell; the Paddington guardians were allowed to receive medical students into the infirmary, in return for special services and advice from St Mary's Hospital. The paupers were permitted to object, but not invited to do so.

The large infirmaries performed operations and accepted acute cases; some of their patients paid fees. The voluntary hospitals were beginning to take paying patients and to pay their consultants. Both could receive medical students. Where lay the difference? Even the definition of 'chronically' ill began to change as medical knowledge advanced. Under these circumstances the doctors in the large infirmaries began to develop a sense of *esprit de corps*: at last a commitment to state medicine was not necessarily a commitment to a second-class service. Dr P.C. MacPherson, the medical superintendent of Portsmouth Poor Law hospital delivered a rousing defence of his establishment at an entertainment for the officers. He claimed that the hospital was now curative, not merely a home for the incurable; that it had 1,200 beds, performed 300 operations annually, and had the latest equipment in x-ray machinery and sun lamps. The nurses then gave a musical performance entitled 'the Romanies', 'and choruses, songs, and dances were given in a charming woodland scene'.[87]

In the *British Medical Journal* the infirmary doctors began to defend their profession. The young residents were often paid a better salary than their equivalents in the voluntary hospitals. Some argued that Poor Law hospitals gave a young doctor valuable experience, and that the pay was attractive to a man without enough capital to buy a practice. The superintendents could command from £600 to £1,600 a year, with a house provided. The small infirmaries, where the master could interfere, still had a low reputation, and were 'worthy of consideration... as a very temporary stop-gap'.[88] The doctors also asserted their independence of the lay staff, for only in the 'separate' infirmaries were they given autonomy. *The Lancet* commented loftily:

[The medical men] have higher education, more profound knowledge of human nature, and wider experience of public affairs than is characteristic of the class, however morally worthy it may be, from which masters and matrons in the Poor-Law Service are drawn.[89]

Life for doctors in the large infirmaries was not dull. The medical officer of Lambeth remembered the 1920s as a period when there was 'plenty of interesting work in great variety', and many distinguished surgeons visited the hospital.[90] Even the unspecialized nature of the work attracted some who resented the growing domination of specialists in the profession. The out-patient departments began to rival those of the voluntary hospitals. The records of Bermondsey Hospital, where the doctor had felt so oppressed in 1891, are in the 1920s almost indistinguishable from the records of a large general hospital, with clinical records and grateful letters from recovered patients.[91] Only occasionally did the Poor Law 'taint' reveal itself; a paying patient complained that a nurse had called her a 'pauper', and a policemen had to be employed to deal with drunken visitors.

Yet the rural workhouses were in much the same condition as before the war. In 1925, 533 out of 699 institutions had less than 100 beds for the sick, and in the small infirmaries the doctors did not keep clinical records.[92] The 70 separate infirmaries provided 30 per cent of all Poor Law accommodation for the sick; the rest still went to infirmaries with close administrative ties to the workhouse. Conditions in all infirmaries were seriously affected by government restrictions on capital expenditure, and throughout the 1920s the guardians spent less in both real and proportional terms on capital developments than they had in the decade before the war.[93] In the depressed industrial areas, particularly in Yorkshire, unions had outgrown their institutions, and there was a serious shortage of sick beds because of the moratorium on new building.

By the 1920s the workhouse doctor could concern himself more with patients and less with paupers, as the able-bodied were removed from the workhouses. His professional, rather than his Poor Law function became dominant. Vagrants were still an important exception: not until after 1929 were doctors required to examine them regularly, and in.the 1920s doctors were consulted only when tramps refused to work. Thus the workhouse doctor's task diverged even more from that of the district medical officer, who was still largely concerned with detecting malingering. The work of the district medical officer, however, declined as national insurance began to replace Poor Law medicine. In the 1920s the guardians employed fewer district officers than before the war, while the hospital service continued to expand.

The war also changed the conditions for nurses, and exaggerated previous trends. Even before 1914 nursing was becoming a major profession for unmarried women. The infirmaries had to compete for staff not only with the voluntary hospitals, but with the new municipal hospitals, private hospitals, and district nursing. War exacerbated the shortage, not only because it drained the nursing service, but because it created new jobs for women at higher rates of pay. Poor Law nurses still had low status, hard work and unpleasant quarters; ambitious young women might well prefer a nine-to-five job in a factory. Demand for trained nurses did not slacken after the war, and the Ministry of Health tried to encourage a ratio of one nurse for every six beds.[94] Nurses with a good Poor Law training often left for another nursing career, and by 1920 it was estimated that about half the district and private nurses in the country were Poor Law trained.[95] A Ministry of Health memorandum commented:

> By treating the nurse as a rather less qualified worker than a typist or factory hand, the standard of the nursing profession has been degraded. Many of the probationers who now offer themselves are of the factory hand type, and enter the service rather for love of the uniform and with a desire to fill in the interval before marriage in what they expect to be a pleasant occupation, than because they have any nursing genius... a wider unit of administration than the union should introduce more breadth of mind upon the subject of women's wages, which have in the nursing profession been regarded as of the nature of pin-money.[96]

The Ministry sanctioned shorter hours and better pay for nurses, and permitted expenditure on nurses' homes while forbidding it for other buildings. In 1924, nearly one third of guardians' capital expenditure was so spent.[97] Yet many nurses in the Poor Law service still had the minimal qualification of one or two years' training, or had trained in an institution which did not give recognized instruction. By accepting these women, the guardians could avoid competing for more expensive and highly trained nurses. The nursing profession had not been able to avoid dilution in wartime, but emerged from the war even more anxious to protect its standards. In 1919 it won the right for which it had long been campaigning—the state registration of nurses.

The Ministry accepted that the second-class status of Poor Law nurses would be abolished by submitting probationers to the examinations of the General Nursing Council. This was accomplished in 1925, when the Council began its first state examinations. In turn, the Council recognized 93 Poor Law infirmaries as training schools for nurses, and pay and conditions of employment improved. In 1927 the average pay of a Poor Law nurse in London was more generous than in the voluntary hospitals.[98] The average working hours also compared favourably with other institutions, but many nurses, especially the night nurses, still worked 60 or 70 hours a week.[99]

By 1929 the improvements in the nursing service had largely accrued to the separate infirmaries, which were soon appropriated by the county and borough councils. The small rural infirmaries were hardly affected, and had a minimal nursing staff throughout the 1930s. The assistant nurses who had been working in 1919 were permitted to register themselves on account of their experience, and the unions continued to employ semi-trained staff. Even in 1933 the local authority hospitals relied on 33.7 per cent of untrained staff (excluding probationers), as compared with 15 per cent in the voluntary hospitals. Professor Abel-Smith has also shown that the public hospitals continued to rely on girls with less formal education than did the voluntary hospitals.[100] By 1933 it cost an average of 54/6 to keep a patient for a week in a general hospital, as against 38/3 in the Poor Law institutions.[101] Much of the difference was accounted for by the understaffing in the rural infirmaries. By this period they had few pretensions as hospitals. Most of them were homes for the infirm with vagrant wards incongruously attached.

The problem was now revealing itself as one which had arisen only in part from the nature of the Poor Law service: it was the problem of carrying for the infirm and senile aged in a society which was committed to institutional treatment. The difficulty of staffing this kind of institution could not be resolved by abolishing the Poor Law. Paradoxically, as medicine became more complex and specialized, care of geriatric patients became even less medically interesting than under the Poor Law. The more highly trained a nurse became, the less likely that she would wish to devote her time to this type of patient. Indeed in 1943 the government responded to the nursing shortage by sanctioning once more the old Poor Law system of a two-year training for a second grade of nurse. The nurses were anxious to dissociate themselves from the lay officers; and they usually contracted out of the Poor Law superannuation schemes in favour of the more expensive

Royal National Pension Fund for nurses.[102] In 1921 the nurses in the Manchester area set up a Poor Law Nurses' Guild, which sent representatives to the NPLOA, but 'it was expressly stated by Miss Burgess, matron of Crumpsall Infirmary, that there should be no question of the National Association becoming a trade union...'[103] At this point the problems of Poor Law nursing merged into the problems of nursing as a whole: anxious for the status of a skilled profession, they were handicapped by the youth and large turnover of their members; above all, because they were women.

Of relationships between the medical staff and their patients, only occasional glimpses emerge from the records. The Poor Law medical staff may have confused patients with paupers, but in the medical world as a whole there was a growing tendency to regard a patient as a 'case'. The workhouse doctor had once been a disciplinarian or a despised hack; in the twentieth century he was more likely to be a competent but distant figure, separated from his patients by the double barrier of social class and professional mystique. Sir Arthur Newsholme was amiably given to letting the cat out of the black bag on such subjects:

> Occasionally... IN HOSPITALS THE DISEASE IS TREATED RATHER THAN THE PATIENT, though this I am confident is exceptional. The story of the negro, who was informed by the hospital doctor that his blood gave a positive Wassermann reaction, and who answered 'Yes, Massa; but I'se also a sick man,' illustrates this occasional lack in hospital work.[104]

The relationship was perhaps more important to the infirmary patient than to one in the voluntary hospital. Robert Pinker has shown that the average length of a patient's stay in the London voluntary hospitals fell from 25.3 days in 1891 to 20.2 days in 1921. By contrast, the most advanced London infirmaries had an average stay of 63.7 days in 1891 and 56.4 days in 1921.[105] Chronic, senile and dying patients accounted for the difference; for them the quality of personal attention was all-important.

Some accounts of patients' experiences survive. Bella Aronovitch spent four years in London hospitals as a young girl in 1929–32; she was suffering from a long and painful illness. After surgery had failed she was (typically) removed from the voluntary hospital to a Poor Law hospital. Her great fear was not the infirmary, but the workhouse itself, where the long-term bedridden patients were sent to make room in the infirmary. The Poor Law hospital in her account is not materially worse than the voluntary hospital. She had little sympathy from any of the doctors, who refused to tell her anything about her illness. The nurses in the Poor Law hospital came from a lower social class than in the voluntary hospital, but were not unkind, although working under difficult conditions. In both types of hospital there was a lack of contact between patients and staff, but the major difference was the understaffing in the Poor Law infirmary. In the voluntary hospital the nurse had time to make tea and light meals for the patients, but in the infirmary everything came from the central kitchen:

> There was actually more food in this Poor Law hospital, though of such poor quality and so badly cooked, most of it was uneatable. . . . The tea, with soda added to make it stronger, arrived in a large discoloured urn, and was poured from a tap on the side . . . It came looking like brown ale and tasted like a brew made from bitter herbs . . .
>
> The cups, plates and other utensils were so weighty, most of us did not have the strength to hold them. There were very few bed-tables, so that most food and drink had to be balanced on the very small space on top of the locker. Many a time I noticed the more feeble patients left their food and drink, simply because they were unable to manage it properly, since the nurses never had enough time to look after all those who needed help.[106]

Even in the 1920s, in much better physical conditions, the 'passive cruelty' which sprang from an overworked staff's inability to give personal attention, still persisted. As in many hospitals, the patients comforted one another.

II

INMATES

8

Workhouse Discipline and the Total Institution

Yellowing files of official documents contain the history of workhouse administration, but the words of the inmates themselves are seldom found in them. The historical image of the workhouse has been created mainly by outsiders, who usually condemned it either for harshness or laxity. Hence any attempt to reconstruct workhouse life must be a patchwork, selected from the letters and reminiscences of the literate poor, or gleaned from middle-class accounts.

Apathy, tedium, listlessness, were the qualities which struck all visitors. Dickens described Sunday in the workhouse chapel:

> Generally, the faces... were depressed and subdued and wanted colour. Aged people were there, in every variety. Mumbling, blear-eyed, spectacled, stupid, deaf, lame; vacantly winking in the gleams of the sun... leering at nothing, going to sleep, crouching and drooping in corners... Upon the whole, it was the dragon, Pauperism, in a very weak and impotent condition; toothless, fangless, drawing his breath heavily enough, and hardly worth chaining up.[1]

This was in 1850: in 1944 a survey by the Nuffield Foundation described life in a former workhouse, now a home for the aged:

> There is usually acute apathy. The residents tend to sit round the walls, unoccupied, and merely waiting for the next meal or for bedtime.[2]

Goffman, who attempts an explanation of this continuum in institutional life, begins with the entrance rituals of becoming an inmate, the reduction of individuality and the staff assumption of power. The inmate must be taught at once to know his place. Rituals of workhouse entrance, carefully devised by the Poor Law Commissioners, remained almost unchanged for almost a century. The applicant presented himself to the guardians, and the meeting might well resemble a criminal trial, for in many boardrooms the applicant stood in a dock. The Whitechapel guardians, for example, were in the 1870s firmly adhering to the Goschen Minute:

> The board-room was large and furnished with the horse-shoe table usually occupying such offices. At the top sat the Chairman, the applicants approaching him by walking up the room between the two arms of the horseshoe table.
>
> 'The House' was the decision usually snapped out by the chairman, often before the applicant had stated his case, or the guardians had had any opportunity of giving their opinions.[3]

The applicant could refuse the offer of the house, thus relieving the guardians of all responsibility for him. If he accepted, he presented himself and his family at the workhouse and was admitted into the receiving ward. Here he waited for examination by the medical officer, who classified him as able-bodied or infirm. The family was broken up, and if it were an urban union, the children might go to pauper schools some distance away, after a little time in the probationary wards to ensure that they were not carrying infection.

Technically, guardians could relieve an applicant only if he were totally destitute, but this created problems about the disposal of any property he might have, including furniture and the tools of his trade. Guardians could annex any property as compensation for the pauper's maintenance; in practice they had qualms about depriving a pauper of everything that might enable him to return to independent life, especially if he had been admitted because of a temporary illness. The Poor Law Commissioners decreed that paupers could own no property, and that guardians were to give only clothing to paupers on leaving the workhouse. But guardians could not see why, if a man were able to return to his trade, they should not give him a start. The Liverpool guardians gave bedding, tools and small sums of money to well-conducted paupers on departure.[4] In 1873 an Inspector recorded the following anecdote of a London board:

> A man who was classed as an able-bodied inmate of the workhouse, and who was on the point of leaving it, applied to the Guardians for a sum of money to enable him . . . to set himself up as a shoeblack. As the grant of this out-relief would involve a violation of Arts 1 and 6 of the Out-Relief Regulation Order, my attention was at once

attracted to the case; upon which the following conversation ensued:
The Chairman 'Here is a knotty point.'
A Guardian 'The Inspector is here.'
Chairman 'I don't care a pin for the Inspector.'
Upon this I represented to the Guardians... that the relief, if given
by them, would in all probability be disallowed by the Auditor.
Chairman 'I don't care a pin for the Auditor either.'
A Guardian 'We should give the relief if the Inspector were not
here, and I hope we shall not make any difference now.'[5]

Guardians connived at property ownership by paupers whose
residence they expected to be short-term; sometimes even agreeing to
store furniture. Alternatively, the paupers could make secret disposi-
tions of furniture and clothing amongst their friends, to be collected
later; though few can have been as well-equipped as Flora Thompson's
acquaintance, who managed to conceal from the guardians 'a
feather-bed, a leather-covered couch with chairs to match and a stuffed
owl in a glass case'.[6]

Inside the workhouse, the pauper's clothes were taken away to be
fumigated and kept for his day of release, while he was bathed and
disinfected and donned the shapeless workhouse clothing. The
uniform was a prime element of discipline, for if worn in the street it
identified the pauper as readily as broad arrows the convict. The
heavy, ill-fitting boots could almost cripple growing children. Some
guardians devised fanciful clothes for certain inmates, though the Poor
Law Commissioners disapproved of the old custom of forcing
unchaste women to wear distinctive dress:

> The Workhouse is not intended to serve any penal or remunera-
> tory purpose [they wrote in 1839]; and it ought not to be used for
> punishing the dissolute or rewarding the well-conducted pauper.[7]

Tufnell reported soon after this that he had dissuaded his unions from
the old practice of dressing unmarried mothers in yellow gowns. The
regulations did not deter the East Retford guardians, for in June 1839
they punished 'Selina Hill an Inmate of the House... [who had]
conducted herself very unbecoming of her sex, she having suffered the
Barbers Boy to have connection with her...' by having 'her hair cut
short and not allowed to wear a cap for three months.'[8]

These old habits slowly died, but clothes remained important to the
workhouse ritual. Paradoxically, even well-meaning guardians who

allowed elderly inmates to wear non-uniform clothes on their afternoons out, reinforced the distance between inmate and outsider. In the 1850s the Lambeth guardians allowed elderly inmates out on a rota: 20 sets of outdoor clothes were kept for the purpose, and handed from one pauper to the next, often wet and uncleaned.[9] By 1898, when most guardians provided 'outdoor' clothes, an Inspector commented:

> It was my experience that the 'undistinctive' character of the clothing formerly supplied to inmates of workhouses to be used when absent on leave was in fact singularly distinctive and conspicuous.[10]

Male inmates were not allowed razors, and were shaved only once a week: bathing was also a weekly ritual, in the presence of staff. Over a century later, Townsend commented on the ill-fitting clothes of inmates of a county home for the elderly; the indignity of being bathed by an attendant; the uniform convenience haircuts for both sexes. It did not require a full-scale pauper uniform to diminish the inmate's control over his appearance; he was always distinguishable from outsiders.

The new inmate was consigned to a dormitory with others of the same class. Beds were usually packed close together, and there were no lockers for personal possessions. Goffman emphasizes the importance of private possessions, however trival:

> ... these places can represent an extension of the self and its autonomy, becoming more important as the individual forgoes other repositories of self-hood ... When such storage places are not allowed, it is understandable that they will be illicitly developed.[11]

Inspectors complained that inmates hoarded pieces of food and other more personal objects, usually in or under the beds. Some smuggled in tobacco and other forbidden commodities. Small possessions could mean a great deal to an inmate, and more latitude was allowed from the 1890s, but even the less personal comforts such as armchairs and cushions often depended on the efforts of charitable visitors.

Work

If an inmate were not infirm he would be set to work, and here began one of the most confusing aspects of workhouse discipline. Workhouses appear amply to demonstrate the argument that total institutions usually do not fulfil their acknowledged purpose. The purpose of workhouse labour was never clear. Under the Old Poor Law parishes used workhouse labour sporadically either for punishment or for profit, but after the Napoleonic wars there was more opposition to inmates competing on the labour market and so (at least in the south-eastern counties), work was more likely to be deterrent. The report of 1834 insisted that inmates must labour, but was surprisingly ambivalent about the purpose of the work. Inmate labour was to provide necessary articles for the workhouse, but was not to be considered a punishment:

> Employment of some kind can, indeed, be always provided, but it appears to us it ought to be useful employment... The association of the utility of labour to both parties, the employer as well as the employed, is one which we consider it most important to preserve and strengthen; and we deem everything mischievous which unnecessarily gives to it a repulsive aspect.[12]

Labour, either indoor or outdoor, should rehabilitate the pauper and fit him for independence. He should have no reward for it other than his maintenance, or he would have no incentive to look for work outside.

The new administrators attacked the common practice of paying workhouse inmates who did special work. Pauper nurses, cleaners, cooks and others expected small sums, or at least an allowance of alcohol, tobacco, or extra rations. The Commissioners ordered guardians to discontinue such payments, and to send paupers who refused to work before the magistrates. The guardians usually resisted: it was more economical to give beer to paupers who carried coffins, pumped water and acted as nurses, than to pay for outside labour. Payments to privileged inmates never entirely disappeared: beer might be discontinued, but was replaced by tea, snuff, food, leave, and (later), sweets, cigarettes and pocket money. The system inevitably created hierarchies amongst the inmates, and workhouses, like prisons, had their 'trusties'. The Inspectors also disapproved of skilled inmates working at their own trades in the workhouse, as this encouraged masters to offer bribes, and so led to illicit sales of food and tobacco.

> A Master [complained Longley in 1873] who can induce inmates to paint and decorate (often with much taste and skill) the Board Room, to make furniture, to grow flowers, or even to make coffin-plates out of Australian meat-tins, is looked upon by

Guardians as having attained the highest pitch of perfection in the discharge of duties.[13]

Female inmates did the routine work and perhaps the sewing of the house; but even in the earlier years this labour could be in short supply. The medical officer of Blean wrote to the guardians in 1842:

> It is my duty to point out to you the total inadequacy of the few women now in the house to do the severe duties required of them without injury to their health, and it is my opinion that women who are on the verge of 70 years should not be called upon . . . for such . . . work as the washing of an establishment of this kind . . .[14]

Able-bodied men, including those over 60, were the chief problem. Northern unions could use the outdoor labour test, but guardians who tried to abolish outdoor relief might face an influx of able-bodied paupers in times of trade recession or in hard winters. The dilemma of the Old Poor Law continued: in hard times the kind of work done by inmates might not even pay for the cost of materials, while in good times able-bodied people would not enter the workhouse.

For this reason the type of work done in many workhouses soon assumed a penal character; it was done not for profit or use, but because it was irksome. Stone breaking, stone pounding and oakum picking were most frequently associated with workhouses, though a few unions encouraged local industries, such as straw-plaiting in Buckinghamshire, or making fruit punnets in Kent. Before November 1845 the Commissioners permitted the grinding of bones to be sold as fertiliser. This could be profitable, but was a loathsome task when bones were 'green' and stinking: the public reacted strongly against it after the Andover scandal. The Andover Committee emphasized that workhouse labour should not be penal or disgusting, or it would deter the genuine applicant from seeking necessary relief.

Stone breaking might be profitable when local roads were under repair: oakum was usually sold to the navy for caulking ships, but was rarely profitable. Both types of work were considered deterrent, though some critics argued that experienced old lags had no trouble in performing their quota rapidly, while new inmates found the tasks hard and painful. Women as well as men picked oakum, tearing all day at old and matted ropes, sometimes denied the use of nails or tools which would have made the work easier. Similar difficulties occurred in finding suitable labour for convicts; and as the same two tasks were commonly imposed in prisons, workhouse labour had a penal reputation.

In cities with large numbers of able-bodied paupers, the Commissioners abandoned the pretence that work should be useful, and sanctioned tasks purely for deterrence. Hand grinding of corn was perhaps the most common work of this type; the guardians installed large mill-stones which could be turned only with great effort. The flour produced was commercially almost valueless, though it could be used for making low-grade workhouse bread. Only the need for discipline justified the use of human energy for this, one of the most ancient of mechanized skills. In the prisons similar principles applied. Early prison reformers had hoped to rehabilitate convicts through useful toil; but it was easier to provide work which had no commercial value, needed little supervision, and was merely punitive. The corn mill was to the pauper as the treadmill to the convict, and both were used as a punishment for offences committed in the institution. Paupers resented the comparison. An unemployed clerk who had entered Lambeth workhouse in 1846 complained of having been set to work at the mill:

> I asked the guardians what was my offence that I should be compelled to associate with felons (in which class a full third of those employed at the Mill are) Mr Churchill replied in a severe tone that *they* knew no difference between *paupers & felons* and ever since I have been treated accordingly.[15]

In typical Poor Law fashion, however, severity of intent was often mollified by laxity of practice. The central authority always urged guardians to employ taskmasters to ensure that work was properly done, but guardians could see little reason for this expense if the flow of able-bodied inmates were merely seasonal. Consequently, guardians and Inspectors often grumbled that workhouse paupers had an easy life and that it was impossible to extract a full day's work from them.[16]

Although the penal work of vagrants and able-bodied inmates has become part of the workhouse image, most work was done by children, women, and the aged. A few guardians achieved profits in unusual trades, including coffin and truss making, while rural guardians could set unskilled aged inmates to gardening. Edward Smith claimed in 1871 that the workhouse garden in Ashby-de-la-Zouche sold enough produce to pay the salaries of all the workhouse officers.[17] Inmates who could do this or perform skilled tasks probably did not need to be in an institution at all, and their misfortunes saved the guardians money; on the other hand, most guardians claimed to house a small number of inmates who could usefully do the work of the house, but who were unable to hold down a steady job because of their drinking habits.

The guardians had to decide whether work discipline should apply to the healthy aged poor, for in the outside world elderly workers laboured as long as their strength allowed. There was no retiring age, and even old age pensions, when they began, applied only to people over 70. But what of those inmates in their sixties who were partially fit or capable or some kind of work? Longley reported in 1871 that Kentish unions were too inclined to indulge people over 60, and not to require specific tasks from them: this he disapproved of.[18] In the 1890s guardians were encouraged to discriminate between the 'deserving' and the 'undeserving' aged poor, by giving privileges to the former and requiring work of the rest. The Local Government Board had thus reversed the argument of the 1830s that the workhouse should not reward virtue or punish vice. Some guardians tried to apply this rule, though they usually tried to classify the aged according to their past lives, rather than according to their behaviour in the workhouse, as the Inspectors recommended. Theoretically, unfitness rather than age relieved a pauper of the obligation to work, and guardians could prosecute an inmate over 60 who refused his task. But guardians were sensitive on this point, for the anti-Poor Law campaign had made capital out of cases of elderly paupers forced to labour beyond their strength. The Brabazon scheme, as previously mentioned, tried to solve the problem by setting the elderly to non-punitive labour separated from the workhouse administration.

By the early twentieth century, the labour test was more commonly offered to able-bodied paupers than admission to the house. In hard times guardians would open the union stone or wood yards where heads of families worked in return for a bare maintenance. Thus, although the name of 'workhouse' was being discontinued, the institutions were still associated with punitive labour, and this created difficulties in employing the infirm, the aged and the mentally defective. In 1961 Townsend criticized residential institutions which did *not* employ the aged inmates, for he saw work as necessary to self-respect.[19] Yet the workhouse tradition had irrevocably linked even household work with notions of punishment. Inmates accepted the Brabazon scheme because it was not run by the workhouse staff and because it provided small comforts from the sale of manufactures. The usual Brabazon work, fancy knitting and sewing, was not part of the utilitarian labour of the house. This may explain why after 1929 elderly inmates often objected when asked to work, and sneered at those who helped to clean the house or work in the garden. In present-day homes for the elderly, residents may discourage one another from doing small tasks on the grounds that they have 'paid for' total care directly, or out of taxes in the past. The pervasive legacy of the workhouse helped to prevent the notion of housework as therapy from displacing that of housework as punishment.[20]

No better example exists of the ambivalence in the Victorian attitude to work. This period, the first in which leisure became possible for large numbers of people, glorified the dignity of labour. Malthus had argued that no man would labour if not compelled by want; the Victorians saw work less as a necessity than a duty. In the workhouse and the prison, these values continually and unsuccessfully struggled against debasement. The institution should have inculcated a respect for labour in order to rehabilitate the inmate, but inmates saw the work as punishment. In some cases work degenerated into open exploitation, especially when the supply of able-bodied inmates diminished. As in lunatic asylums, the more capable long-term inmates became the necessary drudges of the house, and guardians were often reluctant to release them. And yet, in nearly every workhouse could be found aged inmates who worked without compulsion: to act as nurse, wardsman, night porter, or even voluntary cleaner, was to salvage a fragment of identity and self-respect.[21]

Children

Discipline and rehabilitation similarly confused the question of the treatment of pauper children, the only group of inmates to be held blameless for their predicament. In their case rehabilitation was vital, for they must be taught to support themselves: hence the principle of 'less eligibility' did not apply to them. The report of 1834 revealed its Benthamite origins by taking for granted that workhouse children would have to be educated, even though the principle of universal education was then not widely accepted.[22] Because these children started life with a greater handicap than the children of independent labourers, they needed special attention, for under the old system of unsegregated workhouses, they had left 'corrupted where they were well disposed, and hardened where they were vicious'.[23] Moral as well as social redemption was needed, through education and isolation from bad influences. The three Commissioners were less idealistic than the Royal Commission, and argued complacently that without outdoor relief the poor would set their children to work as soon as they were old enough to earn.[24] Tufnell and Kay-Shuttleworth had to persuade the Commissioners that to educate workhouse children would not encourage their parents to become paupers. Nevertheless, pauper children were to be apprenticed as soon as possible, though not under the age of nine.

Tufnell hoped that apprenticeship would be replaced by education in the institution; and legislation in 1844 and 1851 further restricted the terms of apprenticeship, but guardians could still pay a premium with each child to encourage an employer to take him. Tufnell and Kay-Shuttleworth supported district schools because they separated children from adult paupers and hence from 'contamination'. Tufnell did not assume that children would raise themselves above their class; the boys would become labourers, the girls domestic servants.[25] Kay-Shuttleworth was to occupy a larger place in the history of education than in his connection with pauper schools; as the first secretary to the committee of the Privy Council on education he became a major figure in the movement towards universal primary education. It has been argued that he saw education primarily as a means of class control. The state-subsidized voluntary schools, like the workhouse schools, were intended to inculcate middle-class virtues of sobriety, thrift, cleanliness and order into working-class children.[26] One may quote extensively from Kay-Shuttleworth's ideas about education: that he wished to fit the children of the poor for their station in life, and to produce working men who would respect property and the social order.[27] On the other hand, it is difficult to discover *any* system of formal education which does not inculcate a respect for the values of the social leaders. Kay-Shuttleworth did not see society as rigidly hierarchical: he was a Benthamite who believed in the type of social mobility later popularized by Samuel Smiles. To rise above one's station was permissible, provided it were done through temperance, thrift and perseverance, the virtues Kay-Shuttleworth hoped to encourage in workhouse children. To brand him as a reactionary is to underestimate how radical his ideas seemed at the time, especially to the Norfolk guardians amongst whom he first went as Inspector, and who still feared that any education of the poor would lead to rick-burning and sedition.[28]

Kay-Shuttleworth planned a three-part system of mental, moral and industrial training, but guardians usually saw more sense in the last two elements than in the first.[29] With Kay-Shuttleworth as Inspector, the best Norfolk pauper schools taught English history, geography and grammar, as well as the fundamentals of literacy, arithmatic and the Bible. In practice, however, the higher ideal of social discipline was constantly weakened by discipline of a more sordid kind, based on the insensitivity of some guardians, lack of competent teachers, and the demands of the workhouse economy.

The children over whom the guardians exercised fullest control were those without parents or close relatives: around half of all indoor children throughout the nineteenth century.[30] The Poor Law Commissioners had supported district schools rather than schools in the workhouse, but by the early 1860s some of the Inspectors were beginning to question the effect of large institutions on children. In 1862 Andrew Doyle defended the workhouse schools, which he believed had greatly improved since 1834. Unlike Tufnell, he did not accept the idea of 'contamination':

> There are people who seem to think that there is something contaminating in what they call the atmosphere of the workhouse, and who arrive at the conclusion, assuming that every inmate of a workhouse is a depraved and abandoned character, that every child walking into a hall where these people assemble for meals, or into a chapel where they meet for prayer, necessarily becomes contaminated, as it would contract disease if it entered a plague-stricken city.[31]

But Doyle did not wish workhouse children to be sent to local schools, as this would upset workhouse discipline. It should be remembered that for half the children, 'contamination' included contact with their own parents.

Pauper children experienced different kinds of discipline in the workhouses and the pauper schools. In the workhouse school children would be more under the control of the workhouse master, and the guardians might insist that 'industrial training' was the most vital part of their education. Here the school teacher would probably be locked in battle with the master about the children's employment in the workhouse. Industrial training, theoretically intended to occupy about a third of the children's time, could be stretched in its definition to include any housework. The girls could be drafted as full-time seamstresses and laundresses. Rural guardians could provide the boys with profitable work in the workhouse garden, dignified as 'training' for agricultural labour. In 1848 the master of Blean complained that the schoolmaster constantly subverted his authority by objecting when a boy was taken out of school to work in the pantry; the master argued that domestic work would be more useful training for the boy than formal education.[32] Some guardians interpreted industrial training even more literally, as in Reading, where in 1839 the boys were still hired out to employers during the day, while in the 1840s the Blackburn guardians defied the central authority and sent very young children to work as short-time hands in the nearby factories.[33] In 1841, 24 boys in Warrington workhouse were making pins in a room 15 feet by 11 feet.[34] Yet sometimes work might be a relief from incarceration, when workhouse children went out to help with the harvest in country unions.

Children could not leave the workhouse unless an officer accompanied them, and their supply of toys and non-text books often depended on charity. Indeed, apart from sessions in the schoolroom, the lives of the children were like any other inmates'. Discipline produced apathy and dreariness. Even in more generous institutions the children had no personal toys, and the school shared the penal architecture of the workhouse:

> It generally opens on to a yard enclosed by high walls, with a circular swing at its centre, which affords to the children an invigorating and popular exercise... The windows are mostly small and square; and if they should happen to look on an adult ward, they are darkened by whitewashing the glass. During the dark winter days the instruction of the children is much hindered by want of light, while their health and spirits are affected by the closeness occasioned by want of height in the room.[35]

Significantly, in 1864 one of the school Inspectors defended workhouse education thus:

> ... because the schools are smaller, the children more under the command of the teachers, and more disposed to study from the very dulness and monotony of their lives, which renders the drudgery of learning to read, write, and sum, so distasteful to the ordinary schoolboy, a relief and an amusement to the workhouse child.[36]

From 1871 children from smaller workhouses began to attend local elementary schools: whereas in 1870 about 82 per cent of indoor children were being educated in institutions, by 1908 only 42 per cent were so educated, and only 656 children (1 per cent of the total) were still in workhouse schools.[37] Greater integration with the outside world may have helped the workhouse child, but institutional clothes made him easy to identify, and other children could exploit this cruelly.

In the district schools discipline was more formal. Every hour of the child's day was allocated: excursions outside the institution were rare, and usually conducted in regimented groups. Although district schools were run by trained staff rather than workhouse officers and paupers, the distance between staff and pupils was greater because of the large numbers of children. Many district schools had little space for play. The larger the number of children, the more the staff had to resort to corporal punishment to discipline them. Paid instructors provided industrial training for the boys, who could learn carpentry, shoe-making and other trades, but the girls were still relegated to the dreary sewing of the house. In the training ship *Exmouth*, run by the Metropolitan Asylums Board, workhouse boys could begin a career in the navy, while training in the brass bands of city workhouses also served for military recruitment.

As educational institutions, the Poor Law schools seem never to have succeeded. Kay-Shuttleworth had stressed that children should understand what they were learning. His ideals survived amongst Inspectors of Poor Law schools, whether they were employed by the education authority (1847–63, and after 1904), or by the Poor Law authority (1863–1904). Indeed, one of the Inspectors of the 1860s saw workhouse education not as a formula for social control but for social mobility:

> ... this training will open to them many fields of employment from which the totally ignorant are debarred, and ... afford to all the means of rising from the very humble level of society in which they must necessarily take their first steps in life.[38]

In practice the Inspectors found that pauper education was often mechanical. When in the 1870s the children were examined alongside children from the elementary schools, they did worse in subjects which required independent thought, even though the elementary schools were themselves often accused of stifling initiative. The workhouse teachers probably had fewer ambitions than those outside; they would not have taken Poor Law employment if there had been an alternative. History, grammar, geography and arithmetic degenerated into the memorizing of facts. The teachers themselves had been taught the same way, as the types of examination question set by the Poor Law Board for workhouse teachers demonstrate:

> Write out the promises made by God to Abraham, state to whom they descended, and how they were fulfilled...
> Write the conversation between our Saviour and the two Disciples who were going to Emmaus...
> Name the principal countries of Europe, their climates, productions, capitals, and principal rivers and cities...[39]

The Board of Education was still criticising Poor Law schools for their dreary teaching in 1908:

> Rows and rows of fat, clean, well-shod infants sat bored and listless, listening with praiseworthy patience to deadly details about some plant or animal they were never likely to hear of again; they recite in unison what they do not understand...[40]

Children of all classes had books for moral improvement, but workhouse children received a steady diet of them, especially free tracts from the Society for the Propagation of Christian Knowledge. The Blean children in 1849 had a fairly generous collection of textbooks, supplemented by such works as *The Call to Immediate Repentence, Our Protestant Forefathers, Industry and Idleness, Captive Children, The Poor House Penitent, The Swearer's End, Good & Bad Temper, Obstinacy & Passion*. Insofar as exotic ideas crept in, they did so through *The 7 Churches of Asia* and one volume of *Amusing Stories*.[41]

Mrs Senior's attack on district schools was taken up in the 1890s by Henrietta Barnett, who founded the State Children's Association, devoted to dismantling the large schools and encouraging the boarding-out system. Two of the large London schools were broken up in the 1890s and the total number of children in district schools was halved between 1895 and 1907.[42] The Local Government Board would probably have proceeded further against the large schools had not the guardians objected to the waste of their investment in institutions. After the Great War, the only type of education in the Poor Law schools was industrial training, and children went daily to local schools. Chamberlain was sensitive to criticisms that guardians placed pauper children in 'dead-end' jobs, and the Inspectors pressed for the children to have a wider choice of career, or even further education.

For girls, the labour market as well as the guardians' prejudices imposed restrictions. In 1925, nine-tenths of the girls from the West Norwood schools still went out to domestic service, and the *Poor Law Officers' Journal* approved:

> It seems to us the plainest economy to turn the girls in these homes, except the most outstanding and special cases among them, to the calling which provides the easiest means of absorption.[43]

At Bermondsey, boys could learn engineering, plumbing, gas fitting and glazing, but in West London guardians followed an older tradition of sending the boys out as young as possible, without training. Tailoring and shoemaking, the crafts much favoured in the nineteenth century, were still being taught, and sometimes the boys learned only the most mechanical parts of these trades.

Guardians decided when children should leave the workhouse, subject to the factory acts and other legislation on child labour. Just as it was difficult to define old age, so it was difficult to define the age of maturity. Although the Poor Law Commissioners had believed that children should learn to support themselves, workhouse children often had a longer period of education than those of labourers outside. The point of maturity was also that when the child could be taken out of the school and placed in the adult wards: from 1842 this was 15 for boys and 16 for girls. Nevertheless, guardians adopted their own moral distinctions for children as for the adult poor: children with bad habits or foul language might still be found in the adult wards quite late in the nineteenth century. From 1866 to 1897 workhouses could also be used as remand centres for children accused of criminal offences, and guardians were reluctant to place them with the other children. In 1894 remand children in Greenwich workhouse had their clothes taken away from them to prevent their escape, and were virtually confined to bed for a fortnight.[44] If released into the institution, they were usually palced with the adults. As with most Poor Law practices, local habits differed widely.

Children with a parent in the workhouse experienced Poor Law discipline more partially, for they were not permanently resident. The subject of movement in and out of the workhouses will be discussed in the next chapter; but these children had to accompany their parents. By the 1890s guardians sometimes allowed more trusted inmates to leave their children in the house for a few weeks in order to look for work.

Inmate behaviour

Workhouse populations changed continually, making discipline more difficult than in asylums or prisons. The architecture of all three institutions could be much the same; the inmates presented the same abject appearance; the visitor noticed the same smell of whitewash, over-boiled cabbage, and urine. But the pauper could always escape, even if only for a day. On giving three hours' notice to the master he would be released, and his family and his clothes returned to him. The master had a fair idea, based on past experience, of which departing inmates would reappear the same evening, probably the worse for drink. Nothing aggrieved staff and guardians more than their lack of control over workhouse inmates to whom they could deny neither freedom nor readmission. Elderly inmates, allowed formal leave, were less of a problem, but even they were known to come back drunk, for their plight usually aroused compassion in local public houses. If leave were denied, they could apply to leave the workhouse altogether, and the only recourse open to the master on their return was to make them as uncomfortable as possible. The Poor Law Commissioners tried to compel paupers who had returned to the workhouse less than two days after leaving it to give 24 hours' notice of departure, but they had to rescind this order on finding that it was illegal.[45] The inmate could leave without notice, but if he left wearing workhouse clothes he could be prosecuted for theft.

The Commissioners knew how limited were the guardians' powers over inmates, and how easily workhouse discipline might be disrupted by paupers who could leave and return at will. The 'ins and outs' used the workhouse as a kind of hotel, and if they had children, the problem was compounded as the children regularly left and re-entered the schools. Teachers had difficulty teaching transient and permanent children in the same classes, while in stricter unions the transient children spent most of their time without education in the probationary wards, where they were placed to avoid spreading infection in the schools.

In the earlier years of the New Poor Law, many politicians feared the despotic tendencies of the bureaucracy, and denied the central authority the power of incarceration. After 1870, as the workhouses were seen more as refuges for the helpless, Parliament took more notice of complaints about the disruptive effect of able-bodied 'ins and outs'. In 1871 the Pauper Inmates Discharge and Regulation Act allowed guardians greater powers; if a pauper had not left the workhouse within the past month, he could be detained for 24 hours after giving notice; the period of detention was progressively increased so that inmates who had left more than twice in the past two months could be detained for 72 hours. There is no evidence that this stopped paupers from discharging themselves frivolously, though, of course, it limited the number of times they could leave in one week. Potentially, the strongest discipline against these paupers was the guardians' increasing powers to take their children away from them, especially after the Children Act of 1908, but economy-minded guardians rarely adopted this strategy unless children were physically abused or neglected.

In the 1840s the Commissioners had an understandable fear of workhouse violence. Wherever large numbers of able-bodied men and women entered the workhouse at a time of seasonal unemployment, they threatened disruption. In large parishes like Lambeth and Liverpool, the 'dissolute' younger men and women had special refractory wards, which were even more sparsely furnished than the rest of the workhouse, had barred windows, and could be securely locked if necessary. If the master could not impose order himself, he could fall back on the magistrates. Throughout the period of the New Poor Law there was a steady procession from workhouse to gaol, but never more than in the first two decades after 1834. From March 1835 to March 1842, 10,538 paupers were summarily tried for offences in the house. Their offences may be tabulated as follows:[46]

Offence	number	%
Misbehaviour, drunken and disorderly, wilful damage, refusing to work, & c.	7174	68.1
Deserting, or deserting with union clothes	2325	22.1
Theft	613	5.8
Assault, breach of the peace	319	3.0
Leaving family chargeable to parish	107	1.0

Of the offenders 28 per cent received sentences of up to a fortnight; 51 per cent from 14 days to a month; 19 per cent received longer sentences. Only 75 offenders were discharged (0.7 per cent), suggesting how difficult it was to defend oneself against evidence supplied by workhouse officers, and that magistrates supported workhouse discipline.

By 1889 sentences for workhouse offences were less severe: nearly 10 per cent were discharged, and 70 per cent were committed for less

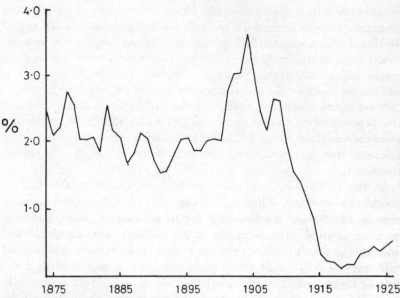

Figure 3. Number of workhouse inmates committed to gaol 1874–1926, expressed as a proportion of the mean number of indoor paupers.

than a fortnight; 16 per cent for two weeks to a month.[47] Yet until the outbreak of war, these offences were a regular feature of magistrates' courts, and furnished the prisons with petty offenders. (See Figure 3).

The figures hint that workhouse discipline was likely to collapse, and that the authorities increasingly relied on the criminal law to support them during the turbulent 1840s. In 1837 only 940 inmates were committed to gaol; in 1842 there were 2596.[48] The authorities argued that workhouse offences were committed only by the dissolute poor, the prostitutes and semi-criminals, who would take advantage of laxity to make the workhouses into places of assignation for their company. Perhaps workhouse offences were an indoor version of the more violent anti-Poor Law campaign. Did the labourers who pulled down the Leeds workhouse or fired the guardians' ricks in East Anglia proceed to further violence once they could no longer avoid incarceration? The records disclose no simple answer. Many workhouse riots took place not when paupers entered the house, but when the administration attempted to tighten up the regulations. Paupers who had accepted one routine were not prepared to see their conditions worsened. Masters who reduced the diet, supervised work more closely, or curtailed customary leave, might provoke this kind of disorder. In Sheffield the able-bodied paupers were released every Wednesday afternoon to look for work; when many of them returned drunk the guardians discontinued their leave, whereupon the inmates rioted and hurled oakum at the approaching police. After that, four policemen usually stayed on duty at the workhouse.[49]

Most of the stories of workhouse riots come from the early years of the New Poor Law, but even in the 1880s and 1890s a remarkably steady average of about 3,700 inmates were annually committed for misbehaviour in the workhouse and destroying clothing. Many of these offences were probably committed by vagrants, who had little to lose socially by being sent to prison, and who were said to prefer the prison food to the workhouse diet. The average of committals rose in the decade before the war, as the authorities counselled stricter measures against vagrants, but by 1916 workhouse offences fell to 548, and remained very low until the late 1920s. The fall was far more rapid than the drop in workhouse pauperism, no doubt reflecting the able-bodied pauper's desertion of the workhouse, but also a greater reluctance to use the law against such offenders. Most sentences were less than 14 days, and a vagrant who had been committed for destroying his clothes in order to be given new ones left prison having attained his object. By the late nineteenth century workhouse indiscipline seems to have been individual rather than collective—but in the close quarters of a workhouse even one unruly inmate could cause much trouble. Here arose that dilemma which the anti-Poor Law campaigners had emphasized: if workhouse discipline were harsh and punitive, there was no reason why the able-bodied pauper should not prefer to go to gaol, like the four girls aged 18 and 19 who in 1840 destroyed a blanket in Faversham workhouse. 'On being ask'd why they did it they said it was on purpose to go Jail,' the master reported.[50] Between 1837 and 1846, 61 paupers from Andover workhouse went to gaol; possibly reflecting the disorderly state of the house, but more likely because they hoped to escape mistreatment and underfeeding.

The central authority argued that reliance on the magistrates was a sign of failure in local administration. If the regulations were strictly followed, and dissolute paupers separated from the rest in refractory wards and cells, insubordination would be quelled; the refractory paupers would apply to leave rather than submit to such discipline. In the early 1870s the Lambeth guardians, who had long been plagued by workhouse revolts, built an expensive new workhouse with strictly segregated blocks for the different moral categories. The architect's plans showed the divisions into 'able-bodied good', 'able-bodied bad,' and so forth; but as the new workhouse was rapidly overwhelmed by the old and sick, this classification could never be effectively pursued.

Summary convictions tell only a small part of the story of workhouse strife. Some masters relied on their own powers to reduce diet and stop privileges. The master of Faversham in the 1840s sent paupers before the magistrates for even slight breaches of discipline:

> Diana Thomas 30 with 2 bastard children Faversham was taken before Genl. Gosselin on Monday last and reprimanded for having said that the bread given her for breakfast that morning was not fit to give to hogs.[51]

In Southwell the master usually stopped the inmates' meat and broth, and gave one pound of potatoes for dinner; since Nottinghamshire diets were more generous than in Kent, he could deprive paupers more effectively that way. The master of East Retford followed an erratic course of his own, sometimes using forbidden punishments which the guardians condoned. A disobedient boy in 1841 was put on bread and water and placed in the 'black hoole'; he escaped, and the master wrote:

'I then tied his hands behind him. But he soon got at liberty. The Strait Jacket was then put on him which he slept in during the night...'[52] (Even this failed to restrain the boy, who disappeared while being taken to the privy.) By the end of the century, when workhouse life became less restricted, offenders were rarely committed to refractory cells, but were deprived of privileges. In London, the Inspector claimed that the worst problem was bad language and insubordination from the able-bodied old men.[53] As in the outside world, the most ruthless punishments were reserved for boys, who were flogged in front of the other children or confined to bed for the day.

The long catalogue of workhouse offences argues that the paupers did not always passively conform to workhouse routine, and the threat of rebellion was always present. The officers' chief power was their ability to manipulate the workhouse routine. An inmate of Blean workhouse wrote the following account of the petty struggle between master and paupers:

> on Sunday last [the Master] came and caut three of us in bed after the appointed time to get up, the man Pattenden he did not punish; Blackman he stopt his food for one day and Martin he gave the full

extent of his punishment forty eight hours on Bread and Warter
... the Master is very cruel to the young Men and Women, for he
first took the milk of that was allowed wen he came here and gave us
the washings of the old people[s] tea leves ... the Poor old men go
out for a walk on Wensday they go out [at] one OClock and if they
come home before a quarter to five they will not be alloud to go to
their Hall, they have to stand shivering in the cold till the bell
Rings ...[54]

In spite of the haphazard fortunes of workhouse life and the
possibility of physical cruelty, the worst enemy faced by most inmates
was the sheer boredom of workhouse life. Modern critics have seen
this as typical of all residential institutions, particularly large ones.
Dickens, Louisa Twining, Emma Sheppard, Rider Haggard, Richard
Jefferies and many other visitors commented on it. What was an
affliction for the old was insupportable for the children, as Will
Crooks remembered:

When Sunday did come it proved to be one lasting agony. He
thought time could not be made more terrible to children anywhere.
They had dinner at twelve and tea at six, confined during the
yawning interval in the dull day-room with nothing to do but to
look at the clock, and then out of the window, and then back at the
clock again.[55]

As late as 1913 visiting hours were restricted to three afternoons a
week, for an hour at a time. In the 1890s games of draughts and other
harmless amusements were allowed, but cards still forbidden. Propriety forbade the guardians to give the aged women tobacco, though
previously both sexes had received snuff. As in most institutions,
tobacco became a form of currency, used by inmates to buy small
favours from one another, and for the officers to reward their
favourites. Elderly inmates with pensions from friendly societies or the
military had to give up their pensions to the guardians, but most of
them received a little pocket money. This gave them an advantage over
fellow-inmates, enough, as an observer wrote in 1903, to make them
'the mandarins of pauperdom'.[56]

Food

In this monotonous world, food created exceptional interest, and
nothing caused more friction between paupers and staff than the
quality of the rations. In all institutions food was an essential part of

reward or punishment, and the central authority saw it as central to workhouse discipline.

> The establishment of a proper dietary [wrote Tufnell in 1836] seems to me a point of preeminent importance, as it alone will prevent paupers entering a workhouse, & thus effectually dispauperise a Union.[57]

Until after the First World War the central authority insisted that all local dietaries be submitted for approval; at first to prevent excessive generosity, but later to protect nutritional standards.

As usual, the regulations rarely corresponded with reality. Diets were graded according to the age and sex of inmates, the able-bodied receiving the plainest fare. The Poor Law Commissioners decided that workhouse diets should be related to the local diet, and so paupers in southern counties fared worse than those in more affluent industrial areas. Bread and cheese or bread and gruel were standard in the south and east, with perhaps a meat or suet pudding and potatoes for dinner three days a week. The only favour allowed the elderly was an ounce of tea with their breakfast and supper. The cooked food had very simple ingredients: each pound of suet pudding had 11 ounces of flour and three ounces of suet, the meat pudding seven ounces of flour, six ounces of meat and two ounces of suet. Anti-Poor Law campaigners claimed that the diets were worse than prison diets, and this was certainly true in Kent, where prisoners in Ashford working on the treadwheel had more bread, soup, and mutton than the workhouse inmates.[58] Prisoners not on the treadwheel had a workhouse-type diet, but able-bodied paupers were supposed to be doing work as heavy as that of prisoners.

Under public attack, the Commissioners had to increase the amount of bread in workhouse diets, but they had little control over the guardians. On one side were the parsimonious guardians who threatened to starve the poor, as in Andover; on the other the northern guardians who were used to a more profuse tradition of workhouse feeding. Inmates in north-east Lancashire had tea, coffee and a meat dinner every day. Blackburn union epitomizes the Lancastrian mixture of squalor and abundance; the diet was liberal, each pauper could take as much as he liked, but the guardians provided no cutlery.[59] The central authority tried to strike a balance: diets were not to be superior to those of the local working class, but were not to be so inferior as to risk charges of pauper-starving. The authorities relied on the monotony of the diet rather than its quantity, as a deterrent; and insisted that officers weigh out accurate portions for each inmate. In the early days little was known about nutrition. The Commissioners took the diet of the independent poor as a rough guide, and allowed fairly substantial amounts of food, but removed from the diet everything which might have made it more palatable.

It is difficult to say whether workhouse paupers were worse fed than the independent poor, partly because of our ignorance about the food values of nineteenth-century ingredients, and partly because the official dietary tables often had little resemblance to the actual diet. The official diets often seem superior in food value to the diets of the poorest labourers: for the quantities of bread allowed in workhouses were higher than the poor could afford, and even the small amounts of meat probably exceeded those in a labourer's budget. In the 1860s Edward Smith found that the poorer workers in Lancashire could rarely afford meat, and that they ate little protein.[60] A modern nutritionist might approve of the coarse workhouse bread, which, usually made of the cheap 'seconds' flour, was less refined than the socially preferred white bread. Its nutritional qualities, however, were offset by the probability that it was hard, stale, and served with such small quantities of fat that it was difficult to eat. Another feature of workhouse diet was that women and children were not as restricted as in poor families, where their needs would come second to those of the breadwinner. In institutions children did not compete with adults; they had a fixed though monotonous diet of bread, butter, cheese and occasional meat puddings.

In 1849 two medical investigators found wide discrepancies in both the quality and quantity of children's food in London workhouses. Rotherhithe, one of the worst, gave children a diet with high liquid content but no milk. They lived largely on bread and milkless gruel; the only solids being four ounces of cheese, $1\frac{1}{2}$ pounds of potatoes, 15 ounces of meat, and 12 ounces suet pudding per week, though with substantial quantities of bread. By contrast, St George's Hanover Square allowed the children a pint of milk a day, as well as treacle on their bread. This was at a time when milk hardly featured at all in the diets of poorer London families.[61]

Nineteenth-century workhouse diets had two distinctive features, one unintentional, the other contrived. Firstly, although in theory they were more ample than the food of the poor, too many middlemen were involved in their supply. Secondly, although the poor were inadequately fed, their preferences differed strongly from the institutional diet, which therefore seemed harsh and punitive. The guardians accepted tenders for workhouse food contracts; but the law did not effectively suppress food adulteration until after 1872, and the tender system ensured that contractors had a strong financial motive to adulterate the food. In 1871 the Local Government Board invited Francis Rowsell, superintendent of contracts for the Admiralty, to investigate workhouse food in London. Although the Board hoped to show that guardians were not sufficiently economical in their food contracts, Rowsell's scientific analysis proved another point. He noted that only the master controlled the quality of workhouse food, and that an underpaid master had too much temptation for collusion with a contractor.

> The regulations [he reported] commit to officers, who are paid on an average £100 a year, the responsibility, with all its temptations, of passing or rejecting goods worth, in the aggregate...£381,000 a year.[62]

As a result, London workhouse food, both for inmates and officers, was often very bad, especially the milk and butter. Of 57 samples of milk which Rowsell tested, only two were unskimmed, nearly all were diluted, and seven were equal quantities of milk and water. It was highly unsuitable for children. Much of the butter was an unhealthy compound of animal fat, horse fat, or other substances known to the trade as 'bosh butter'.

Food adulteration was common enough outside the workhouse, but public institutions were supposed to maintain a higher standard. The central authority urged guardians to test samples before knowing the names of the contractors who supplied them, and that the visiting committee check the food at dinner-time. All this required more interest and vigilance than many guardians possessed, and even if they did not exercise jobbery in their contracts, they sometimes accepted tenders at prices so far below the market rate that it would have been impossible for the contractors to supply anything but adulterated goods. Northern guardians deliberately bought only 'blue' skimmed milk for the workhouse children although it was a vital part of their diet.[63]

Even if food survived the depredations of guardians, contractors and officers, it might be rendered inedible by an unskilled cook working with unsuitable equipment; or it might be well cooked but served cold because the inmates had to be lined up and marched into the hall while it lay on the table. Lay administrators and the medical officers both claimed to regulate the diet, but after the appointment of Dr Edward

Smith the medical Inspectors had the last word and could refuse to sanction diets proposed by the guardians. Smith's own dietary tables, published in 1867, used the best information he had, and assessed food in terms of its 'nitrogenous' and 'carbon' content—corresponding roughly to protein and carbohydrate. He allowed skim milk in children's diets, but increased the amount of meat in the workhouse diet to four ounces per day for five days a week, with an allowance of tea and sugar for breakfast and supper.[64] He also encouraged more generous diets for the sick and handicapped. If paupers had received the amounts he recommended, they would have had more protein food than many labourers could afford; though by modern standards the diet lacked essential vitamins found in fruit and vegetables. Smith's dietaries were used until Downes replaced them in the 1890s.

By the end of the century the medical profession knew more about nutrition, and the central authority tried to conform with the latest theories, especially on the calorific value of food. The gap between the institutional diet and the food of the poor became wider than ever before. Workhouse diets, even for the able-bodied, were by 1900 far more generous than the diets Rowntree discovered amongst the labouring classes in York, or than Maude Davies found amongst agricultural labourers in Wiltshire. Rowntree made the same point that Poor Law authorities had been making since 1834: that the entire wage of the poorest labouring families would not have bought the amount of food per head that paupers consumed in workhouses. The recommended diet for inmates in 1900 included 22 ounces of meat and eight ounces of fish per adult per week: children under eight should have had about nine ounces of meat per week and a pint of milk every day. By comparison, a labouring family in Wiltshire, exercising the most careful thrift, could afford about 11 ounces of meat per head per week, and shared less than a pint of milk a day between five of them.[65]

If the workhouse diet was superior in food value to that of the labouring poor, it was still regarded by long-term inmates as one of the privations of institutional life. The scanty evidence on the diet of the poor in the mid-nineteenth century suggests utter monotony—bread was the staple food, and proportionately more butter was needed to make it palatable. Social investigators who wished to discover whether a worker's income was sufficient to feed his family, did not mention expenditure on more frivolous foods, or if they did so, condemned it. Precisely because their food was dull and unpalatable, the poor tended to spend on unnecessary items, of which alcohol was undoubtedly the most important. Other more harmless foodstuffs were esteemed for the same reason, including tea and sugar. It is harder to document expenditure on savoury items, kippers, bloaters, pickles, cockles, 'a bit of a relish'. Even meat was bought in small quantities as 'a flavouring rather than substantial course'.[66] Holidays and family events required celebratory food as well as alcohol—gilt gingerbread at country fairs, glutinous and dangerously adulterated cakes. Those who observed the habits of the poor noted that resources which might have provided better nutrition if sensibly deployed, were misspent. A slight rise in living standards would be devoted not to broth and cheese, but to tea, sugar, and jam. Sudden depressions did not produce a reduction in unnecessary foods: Boyd Orr noticed in the 1930s what Edward Smith had seen during the cotton famine of the 1860s—if the unemployed could not afford meat they did not eat more bread and potatoes, but continued to buy sugar and relishes to make a bread diet more palatable.[67]

The workhouse diet was stripped of everything which made similar food acceptable to the poor; sometimes even salt was not offered at the table. The Commissioners emphasized that diet must be disciplinary, and for over 40 years the Inspectors tried to uphold this rule. Tufnell extirpated beer from Kentish workhouses, Parker objected to the 'almost unlimited allowance of vegetables' at Newbury, and all Inspectors tried to impose uniform dietaries in their districts. The Inspectors also tried to regulate the manner of serving food; for if inmates were marched to the table and given a weighed portion they would know their place. Parker objected to elderly inmates keeping their own teapots and brewing tea at will, for the continual movement, he said, disrupted the order of the house. The same quantities of tea could be given, but at fixed times, and from one large pot.[68]

Significantly, when the central authority relaxed workhouse discipline in the 1890s, the dietary received much attention. Guardians could reward the deserving aged by allowing them personal teapots, and giving them sugar, tea, sweets and puddings. In 1895 Dr Fuller recommended that all aged inmates be given a 'generous, varied and palatable diet' irrespective of their merits.[69] Twentieth-century workhouse diets included a meat dinner every day, with fish or bacon as an alternative, jam was added to the bread and butter for breakfast, and an institutional milk pudding or jam tart served with the midday meal. But the poor cooking and lack of individual initiative remained. In the 1920s, as in many later hospitals, the old people received the last meal of the day at an early hour, possibly 4.30 or 5 p.m., and were put to bed as early as possible for the convenience of the staff. The discipline which had been consciously devised in 1834 to reduce individual choice had become the unconscious discipline of convenience in the modern institutions.[70]

Total institutions, it is said, produce not only blank mindedness, but a form of institutional dependence. Dr Richard Asher translates this into clinical terms:

> ... 'institutional neurosis'—the syndrome of submissiveness, isolation, loss of individuality, automaton-like rigidity, and loss of all initiative which occurs in people who have been in institutions for a long while. If it occurs in a mental hospital, it is almost invariably assumed to be an end result of mental illness. This is not so. This dreadful thing is caused by institutional life and nothing more...
>
> Characteristically, the hands are held across the body or tucked behind an apron; the shoulders drooped and the head held forward. Entries in the notes (if any are kept) give further confirmation of the diagnosis, thus: 'Dull, apathetic and childish', 'Mute, dirty and withdrawn', or alternatively, 'Has settled down well' or 'Is co-operative, and gives no trouble'.[71]

Did the workhouse sap its inmates of initiative, leaving them unable to cope with life outside? Obviously in the case of younger and healthier people they did not; as will be seen, even the less employable members of the workhouse population tended to leave when they had the chance. When old age pensions arrived, the healthier old people left the workhouses. Handicapped inmates, however, were bound to be dependent on society in some fashion; in the nineteenth century society decreed more frequently that they be dependent in institutions. These, the sick and the infirm, were the long-term residents: if they had no friends outside they had no recourse but the institution. Alternative solutions, such as outdoor relief, were usually resorted to because they were cheaper than incarceration, but could produce shocking results. In 1873 an Inspector reported from Banbury:

> J.T. an idiot, 44 lives alone—earns, and does, and is, nothing. Receives 2s 6d and one loaf. (Qn. How does she live? Relieving officer replies, that he 'has no idea'.)[72]

If the authorities neglected this group, the consequences might be worse than the risk of encouraging them to depend on institutions.

Children were the most contentious group, for critics of the system usually argued that only their own favoured scheme—cottage homes or the like—would prevent the children from becoming dependent on the Poor Law for the rest of their lives. Tufnell believed that children educated in the workhouse rather than in district schools would

> ... fall back, after a few ineffectual struggles for independence, contentedly into pauperism; and constitute no inconsiderable proportion of the adult inmates in the workhouse wherein they were brought up when children.[73]

In the 1870s Mrs Senior and Louisa Twining criticized the district schools for the same reason, arguing that the children were too regimented, and that the girls could learn no ordinary domestic skills in the great barracks. Furthermore, girls from workhouses and barrack schools made sullen servants, were likely to lose their jobs, and return later to the workhouse with their illegitimate children.[74]

Such arguments provoked a number of statistical surveys to see if children from Poor Law institutions really did become dependent and return to the workhouse when they grew up. Mrs Senior claimed that 30 per cent of the girls turned out badly; Tufnell rejoinded angrily that it was only 4 per cent.[75] But in any case, against what standard were the children to be judged? Some of them came from the worst possible backgrounds and were in the schools for only short periods. Even if Mrs Senior's estimates were accepted, they could not be blamed entirely on the institutions. In 1862 some of the Inspectors had carried out their own investigations. H.B. Farnall reported that of more than 20,000 adult inmates in London, only 2.2 per cent had been in workhouse schools. Another return from prisons and reformatories in the same year indicated that only 3.2 per cent of the inmates had been in Poor Law schools, nearly half of them for less than a year.[76]

The evidence did not seem to indicate massive recidivism by ex-workhouse children. Given that the majority of workhouse inmates by the end of the century were old or ill, it was inevitable that some former workhouse children would be amongst them, because this was the common fate of so many of the working class. The main failing of the workhouse schools was perhaps to turn out the children as nothing better than unskilled labourers, likely to earn the lowest wages, and hence most subject to the misfortunes of a harsh environment. Many ex-workhouse children may have relied, like others of their class, on outdoor relief in hard times; but there is no indication that they were so sapped by institutional life that they became a permanent drain on the poor rates.

Even the aged, whose dependence on the institutions might be complete because of infirmity, did not always let the system force them into submission. They established their own hierarchies and currencies, bartered for tobacco, returned drunk from their day off, quarrelled amongst themselves or with the officers. To the guardians these were signs of insubordination—they may equally have been signs of life. In the 1960s Townsend suggested that although many elderly inmates appeared outwardly conformist, they 'appear to cling tenaciously to their individual identity and ideals'.[77] That the inmates subverted the system, either by open defiance or by developing their own rituals, is a tribute to their powers of survival.

9

The Workhouse and the Community

In 1916 the master of West Ashford workhouse reported an inquest on a pauper who had died soon after admission. 'Verdict from neglect & Starvation. No one was to blame.'[1] Legally, if not morally, the master was right. The Poor Law did not reach people who would not ask for relief, nor those who refused it when offered. An Inspector, Henry Longley, stated the official case in 1873:

> ... [he wished] that it might become a matter of wider notoriety that the duties of Relieving Officers are limited to the relief of destitute applicants, and that it is not incumbent upon them to protect the community generally ... against the scandals of deaths by starvation, or to seek out applicants of relief.[2]

Every year from 1871, details of inquests in the London area where the verdict had been death by starvation were laid before Parliament. Longley was gratified that out of 97 cases of starvation in 1872, only one had refused the offer of admission to the workhouse: the rest had not applied for poor relief. In 1908, the first year in which national statistics were published, out of 125 deaths there were 55 vagrants, six neglected children, and six people on outdoor relief. Eighty had made no application for relief, and only 25 had refused indoor relief. The figures, although grim enough, seemed to confirm the original belief of the Poor Law Commissioners—few would die rather than enter a workhouse.[3]

Every year guardians in some union miscalculated in their usual belief that most outdoor paupers had another source of income, and a few paupers on out-relief starved. As late as 1905 the Webbs discovered a case where a relieving officer had given an unemployed man, his wife and twin babies, relief consisting of a little rice, flour, bread and treacle. The only food for the twins, one of whom died, was two tins of condensed milk.[4] This was scandalous indeed, but

222

opponents of the Poor Law claimed that even worse damage resulted because of fear of the workhouse; and that uncounted numbers of people suffered rather than apply for any relief. Statistics of starvation are too crude an index; disease, neglect and malnutrition were less sensational than outright starvation, but they represented human wastage all the same. This was the fate which many recipients of outdoor relief shared with that section of the poor who had to accept the lowest earnings.

Here one enters the most difficult and contentious part of Poor Law history. The horrors of the workhouse became a part of the national folklore. They reached the educated world through the novels of Dickens and the pamphlets of Louisa Twining; they hung on the walls of the Royal Academy in the paintings of Luke Fildes; they provided a sentimental turn at music halls, where Albert Chevalier was an immense success in the 1890s with *My Old Dutch* ('We've Been Together Now for Forty Years'.)[5] They appeared in the dramatically sordid etchings of Gustave Doré; they enlivened many a drawing-room in recitations of Sims's famous poem:

> I came to the parish, craving
> Bread for a starving wife,
> Bread for the woman who'd loved me
> Through fifty years of life;
> And what do you think they told me,
> Mocking my awful grief?
> That 'the House' was open to us,
> But they wouldn't give 'out relief'.
> (*In the Workhouse—Christmas Day*)

At a more popular level there were broadsheet ballads:

> Her lifeless form lies in the grave,
> Her soul has gone to heaven,
> Where Workhouse Cru'lty is unknown
> And *Poverty's forgiven*.[6]

(*Poor Little Greene. The Child whose jaws were bandaged up, while still alive and moving, in St Pancras Workhouse!*)

Critics argued that outdoor relief had little social stigma, although it was humiliating to apply to the guardians and to line up at the relief station every week for doles and bread rations. It was the constant threat of the workhouse, and the social degradation it carried, which forced the respectable poor to bear any hardship rather than apply for poor relief. Many people would literally starve themselves and their children rather than enter the house. A letter from Ann Humphreys of Lambeth to the Poor Law Board in 1855, might be offered in evidence. She had five small children but her husband, though employed, could not earn enough to keep them. She applied to the guardians, who had previously allowed her outdoor relief, but as the head of the family was working and able-bodied, they could not continue it. She wrote:

> ... the other Day I went befor the Board of Gardans to see if they would alow me a little Brade to asiste me at the Present time and I toke my Children with me as they are in want of shouse and Clothing as the Winter is approaching thinken they would give them sum But they would not alow me anything But an order to cume in the House and the answer I made them wase I would suffer Death firs Befor I would Be Parted from my Children until it wase the will of Almighty God to Call me from them
>
> Hopping Gentlemen that you will take it into consideration that it would Be Hard for me to Brake up my Little Shelter after having so many years if I nede to Part from my Children for the little asistance I requier is a Little Clothing and a Little Brad to Asiste me with my Children.[7]

Was Ann Humphreys' reaction a common one? Other inhabitants of the parish had fewer inhibitions. A few months later the Lambeth clerk complained that the guardians were unable to cope with thirty disorderly young paupers 'who are alternately Inmates of the Workhouse and the Gaol'. If the guardians discharged them from the workhouse, they intimidated the overseers until they were readmitted.[8]

Historians disagree on this question, especially over the early years of the New Poor Law. In Nottingham in the late 1930s the poor would sell all they had to avoid entering the workhouse; fear and disgust of the Poor Law drove them to Chartism. During the miners' strike in Durham in the early 1840s, strikers would suffer any hardship rather than apply for relief. While the Norfolk workhouses provided a higher standard of physical comfort than the poor could earn for themselves, the system forced the poor to emigrate from this depressed region in large numbers. They drove themselves to the verge of starvation before they would enter the house. On the other hand, poor relief does not seem to have been regarded as a stigma in the north east, where the almshouse tradition continued and the guardians ran the workhouses leniently. Professor McCord argues further from studies of the north east that the workhouse was not felt to be socially disgraceful in the early years of the New Poor Law. Not until working-class living standards rose at the end of the nineteenth century did the gulf between pauper and worker widen. Derek Fraser claims that it was not the threat of the workhouse, but the Law of Settlement, which deterred many people. The Irish poor avoided applying for relief because they knew it would mean removal back to Ireland; in the depression of 1839–40, public subscriptions were raised in Bradford and Bolton to relieve the non-settled and Irish poor threatened with removal.[9]

Workhouses could be as forbidding as the guardians and their officers made them. Andover workhouse in the early 1840s was a grim deterrent; the local poor would accept starvation wages of five or six shillings a week rather than enter it, while the poor in South Shields apparently felt no such alarm. Nevertheless, there are wider aspects of the workhouses' role in the community: they did not become a national myth because some workhouses were worse than others. The question raises larger historical problems of class relationships, not merely the relations between the ruling classes and the poor, but within the working class itself. Fear of physical hardship or numbing routine, or separation of families and personal degradation influenced local attitudes towards a particular workhouse at a particular time. Fear of social stigma, of the disgrace of becoming a pauper, is a notion more pervasive and difficult to isolate. Until the last decade of the nineteenth century the central authority consciously fostered the idea that the workhouse carried social disgrace, and middle-class observers naturally accepted this. Guardians themselves tried to emphasize the disgrace of pauperism: some of them regularly published lists of names to be pinned to the church door or other conspicuous places. To ask whether the poor also feared the shame of the workhouse is to ask how far they subscribed to the beliefs of their rulers, given that in many workhouses after the 1840s conditions were better than in the homes of the very poor.

Part of the answer to this problem lies in the frequency with which the poor resorted to the workhouse. Casual usage might suggest not only the vulnerability of the poor to changing economic circumstances, but that the workhouse was less degrading than the middle class believed. Official statistics, however, show only the numbers of inmates on two days of the year; they do not indicate how many people entered the workhouse in the course of the year, nor how frequently they re-entered. A solitary Parliamentary return, published in 1861, showed that nearly 21 per cent of adult inmates were long-term, having been resident for five years or more. Of these 14,216 inmates, 42 per cent were resident because of old age of infirmity; 35 per cent because of mental illness; 11 per cent were handicapped, and 7 per cent ill. The remaining 5 per cent included unmarried mothers and alcoholics.[10] Inmates who had been resident less than five years would of course include some who were at the beginning of a longer period of residence.

Evidence on a smaller scale comes from a roll-call of a workhouse in Holborn union. On 1 January 1867, there were 368 inmates who had been admitted more than a year before, and 190 who had been admitted in the past year. (There were few children, because like all London unions, Holborn sent its children to separate schools soon after admission.) 180 inmates (32 per cent) had been in the workhouse more than five years; 56 of them for more than ten years. The age groups of inmates were also recorded:[11]

Age (years)	Admitted before 1 Jan. 1866		Admitted between 1 Jan. 1866 and 1 Jan. 1867	
	Number	%	Number	%
0–15	13	3.5	18	9.7
16–30	35 ⎫		23 ⎫	
31–50	57 ⎬	40.0	38 ⎬	49.2
51–60	45 ⎭		30 ⎭	
61–70	81 ⎫		44 ⎫	
71+	127 ⎭	56.5	32 ⎭	41.1
Total	368		185	(5 ages not stated)

The fate of these two groups of inmates by the end of 1868 can also be stated:

	Admitted before 1 Jan. 1866		Admitted between 1 Jan. 1866 and 1 Jan. 1867	
	Number	%	Number	%
Dead	61	16.6	33	17.4
Removed to other unions or institutions	31	8.4	23	12.0
Given out relief	2 ⎫		0 ⎫	
On leave	7 ⎬	10.9	3 ⎬	35.3
Discharged themselves	31 ⎭		64 ⎭	
Still in workhouse	236	56.5	67	35.3
Total	368		190	

226

From these figures it appears that the most recently admitted inmates were also more likely to have left the workhouse within a year. Instead of taking a census of inmates, as the authorities did, if we look at their movement in and out of this workhouse in the year 1867, there is a much more active picture: 1482 admissions were recorded in the admission book that year, but as these included people who left and re-entered more than once, the total of *individuals* admitted was 1213.

Multiple admissions to Holborn workhouse 1867

Times admitted	No. of people
2	111
3	28
4	10
5	6
6	3
7	1
8	2
14	1

The Holborn guardians allowed leave to elderly inmates, and also sent the old women out nursing when such work was needed amongst the outdoor poor. The 111 paupers admitted twice include people of this kind. The much smaller number who were admitted three or more times were mainly younger, single people, like Martha Andrews, aged 22, who entered the workhouse six times between June and December, usually staying less than a fortnight, or Charles Brattle, aged 21, who entered the workhouse 14 times, never for more than a week at a time, and usually for only a couple of days. Their erratic movements suggest that they had no steady living or regular home; they would have been classified by the authorities as the disreputable poor, prostitutes and riff-raff; but if the number of times they entered is any guide, they were a small minority of inmates.

Taking each recorded admission in 1867, the age groups were as follows:

Ages, (including those counted twice)					
	0–15	16–30	31–50	51–60	60+	Total
Number	392	424	365	118	183	1482
%	26.5	28.6	24.6	8.0	12.3	100

Again, the fate of these inmates by the end of the following year, 1868, is recorded:

	Number	%
Dead	99	6.7
Absconded	21	1.4
Emigrated	9	0.6
Sent to friends or other care outside	27	1.7
Sent to another institution	131	8.8
On leave	21	1.4
Sent to supplementary workhouse in Holborn	31	2.1
Sent out to domestic service, nursing	71	4.8
Removed to another union	22	1.5
Wives leaving with husbands	36	2.4
Children leaving with both parents	37	2.5
Children leaving with mother	160	10.8
Given out-relief	388	26.2
Discharged themselves	327	22.1
Still in workhouse	102	7.0
Total admissions	1482	100

These figures reveal some of the patterns of London workhouse life at this time. Most of the children in the house came from fatherless families: 61 of them were born in the workhouse in 1867, mostly to unmarried women. The large group of inmates sent out on outdoor relief indicates that many entered because of illness: as soon as they were able to manage for themselves, the guardians could support them more cheaply outside. The workhouse acted as a clearing house for more specialized institutions: most of the inmates sent to other institutions were children, but 31 aged people went to another workhouse in the union. Of the 102 people admitted in 1867 who were still in the workhouse by the end of 1868, nearly half were over 60, and probably had little hope of leaving. If we assume that as many as 307 people were still in institutions by the end of 1868, including those who had been removed to other unions, those on temporary leave, and children in the schools (though many of these may well have left the second institution in 1868), then it still seems that about three quarters of the people who entered this workhouse in 1867 used it only as a temporary expedient—including the 99 who were *in extremis*. A static census of the workhouse shows an aged population: half the inmates on 1 January 1867 were over 60 years old; but this does not show the constant movement of younger people through the workhouse in the course of the year. For some inmates the workhouse was literally a place of last resort; for most, a temporary lodging.

Writing of the poor in eighteenth-century France, Olwen Hufton uses the phrase 'an economy of makeshifts'. The wretched small-holders of the villages, the common labourers of the towns, could rarely hope to earn a steady living by regular work. In France, casual employment, seasonal migration, charitable relief and begging spun out the slender lines of existence. The historian cannot separate the 'honest' poor from the professional beggars and vagabonds, nor draw a rigid boundary between the labouring classes and the dangerous classes.[12] Indigence shaded imperceptibly into crime and prostitution. The poor could not afford to be too nice about certain moral distinctions, nor regard beggary and the acceptance of charity as shameful. The same comments apply to the Parisian poor well into the nineteenth century.[13] No comparable study exists for Britain, where greater affluence may have encouraged observers to define the respectable and the disreputable poor more strictly. Yet recent works suggest that until at least the mid-nineteenth century, most crimes against property in Britain were committed not by a criminal class, but by people who normally worked for a living.[14] Furthermore, the crime rate rose in years of economic hardship. If a section of the working class used this expedient to alleviate poverty, who can doubt that the workhouse was yet another makeshift, preferably of a short-term nature? The Commissioners of 1832 had objected to the Old Poor Law because it did not adequately distinguish the pauper from the labourer; in the face of economic hardship, even the deterrent workhouse system could not immediately separate the two. The distinction was, in many cases, fallacious.

In the earlier decades of the New Poor Law, those on the fringes of the labour market had to contemplate the workhouse whenever any local or personal disaster struck. Illness and old age were the two main reasons for entering it, but workhouses also developed a rhythm of their own, which fluctuated with the local economy. In fact there are two overlapping patterns of workhouse relief: the sudden emergencies and the seasonal ones. Irregular events, such as epidemics, exceptional-ly hard winters, or a crisis in local industry, could suddenly raise the numbers of applicants for relief. This erratic effect shows up in local rather than national statistics, though of course periods of widespread depression, such as the 1840s, could affect the national figures. Sudden catastrophe, however, also stimulated charity, which acted as a counterbalance to the Poor Law: the best example of this is the

Lancashire cotton famine, when huge sums flowed in from all over the country to alleviate distress, and the authorities avoided using the workhouses. Seasonality of relief showed up most clearly in the casual wards which housed the migrant workers, but it could be seen also in the workhouses. Rural workhouses until the First World War (and even afterwards) had more occupants in the winter months than in summer: this is reflected in the national censuses of pauperism, where the figures of the indoor poor are always higher on 1 January than on 1 July. Winter threw many agricultural labourers out of work, especially if they were paid by the day, and both guardians and employers favoured the married men with families when employment was scarce. Single people, denied work and outdoor relief, might well have to enter the workhouse at this period if they were not aided by their families, by charity, or by their own savings. Family earnings were low in winter, and personal savings would drain away if there were any personal catastrophes such as illness.

In the large towns the pattern was more complicated. The unskilled labour market was also affected by the seasons, but Stedman Jones argues of London that winter still afflicted the poor most severely. In winter the fashionable world returned to London; its wealth provided a long chain of employment, and certain types of unskilled labour, such as coal-heavers, were more in demand in the winter season. To counteract this, outdoor trades such as building and riverside work were disrupted in bad weather. Summer could bring epidemics, including cholera, but in winter the homeless poor could not all sleep outdoors. Large towns, particularly London, were centres of charity, usually most active in winter. The sum of these conflicting agencies was, however, to fill the workhouses in the winter months; Holborn, Lambeth, Bromley, Bridge and Blean, with their widely different economies, had similar patterns of seasonal relief, excepts at times of a local catastrophe. From October the workhouses began to fill, and numbers remained high until March, when they began to decline. Irrespective of the location, the workhouse threatened the poor most in winter. The exception was the casual wards, for, like the rich, the migrant and casual poor tended to leave London in summer.[15]

Although workhouse accounts of individual inmates are often incomplete, a brief survey hints that not only the able-bodied poor produced these seasonal variations. The term able-bodied may be misleading, but one may assume that when a medical officer classified a pauper as aged or infirm, he was less likely to err. In Lambeth, Bromley and Bridge, in the occasional years when complete records survive, it seems that both old and young were likely to leave the workhouse in summer. In Bridge, all the old men who were capable discharged themselves to go to the hop fields; in Lambeth, certain aged men also left the workhouse in summer, though to what purpose was not stated. The average number of aged and infirm men in Lambeth workhouse from January to March 1874 was 265; for June–August it was 220. The aged women showed no such propensity to escape, probably (as will appear), because of their greater infirmity.[16] The old may have been able to support themselves for short periods; but more probably, in the good season their families were earning enough to remove them from the workhouse, or to offer them a lodging. The Victorian economy was highly labour intensive at certain seasons, when the labour of children and older people would be used. After the harvest, or as the season ended, the feeblest were thrown aside. Then there was family help, charity, begging, outdoor relief. At the end of these expedients stood the prison and the workhouse.

Did the patterns of workhouse relief change before the First World War? The Royal Commission of 1905, like its predecessor, objected to the casual usage of the workhouse by the disreputable poor, 'a troublesome class who make a convenience of the workhouse and whose improvidence is born of the knowledge that that institution is always at hand.'[17] The Commission made the first official attempt to chart movements in and out of the workhouse, for a sample number of unions representing about 12 per cent of the country's paupers. In the year ended September 1907, 83.7 per cent of the indoor paupers had received relief only once during the year; 13.5 per cent two to four times; 2.8 per cent five times or more.[18] The 'ins and outs' were obviously a small minority, though they created administrative irration; nor were they all young people. The Commissioners recorded with distaste that one woman aged 81 had entered the workhouse 163 times in the year 1901. In her case the workhouse was unavoidable, but the will to escape was strong. Nearly a third of the inmates in 1907 had used the workhouse for less than four weeks; another 18 per cent for less than 13 weeks; but just over a quarter had been in the workhouse for the whole year. The Majority Report concluded that, apart from the small group of ins and outs, workhouse inmates had entered because of illness and infirmity, and that few could more properly have been dealt with by outdoor relief.[19]

It appeared that the number of individuals entering the workhouse during that year was about 2.26 times higher than the number on 1 January 1908. (The same proportion applied almost exactly to paupers on outdoor relief). The official figure for indoor pauperism was 7.3 per thousand in that year: in fact, about 16 people per thousand had entered the Poor Law institutions at some time in the course of the year. Therefore, the numbers of people who at some time in their lives actually entered, or were threatened by, the workhouse, would always be far more than the annual census of pauperism implied. In the early years of the Poor Law, when there were fewer alternatives to poor relief, the workhouse must have cast its shadow over a large section of the working class. Figures for Holborn in 1867 may be used again. A workhouse which held 553 on 1 January actually passed 1213 people through its doors in the course of the following year; and there would be fresh inmates the following year. In the course of a decade, a considerable proportion of the local population would experience this institution.

Poor Law policy in the later nineteenth century diminished the effects of sudden catastrophes on the workhouses, but left underlying patterns unchanged. Increased use of the labour test and outdoor relief, as well as non-Poor Law expedients such as unemployment insurance, reduced pressure on the workhouses in times of depression. The casual wards, it will be seen, became a more sensitive barometer of the national economy than the rest of the workhouse. Yet the seasonal pattern of workhouse relief appeared even in the 1920s, and a substantial group of long-term residents (probably more than one third), was still balanced by a shifting temporary population.

The records of Bridge union, which are relatively full, give an indication of changes in this small Kentish workhouse. Bridge was almost exclusively agricultural, though its economy prospered more after the mid-nineteenth century, when the railway connected the parish of Chartham with London and the coast. Its population increased gently—only about 5 per cent per decade in the nineteenth century—and its workhouse, which in the 1830s had been a regular expedient for unemployed labourers, gradually decayed. The workhouse was most used in the 1840s, when it held an average of nearly 200 paupers, but this diminished to 96 in the 1890s, 56 during the war, and around 60 during the 1920s. Unions where the workhouse became a hospital, as in Lambeth and Bromley, had to house inmates whose numbers continually increased, but the Bridge workhouse did not become a hospital, and so it contracted. Unlike Holborn it was quite unspecialized, and did not send inmates to special institutions until after the First World War, except for some urgent hospital cases.

We may study the records of Bridge inmates for two-year sample periods in 1837–38, 1887–88 and 1927–28. The most striking features of the earlier period are the large turnover of inmates, the numbers of multiple admissions, and the use of the workhouse by younger people and family groups.[20]

		1837–38	1887–88	1927–28
Individuals admitted		352	198	100
Entered workhouse twice	adults	41	39	9
	children	26	19	4
Entered three times	adults	18	11	—
	children	14	2	—
Entered four times	adults	4	3	—
Entered five times	„	2	1	—
Entered more than five times	„	2	2	—
Family Groups				
With both parents	adults	22	6	—
	children	33	10	—
With mother only	adults	32	13	6
	children	84	31	12
With father only	adults	4	—	—
	children	12		
Childless couples	adults	10	4	—

Age Groups (% of total individuals admitted)

Ages	1837–38		1887–88		1927–28	
	men	*women*	*men*	*women*	*men*	*women*
0–15	50.7		23.8		18.0	
16–40	8.5	14.6	9.1	19.5	2.0	12.0
41–60	7.3	4.8	11.9	2.4	15.0	5.0
60+	10.4	3.7	25.2	8.1	34.0	14.0

The samples suggest that the workhouse was used less by families and by young people in the later periods; after the First World War it was inhabited almost entirely by the elderly and a few unmarried mothers. Amongst the young people, women were more vulnerable than men, usually because they had dependent children, although a few were young servants out of work who returned to the workhouse because they had nowhere else to go. Family groups were decreasing by the late nineteenth century, though 'ins and outs' did not quit the workhouse until later. Inevitably, an ageing workhouse population produced a higher death rate. In 1837–8 and 1887–8 the death rate amongst adults was almost the same—just under 10 per cent of those who entered in the two years. In 1927–28 it was 22 per cent.

The Bridge figures also show clearly a feature which appears in the national decennial census. Younger inmates were likely to be women; elderly inmates were mostly male, though by the end of the period, elderly women were entering the workhouse in larger numbers. (See Figure 4). Whereas in the nineteenth century children and elderly men were the largest groups of inmates, institutions under the Welfare State have a majority of children and elderly women.[21] The transition came slowly, and the reversal of sexes amongst the elderly was not apparent until after 1930; even then, there was a higher proportion of old men in local authority homes than in other types of homes for the aged.[22] The statistics hint at changes in English family life. In the nineteenth century, old women did not enter the workhouse unless they were too infirm to care for themselves, and became a burden to their families, even though there were more elderly women than elderly men in the population. Hence they were less able to leave the workhouse to find seasonal employment. In 1836 Tufnell was surprised at the surplus of aged men in East Kent workhouses—one third more than the old women. 'Old women', he wrote, 'in fact, are not nearly so helpless as old men'; they were useful to their families as long as they could do household tasks and look after children.[23] This is the corollary of what Michael Anderson discovered of family structures in Lancashire. Where wives worked, an aged relative would be useful to care for the children, but with rigid sexual divisions of labour, old men were unaccustomed to such household work.[24]

In agricultural Kent, married women did not often work full-time, but families did not keep elderly relatives merely for economic reasons. Family pride might operate to keep an elderly parent out of the workhouse, but affectionate ties with the mother were likely to be stronger. In a culture where the breadwinner often took most of the food; where he annexed earnings for his own pleasures; and where paternal discipline could be harsh, fathers did not always inspire affection.[25] Although these glimpses are fragmentary, the disproportionate number of old men who ended their days in the workhouse suggests that some working families were not reluctant to hand over a former tyrant to the Poor Law, even if he were not altogether infirm. By the mid-twentieth century, when institutional care for the infirm was no longer confused with deterring pauperism, more old women entered homes, reflecting their natural majority in the population. The census also shows clearly that old people who were single or widowed were more likely to enter the workhouse, just as they were more likely to enter a home in the 1960s.

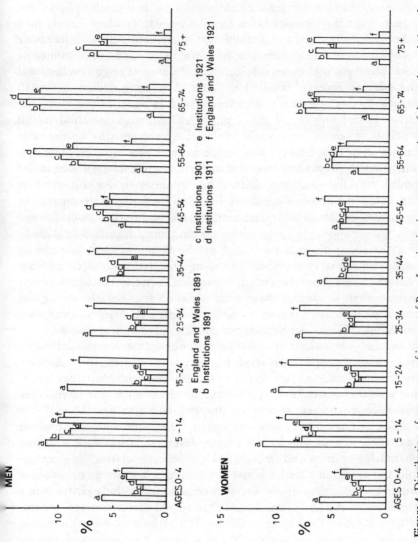

Figure 4. Distribution of age groups of inmates of Poor Law institutions as a proportion of the total population of these institutions in four census years; compared with the same distribution in the population of England and Wales in two census years.

The high turnover of inmates in the early decades of the Poor Law indicates that poverty could not afford to be too mindful of social disgrace, though no one used the workhouse longer than he needed. In any case, if many of one's neighbours were in a similar plight, the threat of social rejection cannot have been great. Incidents cancel each other out. In Basford a sick child died of starvation because its father would not enter the workhouse; but rural unions in Kent continued to take into the workhouses one or more children of large families, and the parents accepted this. The West Ashford guardians in 1840 reported a case of a family with seven children under 14 years old; the father earned only 12 shillings per week. Keeping one child in the workhouse school for a while could relieve the pressure on the rest, but the Poor Law Commission strenuously objected to such practices, and tried to persuade guardians to force the whole family into the house.[26] To these families, distress had to outweigh shame or fear. In the 1840s, applicants were more likely to be deterred by separation from families, intolerable constraint, and fear of those local workhouses which were known to be scandalously mismanaged. Indeed, it is likely that the social disgrace envisaged by the Commissioners bore most hardly on the stray members of the middle class who were unlucky enough to find themselves in the institution. Letters of complaint from many unions show that there were always a few inmates with good education who had not been saved by the many charities for distressed gentlefolks. Clerks, with moderate education but limited salaries, were particularly at risk; but most union workhouses contained small tradesmen or professional men, sometimes even former guardians or workhouse officers. A relief list of the Medway Union in 1849, amongst a majority of labourers and semi-skilled workers, includes two tallowchandlers, two linen drapers, and a grocer.[27]

Middle-class inmates aroused mixed feelings in the guardians. In 1841 the Lambeth guardians were perplexed by an applicant who was obviously, in dress and manner, of the superior classes. A guardian told the applicant that he himself would 'cut his throat, or sweep a crossing rather than apply for Parochial Relief': (the guardian later explained to the Poor Law Board that he had meant this as a general reflection rather than specific advice).[28] The Board's correspondence was also enlivened for many years by letters from James Nicholls, an inmate of Lambeth who had formerly been in the legal profession. He frequently organized petitions of complaint from the inmates, and became sufficiently famous to rate an obituary in the *South London Press*.[29]

Nicholls showed the middle class to what depths they might fall if they broke the conventions of thrift and respectability; the unskilled working class had less far to fall, and feared the workhouse for more tangible reasons. They would use it also for their own ends, like the unmarried labourers in some unions who entered the workhouse for that one night of the week when a meat dinner was served.[30] Fear of social disgrace does not enter into this calculation. Working-class families might hope to support an aged relative with the aid of outdoor relief, which to them held no disgrace; hence a dependent relative could become a pawn in a game of blackmail between family and guardians over who should pay for his keep. Joseph Arch's account from the 1870s strikes a conventional note. His behaviour, except for his application for outdoor relief, would have been approved by a middle-class reader:

My father was a ratepayer for 32 years and never troubled the parish for a farthing. When the poor old man was taken ill, of course my wife had to attend on him. She was pleased enough to do it... but she had her little family to see to, and she had been accustomed to bring in about two shillings a week by going out charring...

Arch applied to the guardians for a small sum to compensate his wife for her loss of earnings while she nursed the old man—he did not like to think of it as outdoor relief.

Well, they refused me that, and said that my father could go into the workhouse, and I could pay one-and sixpence a week towards his expenses.

My blood boiled up at that. What! My honest, respectable old father turned into the workhouse to end his days—never! I up and said to these gentlemen,

I'd sooner rot under a hedge than he should go there!'
And he did not go—he died under the old Arch roof-tree, and he breathed his last breath in my arms.[31]

Similar tales were still being recounted in Edwardian days, but where family ties were less strong and the sense of respectability less developed, the blackmail could be the other way. In 1859 the Blean guardians received the following letter:

Gentlemen,
I beg to inform you of the state of Rosa Ann Harvey that I Henry Harvey took out of the workhouse on the 13 of January 1859 I was

quite ignorant of the state that the poor child was in poor dear child red head when we got her home was neerly swarmed with Lice and that is not all for she had a great many sores and scars about her we got some mediciam for her but did not get the rid of it and if I had not kept something over her hands she would off scrached herself to pecies . . . has I took her without a farthing to help maintain her and without a bit of close to put on her . . without being put on our gaurd . . and iff their is not any thing alloud I must forward the child back again has we have nothing but our daily labour to depend on and now with the expence of these too very bad troubles we cannot stand against it.

Gentlem please to answer this letter by return of post and if we are not alloud any thing the child will be sent back in a few dayes.[32]

Harvey, unlike Arch, had no legal responsibility to maintain this more distant relative, and he must have known it would cost the guardians more to maintain her in the workhouse than to allow some outdoor relief.

By the late nineteenth century standards of living were rising for at least part of the working class. Universal education, more spending money, and the growth of new leisure activities outside the public house, as historians have surmised, probably widened the gap between the 'rough' and 'respectable' elements of the working class. The suburbs of large cities themselves encouraged social distinctions, with the development of housing estates built for the 'superior' artisan and the lower middle class. Even in the apparently undifferentiated urban slums, as Robert Roberts recalled of Salford, nicely balanced social judgements could be made, even between one identical house and another. The lace curtains at the window, restrained language (in front of the family), moderate indulgence in drink, above all, the cleanliness of house and family—all attested the growth of respectability. Schools reinforced these distinctions; a child with lice in his hair would be sent home, his family disgraced.[33] There was an elaborate system of credits and demerits: a daughter who married into the middle class raised the prestige of the whole family; a relative in the workhouse or in prison lowered it. The school board visitors who gave Charles Booth his information on London in the 1880s, going from house to house, used similar tests to class a family as 'respectable' or 'degraded'. It is not necessary here to pursue the argument that the working class, particularly the skilled workers, had accepted middle-class standards; it is possible that they devised their own code which was related to, though separate from, middle-class ideals. Yet in this finely graded hierarchy, arising from a more affluent society, the workhouse was almost the social nadir, only one rung above the prison. The more pretensions a working family had, the more the workhouse seemed a threat.

In the early years of the New Poor Law, a working-class family allowed a relative to enter the workhouse regretfully, but not with any sense that they had become social pariahs. Dickens sentimentalizes the situation in the Plornishes (*Little Dorrit*), who live only for the day when they can afford to take the aged father out of the workhouse, while the father nobly refuses to become a burden on their indigent family. Their plight is meant to excite compassion, not criticism. Michael Anderson and others have argued against Engels that the Industrial Revolution did not destroy family ties. The extended family, living under one roof, had disappeared long before industrialism, but close community with one's kin was valued nevertheless. Yet indigence is a powerful solvent of family affection. No historical method can show how many people entered the workhouse to the regret of their families, or how many had seen all ties broken. Each workhouse had its complement of deserted wives and children; the Kentish unions even combined to offer a reward for the apprehension of these husbands. The authorities sometimes joked that elderly couples were delighted to be separated at last—Thomas Hardy wrote some sour verses on the subject:

> [The old man reflects]
> 'Life there will be better than t'other,
> For peace is assured.
> *The men in one wing and their wives in another*
> Is strictly the rule of the Board.'
>
> (*The Curate's Kindness*)

The old man is then horrified to find that a well-meaning curate has arranged for him to share a room in the workhouse with the wife. But the sorrow of families too poor to keep their relatives out of the house was compounded because they were now involuntarily associated with broken families of the 'lowest class'.

Middle-class critics of the Poor Law also began to change their tone by the 1880s. Previously they had concentrated on harsh conditions in workhouses; now they emphasized the social disgrace, particularly enforced mixing of the respectable with the disreputable poor. Workhouses threatened the old most of all, and it was abominable that

239

a respectable working man should have to end his life in the company of all the riff-raff to whom guardians refused outdoor relief. Booth himself made the point forcibly:

> The aversion to the 'House' is absolutely universal, and almost any amount of suffering and privation will be endured by the people rather than go into it. Loss of liberty is the most general reason assigned for this aversion, but the dislike of decent people to be compelled to mix with those whose past life and present habits are the reverse of respectable is also strongly felt.[34]

Others took up the point. Both factions of the 1905 Commission made it a substantial part of their criticism of the workhouses, hence their suggestion for segregated buildings. Other interest groups such as MABYS objected that young women who had made 'one mistake' in producing an illegitimate child were forced to mix with prostitutes. Edith Sellers wrote a melodramatic piece for *The Nineteenth Century* (1903), in which she described respectable old people in country workhouses, sometimes in quite comfortable surroundings, whose lives were made miserable by their proximity to former criminals, howling idiots, and the 'hopelessly immoral'.[35] Like a rotten apple, even one such inmate could ruin the lives of the rest. In response, the Local Government Board tried unsuccessfully to encourage special treatment for the respectable aged poor in the workhouses, but attempts foundered on definitions of respectability. In any case, as one Inspector remarked, even a virtuous pauper could be a very disagreeable fellow-inmate.[36]

These were middle-class comments, no doubt, but working-class critics also scorned contact with the disreputable poor. Concluding his reminiscence, Joseph Arch wrote, 'it was the unfortunate pauper, not the drone pauper, our hearts bled for'.[37] Joseph Ashby of Tysoe, born illegitimate, whose mother had depended on outdoor relief during his childhood, was severe on the 'undeserving' poor when he later became a magistrate and a guardian.[38] Even the open-handed Poplar guardians, who hoped that their farm colony would rehabilitate the able-bodied poor, detested the idle tramps.[39] Before one sneers at these advocates of respectability, it must be remembered that their fears were not groundless. Every year there were cases of assault and violence in the workhouses, not only by inmates on the officers, but by inmates on one another. As in prisons, certain inmates would try to dominate the rest by force, especially in the monopoly of scarce resources. Workhouse punishment books record some of these events.

In Faversham in the 1840s some of the young men terrorized the old ones and stole their meat rations. In Blean in 1897 a pauper was sentenced to two months' hard labour for attacking one inmate with a poker and another with a bread knife.[40] Will Crooks remembered Sundays in the able-bodied men's ward in Poplar when he was elected guardian in 1892:

> ... as near an approach to hell as anything on this earth. It was everyone for himself and the devil take the hindmost. If a fellow could fight, he got as much as he wanted. If he could not, he got nothing.[41]

As young male inmates of the workhouses diminished in number, violent offences were less common, but offences committed by, or against, the mentally handicapped, remained a problem. Conditions in enclosed institutions no doubt bred such offences, but continued to terrify the aged poor. No amount of extra food or liberty could compensate for it. Even under the Welfare State, Townsend discovered that local authorities still essayed a rough moral discrimination in homes for the aged. Middle-class and 'respectable' inmates were more likely to be sent to the new, better equipped, local authority homes. Former tramps and less reputable inmates were kept in the old workhouse buildings.[42] Threat of relegation from one type of home to another was a useful element of discipline.

The most familiar aspect of popular revulsion is the working-class attitude to pauper funerals. The Poor Law Commissioners precipitated this hatred by their early rule that paupers be buried as cheaply as possible, and that the bells be not rung at the funeral, to save expense. Public outcry against this was such that the Commissioners had to compromise by arguing that burials should not be worse than, or superior to, those of the lowest classes.[43] The Church itself compounded the distress because an incumbent of the parish in which the workhouse was situated could refuse to bury a pauper from another parish who died in the workhouse. Where churchyards were crowded or the incumbent's fee was low, unseemly squabbles broke out over the disposition of the dead poor, akin to the Law of Settlement for the living. Even where the guardians intended to do things decently, their contract system allowed abuses; tradesmen provided coffins of poor quality, or which were too small. In 1855 a clergyman complained to the Bromley guardians that a pauper child had been buried in a disgraceful coffin, 'any tradesman would be ashamed to send so rough a packing case for the most common articles.'[44] In 1850 a Parliamentary report criticized the St Pancras guardians for their parsimonious burials:

> These burials take place twice-a-week, on Tuesday and Friday (the object of which is stated to be the saving of expense of conveyance), when the whole number are put into the grave together, and one service is read over them as is not unusual.

Paupers in the adjacent workhouse could see the coffins being stuffed into the overcrowded earth.[45]

Death, perhaps more than any other event, required its celebrations, regardless of expense. The popularity of burial clubs, particularly to provide against the frequent deaths of children, is well known. Even in the early twentieth century the poor of Lambeth, fearing the indecencies of a pauper funeral, paid into burial clubs for their children out of inadequate incomes. By this time, most guardians provided more respectable funerals, but this was not enough to satisfy working-class needs. The painted tin-plate mountings for a pauper child's coffin, gilded with the motto 'There's a Home for Little Children/Above the Bright Blue Sky', cost about four pence in the late 1860s, compared with the five pounds or more which a gentleman's family might spend on similar decorations.[46] Expenditure on the trappings of death varied exactly with social status, and the meanness of a pauper funeral could drag a family down. Relatives who had been prepared to allow an aged pauper to enter the workhouse would suddenly appear to pay for his funeral when he died, to the annoyance of guardians who felt that the money could have been better spent in his lifetime. The etiquette of burial entered deep into Victorian society, and the economies of a pauper funeral offended strong emotions.[47] As a result, there were undoubtedly many old people who resisted the workhouse even though they were unable to care for themselves: their antipathy also extended to the infirmaries. Betty Higden may not have been typical, but she did exist.

The efforts of the Charity Organization Society exacerbated the problem in the late nineteenth century. Although the COS did not have the widespread political influence it desired, it did manage to take over a number of boards of guardians. COS members were likely to be active in their community, willing to take part in local government, and by the turn of the century they had considerable hold over some large urban unions, particularly in London. Once in office, they followed official policy of denying all outdoor relief to the able-bodied, and offering the workhouse to widows and elderly people if their home circumstances were believed to be insanitary or immoral. The effect, as the Webbs pointed out, was to encourage these people to become even more insanitary and immoral, for they refused the workhouse and had to manage as best they could without any help. The Webbs engaged Miss G. Harlock in the course of their work for the 1905 Commission, to investigate the fate of people who had been refused outdoor relief in certain unions. These included Bradford, Manchester, Hackney and Paddington. In Bradford, Miss Harlock followed up 41 people who had been refused outdoor relief, and six who had been refused any relief: she concluded that over half had experienced physical and mental suffering as a result, while others threw their families into serious financial straits. The guardians had refused relief for both moral and health reasons: women with any stain on their characters were offered the workhouse, including one aged 70 who had been living with her lodger for 20 years. An aged couple had been offered the workhouse infirmary simply because they could not look after themselves; their refusal was based on past experience.[48]

It's not so nice there; [the old man said] they are all so ill in that ward, and many of them bad-tempered on account of their disease. And some of them groan and groan, and you can hear them dying, and then the dead ones are carried out by your bed, and you can see and hear it all... They say we must go into the house, and there they would separate us, me and her, after we have lived together 40 years.

It was alleged that if unions like Hackney and Whitechapel refused outdoor relief, they simply passed their burdens on to more generous areas like Poplar: by this time only a short period of residence was required to achieve settlement, and people moved from one part of London to another to obtain outdoor relief. Medical and relieving officers sometimes exceeded their authority and forcibly removed bedridden old people to the workhouse, like the old woman in Leeds, who was snatched from the mounting pile of filth in her lodging and carried off to the infirmary, swearing vigorously at the health inspector.[49]

Apart from fears of hardship, regimentation or social disgrace, the workhouse created other types of bitterness. Even after the anti-Poor Law campaign had subsided, the workhouse was a focus for class hostilities. The Poor Law Commissioners were not reticent in their belief that the workhouses would break the power of organized labour: they quoted with approval a letter from a northern manufacturer which argued that the Poor Law scheme for sending hands from southern unions to the industrial areas would destroy the trade unions.[50] The workhouse could also be used to manipulate wages: Anne Digby shows how farmers in East Anglia used the threat of the workhouse to compel labourers to accept low wages; in return the labourers burned ricks.[51] By the time Joseph Arch began to unionize the agricultural labourers in the 1870s, there was a long history of bitterness against the Poor Law. In industrial areas, employers also used the law. In 1860–1, during a lockout in the Nottingham lace-making industry, the employers (aided by the guardians) tried to employ non-union labour from the workhouse; but the trade union committee supported the paupers instead from its own funds.[52]

Guardians and employers were often likely to be the same men, or closely connected. During the 1870s, as the trade recession set in, strife began again in the industrial towns. By this time the trade unions had some legal recognition and a more highly organized membership, but at the same time the northern guardians were implementing the Poor Law more severely than in the 1840s. Where the workhouse was not large enough to cope with strikers or the unemployed, the guardians imposed harsh versions of the labour test. In 1879 there was a battle of wills in Bradford, where the unemployed first tried to crowd out the workhouse by applying for relief *en masse*, and then collected in a mob to intimidate the guardians. Encouraged by the Inspector, the guardians refused to offer relief other than in the workhouse or in return for stone breaking. Here charitable donations healed the breach, though the Inspector complained of sentimental charity which helped workers who ought to have been saving against such depressions.[53]

Incidents in Wales, however, set their seal upon all future relations between guardians and the trade unions. In Merthyr Tydfil, the industrial heart of Wales, the falling price of iron and coal drove employers to reduce wages and led to a series of bitter strikes. The strike of 1875 was accompanied by an employers' lockout; the guardians, themselves mainly ironmasters and coal-owners, at first refused all relief to single men. In February 900 men attacked the workhouse, overcrowded it, and the board had to offer indoor relief. Other able-bodied men did task work, but when the guardians ran out of suitable tasks, the Dowlais Company offered work at the collieries, which would have effectively used the labour test to break the strike. The men refused, but were starved out; by May the strike was broken.[54] The savagery of the Merthyr dispute created a debate which has never been settled—whether public authorities ought to relieve strikers, men whose unemployment is (in a sense) voluntary. At the Poor Law conference of 1878, passions ran high. Chadwick, in the chair, argued that guardians had no duty to consider the causes of destitution, but merely the most proper way of relieving it. For able-bodied men, relief clearly should be the workhouse or a labour test.[55] A working-class guardian from Maidstone, a member of the Kent and Sussex labourers' union, stated that guardians in his area often refused relief to union members, telling them to apply to their union. Other guardians argued that a rigorous use of poor relief would discourage strikes in the first place. Chadwick was magisterial:

> Capital, as such, has no place at the board of guardians; only a civil service and a duty has place there, to see to the correct administration of the law, which allows only of relief in absolute and entire destitution. The guardians have nothing to do beyond that. They have no right to operate upon wages.[56]

Chadwick, in his austere fashion, had always believed that the Poor Law, operating in a world where wages were mechanistically determined, would help resolve class conflict: he took no account of human nature. Nevertheless, under the Poor Law, strikers had a slight advantage. Guardians, even as hostile as those in Merthyr, could not ultimately refuse all relief to them, even though they could hedge it about with conditions such as the workhouse, or a labour test. Since many strikes were now on an enormous scale compared to those of the past, strikers relied on their own weight of numbers to compel the guardians to give unconditional relief. Plainly, a thousand men and their families could not be lodged in a workhouse, and to provide work such as stonebreaking would be even more costly than to give unconditional relief. In the difficult 1880s the matter slumbered briefly. Trade disputes such as the London dockers' strike aroused more public sympathy than before; charity was stimulated; Chamberlain issued his circular on public works for the unemployed. But South Wales was not pacified. In 1898, after further price and wage cutting by the employers, a five months' strike began.

This strike was even more costly to the poor rates than the previous ones. The guardians, who still represented the employers, nevertheless accepted that they must give outdoor relief to strikers in return for stonebreaking, and the Local Government Board sanctioned this.[57] When the strike ended, the coal-owners decided to test the legality of such relief, and began two actions against the Merthyr guardians. They claimed that it was illegal to support men who were capable of supporting themselves, and who could obtain work if they accepted the employers' conditions. After much wrangling, the Court of Appeal in 1900 issued its judgement—known as the Merthyr Tydfil judgement—in which it supported the employers up to a point, by arguing that guardians could not legally relieve an able-bodied man (whether on strike or not) who could obtain work, unless he were too exhausted by privation to be capable of labour. They also allowed the compromise which was to remain long a feature of public assistance: that the wives and families of strikers could claim poor relief, for they were innocent victims of the husband's destitution. This left out unmarried strikers, who were not eligible for any relief until they became debilitated, and who could not share the relief given their families. The effect of this judgement was to allow inadequate outdoor relief to strikers through their families.

Relations between guardians and trade unions were not always discordant. By the end of the nineteenth century, some guardians refused to accept contracts with employers who did not pay union rates. Labour-controlled guardians were obviously most prone to this arrangement, but 'progressive' London unions like Lambeth also accepted it because they argued the poor rate would always have to bear the consequences if workers were underpaid.[58]

The New Poor Law was passed at a time when strikes and trade unions existed in a legal limbo; the Commissioners had not contemplated that they would become a national issue. To trade unionists after 1900 it seemed that a legal judgement (unsupported by legislation) had manipulated the Poor Law as an anti-strike weapon. As previously discussed, this was crucial in 1926. The Poor Law, which had arisen out of class conflict, ended as it had begun, hated by the labour movement. The workhouse, the most tangible symbol of the Law, naturally inspired the harshest criticism, which even its greater comfort and new hospital facilities could not allay.

Thus the reputation of the workhouse developed. After it ceased to threaten cold, hunger and mistreatment, it threatened social disgrace. It stood opposed to the family, to working-class culture, to the aspirations of organized labour. Yet even as these objections crystallized in the late nineteenth century, the workhouse was becoming a refuge. Its actual, as opposed to its theoretical, relations with the able-bodied poor became yearly more tenuous. Like the Poor Law in 1832, it seemed intolerable that the workhouse should survive, and impossible that it should be abolished.

10

The Casual Poor

One group of workhouse inmates was always treated differently from the rest. Whereas most of the regular inmates experienced improved conditions during the nineteenth century, the casual poor shared few of the benefits. The Poor Law Commissioners stated their attitude towards them in 1841:

> There is, however, a class of paupers who contrive to enjoy the physical comforts of the workhouse, without performing the labour or submitting to the discipline which are . . . necessary conditions for obtaining these advantages.
>
> These paupers do not, as a class, possess or deserve the compassion of the public . . . These are the *mendicant vagrants*, who are known to be generally persons of dissolute character, to lead habitually a life of laziness and imposture, and not infrequently to resort to intimidation and pilfering.[1]

Vagrants were one rung below the able-bodied settled poor. If they applied for relief they were entitled only to a night's lodging in the workhouse, but a lodging of the most primitive kind. When the New Poor Law was enacted, some guardians assumed that, since casuals were not mentioned in it, there was no longer an obligation to relieve them. After a number of cases in which casuals died after being denied access to the workhouse, the Commissioners ordered guardians to relieve all who applied, and to provide casual wards for their reception. Few guardians spent much money on building for the casual poor; and casuals normally slept in makeshift sheds and outhouses. In many workhouses they had no beds—sometimes not even straw to lie on—and in some the men and women were promiscuously lodged together. Guardians gave them bread and water for supper, but often gave no meal in the mornings: their whole aim was to be rid of casuals as quickly as possible.

The casuals are the most mysterious of all workhouse inmates, and vagrancy is by its nature one of the least quantifiable of social problems. Poor Law administrators were concerned only with those vagrants who applied for relief at the casual wards, but this was only a proportion of the homeless poor. The published statistics showed how many had applied to casual wards on the nights of 1 January and 1 July; they could not show how many had slept in barns, haystacks, doorways, brickyards and railway arches, nor those who had found refuge with a charitable organization. The July figures were swollen with town poor moving into the country for casual work, while the January ones were diminished by the opening of charitable shelters in winter and the public's tendency to be more generous to beggars at Christmas. A casual with a few pence in his pocket had the choice, in the towns, of spending the night in a common lodging house rather than the casual ward. Over long periods the vagrancy statistics were affected by the closing of lodging houses in some towns, where the land could be sold for more profitable uses.

'Vagrant' and 'casual' were almost synonymous terms to the authorities, but this simplified a complex problem. There was a great difference between the aimless tramp who rarely worked and the van-dwelling gypsies and tinkers who were unlikely to seek the casual ward except in sickness. Certain unions, like Bromley, who were on the road to harvest areas where casual labour was needed, always had a summer influx of seasonal migrants who were not habitual wanderers, and who used the casual wards as a stopping place: these people usually travelled in family groups. Kent received many of the London poor for the hop season, and the average of casuals relieved on Friday nights in August in workhouses in 1904 was 1,087 compared to the average for the whole year of 559. Some parts of the country saw few vagrants, and Cornwall with its lonely and scattered workhouses averaged 18 casuals on Friday nights in the same year.[2]

In the mid-nineteenth century, trampers included seamen who had spent their pay and were off to another port, navvies moving from gang to gang, and Irish seasonal labourers making their way home, as well as the destitute Irish who emigrated permanently during the famine. All of these might use the workhouse occasionally, and they were not always destitute. Seasonal labourers might use the workhouse to save money, having sent their wages ahead of them, or having delegated one of their number to take care of the money while the rest applied to the casual ward. Others were destitute, but not vagrant in the true sense of the word. London and the larger cities contained many homeless paupers who picked a living from the streets. Charity and the casual wards kept them barely alive, and at the end their bodies would be sent, unidentified, to the anatomy schools. Munby, the diarist, observed them:

> Walking through St James's Park about 4 p.m., I found the open spaces of sward on either side the path thickly dotted over with strange dark objects. They were human beings; ragged men & ragged women; lying prone & motionless, not as those who lie down for rest & enjoyment, but as creatures worn out and listless. A park keeper came up: who are these? I asked. 'They are men out of work, said he and unfortunate girls; servant girls, many of them, what has been out of place and took to the streets, till they've sunk so low that they cant get a living even by prostitution.'[3]

The authorities knew that vagrancy would always increase at the end of wars as returning soldiers wandered in search of employment: this had been true in Elizabethan times, and it was still apparent in 1901 and in 1918.

The tramp, for so long a familiar sight on the highroads, aroused two separate images in the public mind. One was of the sturdy beggar who found vagrancy preferable to employment, whose life was hard but free and full of interest, and who would turn to crime when it suited him. The other was of a defeated man, incapable, old or sick, searching desperately for work. Vagrancy has an enormous literature, which is divided between these two types, and throughout the period, life on the road attracted many disguised journalists, clergymen, novelists, and reformers of all kinds. George Borrow's books fashionably romanticized the gipsy life; Jack London and George Orwell also wrote famous accounts of the casual wards which, although written 30 years apart, differ little in essentials.[4] London noted the preponderance of the old and incapable in the wards, Orwell the young unemployed, but many of the public reared on romantic picaresque novels uneasily suspected that vagrancy was happier than the settled life; an attitude which perhaps encouraged indifference to the vagrants under the Poor Law.[5] It was not certain whether tramps ought to be considered as paupers or as criminals, hence many of the inconsistencies in their treatment. Homeless and workless people had no official recourse except charity or the casual ward, for if they were caught begging or sleeping in the open they risked a fortnight's hard labour under the commodious Vagrancy Act of 1824. Repeated offences commanded even longer sentences. In fact the administration of the law depended entirely on the zeal of local police and the views of magistrates, who might not wish to crowd the gaols with such people.

The confusion about the status and treatment of vagrants was embedded in Poor Law policy, and for nearly a century the authorities fruitlessly attempted to find ways of sorting out the genuine work seeker from the shiftless vagabond. If the casuals were the least deserving of the undeserving poor, their treatment should be harsher, their diet more limited, and their task stricter than other inmates'. But if some of the casuals were genuine unemployed workmen seeking help, how could this harsh treatment be justified in their case? Again, if the workhouses were so strict that they deterred the idle tramp from seeking admittance, would he not resort to begging and other criminal acts in preference? The authorities found no satisfactory answers to these questions, and by the end of the nineteenth century they were considering the possibility of incarcerating the casual poor.

For much of the nineteenth century, however, the central authority had to concentrate on persuading guardians to provide even passably sanitary conditions in casual wards. There was an ancient fear that vagrants carried disease, and this revived strongly during the cholera epidemics. The central authority wished to have casuals bathed and their clothes disinfected, and to have them put in harsh but clinically clean sleeping quarters. By the mid century they also favoured casual wards with separate cells, where the casuals could be prevented from communicating with one another; in separate cells casuals would not be able to riot, and the authorities suspected that dirty but sociable wards were not sufficiently deterrent. The Poor Law Board also encouraged guardians to pay the police to act as additional relieving officers; habitual tramps would not wish to apply to a police station in order to obtain a night's lodging. From the earliest days the central authority hoped to impose uniformity on the casual ward system; since vagrants, unlike the settled poor, had some choice of workhouse, they would naturally gravitate to workhouses where discipline was lax, better food was provided, and no questions asked. Experienced tramps had their own grapevine, and by graffiti and word of mouth they would inform their fellows of any changes or advantages in certain casual wards.[6]

Sometimes an Inspector would influence his unions into unifying their treatment of casuals; in the 1860s Basil Cane persuaded most of the Kentish unions to demand that casuals pick oakum in return for their lodging, and that the police be employed.[7] He was not able to unify the diet in the casual wards, which varied from ample rations to none, nor the sleeping and bathing arrangements. Some casuals still slept in the stables which the guardians' horses occupied during the day. Cane argued that the Poor Law Board needed a general theory of the management of casuals. Meanwhile the casuals continued to terrorize officers in small rural workhouses which were on the highroads, and to be terrorized in turn by martinet officers in the urban unions and the foul conditions in the wards.[8] Attention focused on the riotous, rick-burning casual, but his acts were often acts of desperation.[9] Critics of the system argued that the casual would tear his clothing in the workhouse or commit a petty crime in order to spend time in the more comfortable gaol where he was better fed. Where workhouse conditions were known to be harsh, magistrates might be more lenient with tramps who committed workhouse offences. In any case, the system pressed most heavily on the helpless casual poor, who were exploited both by the workhouse officers and the more experienced tramps.

From the late 1860s a 'theory' of casual wards began to develop, but it remained confused by the very nature of the problem. The Poor Law Board experimented first in London, where the Houseless Poor Act of 1864 provided central finance for Metropolitan casual wards and thus encouraged guardians to provide better accommodation. The police were instructed to round up people sleeping in the open and direct them to the wards. Yet the system was incomplete without powers of incarceration and compulsory labour; and in 1871 the Pauper Inmates Discharge and Regulation Act allowed guardians to detain a casual pauper until he had performed a morning's work. If a casual applied to the same workhouse more than twice in a month, he might be detained for two nights. The Act also defined the London wards as one institution, so that the London houseless poor might be discouraged from moving from ward to ward. The Act was inconsistent, for it was based on the assumption that vagrants ought to be seeking work; but if vagrants were not released from the workhouse until 11 a.m., they would not be able to find employment that day. In 1882 the Casual Poor Act remedied this and allowed further detention: all casuals were to be kept in the workhouse for two nights to perform a task, but released early on the morning of the third day. Longer periods of detention were allowed for habitual applicants, and casuals who refused to work could be committed to gaol.

Both these Acts were passed at times when vagrancy was believed to be increasing, though the authorities had only the twice-yearly Poor Law statistics for information. It is impossible to say whether pressure on the casual wards did reflect an increase in vagrancy generally. Groups like the anti-Mendicity Society and the Charity Organization Society tried to discourage the public from giving alms to beggars; lodging houses were subject to stricter regulations and could accommodate fewer people; the casual wards were offering slightly less repellent accommodation in London and some of the large cities. All this may have encouraged casuals to use the Poor Law rather than other forms of relief. Legislation against casuals was always followed by a drop in the numbers of applicants to the casual wards for a few years, and the authorities used this fact to argue that the idle vagrants must have been forced into employment. Although the historian is not in a position to explain the causes of vagrancy with any exactness, the nettle must be grasped. The most thorough statistical inquiry was conducted by the Departmental Committee of 1904, which reported in 1906. Although the Committee recognized that vagrancy seemed to increase in times of trade depression, they would not accept a definite link between vagrancy and unemployment. Only the worthless, they argued, would ever become vagrants, and deterrent conditions would force them back into the labour market.[10] If this were so, one would expect the vagrancy figures (limited as they are) to follow a different pattern from the larger figures of total pauperism, which were acknowledge to fluctuate with the trade cycle. At the time there were no national figures for unemployment, except for the statistics collected by the Board of Trade, which recorded the percentage of unemployed in certain trade unions. These unions were mainly of skilled workers, but unemployment amongst the skilled had a 'downward' effect on the labour market, as unemployed skilled workers would compete with the less skilled for casual employment.

In Figure 5, 1904 is taken as a convenient base year, in which both unemployment and vagrancy were engaging government attention. The large fluctuations in the vagrancy and unemployment figures reflect both poor methods of counting and the fact that relatively small numbers are involved (8,519 vagrants, and 6 per cent unemployed.) Total pauperism, with its larger figures (869,126 paupers in 1904) and more accurate methods of counting, produces a smoother curve.[11] Pauperism is also related to unemployment, not necessarily because of more able-bodied applicants for relief, but through the inability of unemployed families to support an aged or sick relative, or to keep up insurance premiums. Not surprisingly, each series shows a sharp drop just before the start of the First World War, stays low during the war, and then rises very sharply during the 1920s. The movement of the

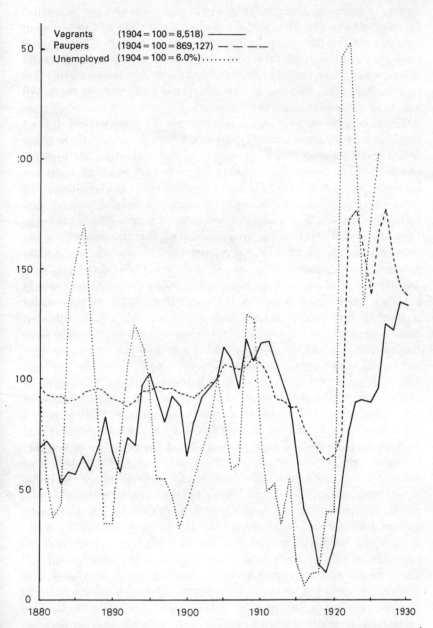

Figure 5. Number of vagrants relieved on the night of 1st January 1880–1930, compared with total number of paupers relieved on the same night, and with the average percentage of unemployed in certain trade unions 1880–1926.

253

figures of unemployed is followed about a year later by the pauperism figures, and in a year after that the vagrancy series. It is not possible to estimate the average time lag between the three series because the unemployment figures represent the average for the whole year, whereas the other two represent only the first of January; hence the two-year time lag between peaks and troughs in unemployment and vagrancy is probably an over-estimate.

The period before 1914 shows less extreme fluctuations, but it is just possible to see that the larger peaks and troughs in the three series follow each other in the order suggested above. A more quantitative check is provided by computing the cross-correlation functions between the three series.[12] Taking the period 1880–1914 inclusive, the cross-correlation function between unemployed and vagrants shows a similar peak of 0.125 at a delay of two years. On each side of the peaks the cross correlations are negative, indicating that the fluctuations are then anti-correlated. However, the cross-correlation function between paupers and vagrants shows a strong peak of 0.72 between zero delay and a delay of one year, indicating that the series tend to move closely together, with fluctuations in the number of vagrants on average lagging slightly behind fluctuations in the number of paupers. The same computation for the period 1880–1926 yields similar results: there is a peak of 0.8 for one year's delay for unemployed and paupers; and a peak of 0.4 after a two-year delay for unemployed and vagrants. The peak values are much higher than before, reflecting the dominance of the period 1914–1926, when all three series move closely together.

The statistical analysis indicates that fluctuations in pauperism and vagrancy tend to follow similar fluctuations in the number of unemployed. Such feeding of the statistics of human misery into the computer does not of course prove that unemployment causes vagrancy, but does give some basis to the promptings of common sense that a relationship is very likely. They also indicate that vagrancy and pauperism were not two separate problems, as the Poor Law authorities believed. Other authorities in the early twentieth century rejected the simple Poor Law analysis. Beveridge used the figures for vagrancy as one of the available methods of calculating unemployment; he adopted a somewhat Marxist analysis of the unemployed as the 'reserve army' of labour.[13] The apparently unemployable could be absorbed back into the economy in favourable times. The Webbs also agreed that unemployment and vagrancy were closely connected,[14] but like Beveridge (and indeed, like Marx) they argued that under the variable numbers of marginal men was a hard core of incorrigible vagrants, who formed part of the nineteenth-century concept of the 'dangerous classes'. Poor Law policies continued to concentrate on this hard core.

Guardians themselves often wished to distinguish between the respectable unemployed and the idle tramp. In 1867 J. Barwick Baker, a Gloucester magistrate and guardian, devised a system which was used by unions in parts of the West and Midlands. Baker suggested a way-ticket system, by which the casual seeking work would have a ticket entitling him to favourable treatment in the casual wards along the route to his destination. These men would also be given bread and cheese for a midday meal, so that they would not have to beg; while the undeserving casual should be made to perform a task before he was released.[15] Support for this measure impelled many guardians to join in the Poor Law District Conferences, and the Local Government Board also encouraged way-tickets from the 1880s onward. Yet few men genuinely seeking work would be so certain of their destination that they could plan their route in this manner; not would all guardians accept the expense of a more orderly system. The Acts of 1871 and 1882 were not enforced, and guardians often disregarded both strictness and sanitary regulations in favour of cheapness. They would not detain a vagrant for two nights if it were cheaper to send him away unfed the day after arrival. Even in 1904, during a period of much concern over vagrancy, many unions did not detain vagrants, and after the war they became even more lax, as the following figures show:[16]

	1904	1924
Unions detaining for the regulation two nights	116	188
Unions not detaining for two nights	129	250
Unions claiming to detain 'occasionally'	168	85
Unions detaining only male vagrants	86	no figures

In the years before 1914 the applicants to the casual wards were changing. They still included seasonal immigrants; but with the gradual decasualization of many types of labour, the wanderer for whom tramping was a necessary part of his work, or the inevitable outcome of unemployment, was dying out. The homeless man who had irregular work was more likely to seek the common lodging house, if he had any money, than the uncomfortable casual ward where he might be detained. Labour exchanges, cheap travel and the newspaper advertisement all provided the work seeker with better opportunities than the uncertain journey from workhouse to workhouse. By 1914 it is probable that the wards attracted the most hopeless section of the unemployed, and were refuges for the socially incapable and those for whom the wandering life offered an escape from personal problems. Women and children on the roads were declining in numbers, though admittedly they were less likely to use the casual wards because they had more success as beggars. Women and children made up about 15 per cent of applicants in 1891, and 11 per cent in 1905: by 1928 they were only 5 per cent.[17]

The 1904 Committee, without any detailed survey of the health or ages of casuals, decided that most of them were of working age and should be forced into employment. That this was possible seems to be demonstrated by the enormous decline in vagrancy during the war, when the army and the labour market were both prepared to accept tramps, and 284 provincial unions closed their casual wards. Yet it seems that only in such exceptional circumstances were tramps reabsorbed into the economy without special efforts being made to rehabilitate them. The Committee ignored the well-known inflexibility of the labour market in absorbing men over 40, or those with any kinds of disability. They noted that 70 per cent of male casuals in 1905 were between 35 and 65 years of age, and therefore capable of work, but they did not consider the other social factors which made employment difficult for this group. Nor did they investigate the physical state of the 24 per cent of casuals who were under 35 years old.[18] A second departmental committee on vagrancy in 1929 attempted a more detailed study of vagrants; in a sample of casual ward applicants, 50 per cent were found to be over 40 years of age, and 15 per cent over 60.[19] This may be compared with a comment made by an Inspector in 1920:

> Men tramps cannot be divided into able-bodied men and sick men. For the most part they are elderly semi-competent, semi-incompetent men—midway between able-bodiedness and infirmity.

This was in spite of the high unemployment after the war, when it was argued that casuals were younger than in pre-war days.[20]

Casuals thus suffer from the same problems of definition as the 'able-bodied' inmates; though there was no way of telling whether disabilities were a cause or an effect of vagrant life. The 1904 Committee accepted that there must be some disabled and feeble-minded men amongst the vagrants, and that they ought to be taken into care; but they still concentrated their recommendations on the 'able-bodied' man. Indeed, the report contained two contradictory statements; firstly that the tramp who lived in casual wards was usually fairly clean and healthy because of the regular food and baths he could expect; secondly, that many tramps who were sent to prison were certified unfit for hard labour 'as the vagrant is seldom wholly sound in body'.[21] Two years later, the report of the Royal Commission on the Feeble Minded included some evidence from Manchester, where a medical officer had examined 3809 tramps and found 161 (4.2 per cent) of them to be mentally defective.[22] He concluded that milder cases of mental handicap, or cases who had been supported by relatives until late in life, were likely to end up in the casual wards after the deaths of their supporters. The Commission argued:

> To control this wandering population of mentally defective persons, who are many of them dangerous, morally and physically, and criminal in their characteristics, it seems to us there should be systematic notification—identification, if necessary, by finger-prints, and some authoritative control...[23]

The 1929 Vagrancy Committee attempted a more systematic study, and appointed Dr E.O. Lewis to investigate mental deficiency amongst tramps. Lewis was trained in psychiatric medicine, and examined a sample of 592 casuals who believed they were receiving a standard medical examination. He considered that his cursory inspection would underestimate any possible deficiencies, but still noted the following:[24]

	%
Feeblemindedness	15.7
Insanity (including senility)	5.4
Psychoneurosis	5.7

This would not compare with modern medical analysis, given that Lewis was dealing with possibly inarticulate and hostile subjects, and his sample was small, but it does indicate that a significant proportion of casuals probably suffered from mental disturbance of a kind which made them difficult to employ.

Alcoholism is also a question which must arise in connection with vagrancy. The 1904 Committee believed that the more drunken and dissolute section of the working class were most likely to become tramps. No clear distinction was made between heavy drinking and alcoholism; drinking, like unemployment, could be discontinued at will. Alcoholism may be connected with homelessness, both as cause and effect, but the life of the casual ward, especially if the casual were detained for the regulation two nights, was inimical to the alcoholic, which may be why so few of the social investigators remarked on it as a serious factor. The inebriate was unlikely to be capable of energetic movement from ward to ward; yet if he returned to the same ward too often he risked prison, and he was also threatened with incarceration under the Inebriates Act if he committed an offence. Vagrant alcoholics were likely to sleep rough. In 1929 Lewis thought that 75 of his 592 casuals showed signs of chronic addiction. A modern researcher would also study the home background of tramps; in 1929 nearly all of them claimed to be single or widowed. Some may have been lying, but in all probability they had no homes to which they could return.

The report of the 1904 Committee reflected the ideas of the COS in many ways, particularly that the chief cause of vagrancy was indiscriminate charity. Free refuges were 'a source of positive danger to the community'. The Committee concluded that 'the vagrant cannot be suppressed, but must be specially treated for his mode of life and his disinclination to honest work'.[25] Since the public often believed that vagrants were honest unemployed men, or that they would be barbarously treated in the casual ward, the answer was to devise ways in which an honest worker would be removed from the wards, while the clean but rigorous conditions in the wards would seem the most appropriate place for habitual beggars. The Committee wished to remove casuals from the Poor Law and hand control of the casual wards over to the police, thus firmly associating vagrancy with crime. They also recommended labour colonies for habitual vagrants, and drew up elaborate regulations for them, based to some extent on the voluntary colony at Hadleigh run by the Salvation Army. Unlike the Army's colony, the official labour colonies were to have powers of compulsory detention, but the Committee was so impressed with the Army's efforts that they were prepared to leave the administration of labour colonies to voluntary agencies. This was a suggestion not likely to command much political support, for, as an Inspector commented:

> Civilized governments do not farm out their prisoners; and if the liberty of the subject were entrusted to the Salvation Army, the public would think it possible that the treatment of the men might depend on the fervour of their Hallelujahs.[26]

Although the government came close to accepting labour colonies,[27] the Committee's report had no effect.

The authorities could not depend on the police and magistrates to enforce the Vagrancy Act, and so prevent casuals from existing outside the workhouse. Although the number of vagrants was probably higher in 1929 than in 1899, the number of prosecutions for begging and sleeping out of doors dropped sharply, and tramps who came before a magistrate were more likely to be discharged or bound over.[28] Although habitual vagrancy was technically a crime, it was not accepted by everyone that vagrants were criminals, and the Master of the Supreme Court wrote in 1901:

> It is possible that pauperism and crime are alternate episodes in the lives of some, and that of certain families some members become criminals, others receive poor relief; but there is no reason to believe that vagrants are 'essentially a criminal class.'[29]

The First World War and its economic aftermath made it more difficult for the Poor Law authorities to argue that vagrancy was unconnected to other social problems. The Ministry of Health, however, had little to advance on the policies of the Local Government Board, and the 1920s saw strenuous efforts to maintain the deterrent policy in spite of growing attacks from the Labour Party and from within the Poor Law administration. Many people believed that since so many vagrants had been absorbed into the war effort, they must necessarily be classed as deserving. With the vagrancy figures rising rapidly after 1918, some guardians tried to give preferential treatment to vagrants who had been in the services, but discrimination was as difficult as ever, and war medals easily purchased. The Ministry of Health decided that ex-service tramps were merely returning to their former life: despairing of either reforming the casual or locking him away, the Ministry preferred to see him moving on in an orderly manner, not loitering, and keeping out of London. 'The aimless wanderer cannot be abolished, only discouraged', wrote a senior Inspector in 1924.[30] He was trying to decide which of the closed casual wards should be reopened and was plotting them out at intervals of about 15 miles. He hoped to produce a *cordon sanitaire* around London, which, with its numerous charities, refuges, and easy anonymity, acted as a magnet for vagrants. Roundell wished for more enforcement of the law to stop tramps staying in the same place; this he called 'canalizing' vagrants. Yet this immediately raised the old problem that if the Poor Law made life difficult for casuals they would use illegal means to exist outside it.

Even by the 1920s, the conditions in casual wards had changed far less than in other sections of the workhouse. Vagrants gathered outside, where they waited to be admitted at 4 p.m. in winter and 6 p.m. in summer. They were met by a 'tramp major', often a workhouse inmate or retired tramp, who searched them and removed their personal belongings. Tramps were adept at storing forbidden goods like sugar and tobacco in their boots, which by time-honoured custom were not searched. In the better wards they could have a hot bath and use clean towels, and afterwards would receive a clean shirt while their own clothes were being disinfected. They had a meal, and hoped for a bed or hammock with a supply of blankets. In fact many guardians still disregarded elementary sanitation in the casual wards. In 1924 the Inspectors surveyed the wards, and listed 217 as 'good', 180 as 'medium' and 92 as 'bad'.[31] The worst wards might have plank beds or no beds at all, and men lay on the floor in their dirty clothes. They might have no provision for washing, filthy linen, and a communal bucket instead of a W.C. The middling wards often had towels shared between several men, and inadequate disinfection. A complaint about the Cannock ward in 1923 may serve as an example of the worst type:

> Shirts are verminous. On many occasions men sleep in stables. Inmates who are taken ill have no facilities of notifying the officials. Sanitary arrangements bad, food utensils filthy, blankets old and verminous. One bath only in use, men who may have skin diseases dry themselves on the one and only towel provided.[32]

The survey did not inquire whether men were made to spread their margarine with their fingers, not did the Inspectors ask what the men did when they were not working.

The dietary and the task in casual wards set the vagrant apart from the regular workhouse inmates, and were the twin pillars of deterrent policy, yet here the theory and the practice diverged. In 1882 the Local Government Board recommended a dietary for vagrants: eight ounces of bread and one pint of gruel or broth for breakfast and supper; eight ounces of bread and 1½ ounces of cheese (or six ounces of bread and one pint of soup) for dinner on the day of detention.[33] This compared unfavourably even with the diet of the able-bodied workhouse inmate: and elderly vagrants received far less than elderly inmates. The diet of workhouse inmates was glutinous and unwholesome, but vagrants had even more monotonous fare: many guardians gave less than the regulation diet, and in 1904 over half of them gave the vagrants only a piece of bread for breakfast and supper.[34]

The 1904 Committee was influenced by Dr T.B. Hopkins, who did not think the regulation diet adequate either for stonebreaking or for walking 10–12 miles a day, and recommended the addition of margarine, cocoa and potatoes. The Local Government Board, however, did not change its regulations until 1914, when it proposed a diet of 'the minimum nutriment necessary for physical health', composed of food which was easy to store and took little preparation. The vagrant was now allowed an ounce of margarine and a pint of shell cocoa with his bread for breakfast and supper—shell cocoa being an infusion of cocoa husks with little nutritive value. For dinner he could have an extra half ounce of cheese, and four ounces of potatoes, with salt.[35] The Board also accepted that the vagrant could be given food for a midday meal on discharge from the casual ward, as a precaution against begging. The new dietaries for the able-bodied inmates included meat or fish on five days of the week, while in 1920 the Ministry of Health relinquished control over the details of local workhouse diets for regular inmates. The diet of vagrants, however, remained under central control lest local variations should encourage vagrancy.

As unemployment and vagrancy increased in the early 1920s, Labour MPs began to ask Parliamentary questions about casual wards. They assumed that among the swelling numbers of vagrants there must be many ex-servicemen who were not being lodged as befitted war heroes. The Ministry was more interested in restoring cleanliness and order, both of which had suffered during the war; a committee of senior officials began to draw up a new order to consolidate the regulations. The committee was unwilling to admit that the diet in casual wards was inadequate: since vagrancy was supposed to be a temporary state in the search for work, the diet should not be sufficient to keep a professional vagrant in health. Dr M. Greenwood wrote in a revealing memorandum: 'I think we should have to condemn these dietaries as inadequate *if it were the practice to maintain any large numbers of paupers on this scale for long periods.*'[36] Yet Downes had noted in 1913 that the dietary was not adequate for habitual vagrants, who would indeed be better fed in gaol.[37] The existence of habitual casuals was recognized in all the regulations except the dietary, which in any case could not be enforced on the unions.

Work was the second main element of deterrence. Here again the intentions of the central authority were often foiled by guardians who found that it was uneconomic to provide vagrants with a task, both because of the cost of materials and the extra burden on workhouse staff who had to supervise it. Since 1882 the allotted task for a casual had been breaking up to 13 hundred weight of stone, pounding up to two hundred weight of stone, picking four pounds of unbeaten or eight pounds of beaten oakum, or doing nine hours of such duties as chopping wood, grinding corn, or pumping water. Tramps were not supposed to be given tasks which were beyond their age or strength, but the medical officer was rarely consulted unless a casual refused to work. By 1924 guardians had discontinued these old punitive tasks to a large extent, and preferred to give casuals odd jobs, since the workhouses had few able-bodied inmates. Only 122 unions asked casuals to break stones, as compared with 438 unions in 1904.[38] Only 22 unions asked vagrants to pick oakum. The motive of economy may have been as strong as that of humanity in the guardians' attitudes to these tasks, but the two combined to make a different atmosphere from that of the pre-war days recollected by one guardian:

> In one place was the heap of granite stones by the side of an iron grating, and as the Clerk remarked, there were the stones and there was the grating—before the vagrant left the cell he either had to pass the stones through the grating or eat them.[39]

The able-bodied workhouse inmate in the nineteenth century had been on much the same footing in regard to tasks as the casual, though with the advantages of more comfortable lodging and better food. By the 1920s punitive tasks were disappearing for both of them. The Ministry of Health objected to losing this deterrent to vagrancy, and the Casual Poor (Relief) Order of 1925 strongly affirmed traditional policy, including the diet of 1914 and the tasks of 1882. On this occasion the public reacted far more strongly than to any previous order concerning vagrancy. By the mid-1920s the Poor Law policy on casuals was under attack, not only from MPs anxious to shield the deserving unemployed, but from the men and women who actually administered the law. The revised regulations of 1925 provoked strong protests from local officials: the Clerks' Association and the National Association of Masters and Matrons of Poor Law Institutions wished to drop any mention of oakum picking, which was being discontinued as a task in prisons. They also wanted an end to shell cocoa (a nuisance to make), and to reduce the hours of work for casuals from nine to eight. The masters and matrons spoke of workhouse realities: they said that Sunday detention was difficult because most casual wards had no facilities to keep the men occupied; that tasks could not be imposed because there were not enough officers to supervise them; that guardians were indifferent to the problem; and that it was impossible for them to distinguish a habitual vagrant from a genuine unemployed worker. They argued that magistrates would not uphold the regulations:

> We regret to note the re-establishment of oakum picking as a task which, apart from being degrading, we think would not be supported by magistrates were casuals proceeded against for failing to perform their allotted task.[40]

The joint vagrancy committee of Glamorgan, Monmouth and Brecknock resolved that casuals should have the ordinary dinner for able-bodied men, and that six hours work a day was enough.[41]

The Ministry reluctantly abandoned shell cocoa (which had become unobtainable), and accepted the eight-hour day, but clung to the other regulations. 'The dietary', they argued, 'is not and never has been designed for permanent sustenance, but is suitable for all the requirements of a person who is travelling in search of work.'[42] To the charge that oakum picking was a penal task and also useless now that ships were no longer caulked with oakum, the Ministry replied that it had the advantage of being simple enough for anyone to do, and that oakum was still sometimes used for surgical dressings. The new order, however, caused an outcry amongst Labour MPs, and oakum picking was attacked in the press as degrading and punitive.[43] George Lansbury took up the cause enthusiastically, demanding that stone pounding equipment be placed outside the Commons so that Members could see the kind of task given to 'half-starved men'.[44] Chamberlain was embarrassed by complaints from the Bishop of Lichfield and various Poor Law organizations, and the Ministry became defensive. A.B. Lowry and C.F. Roundell, who had been responsible for the order, argued that the tasks were intended to discipline, not degrade, but Lowry acknowledged that 'The objections to the tasks . . . are to a large extent sentimental but for that very reason they have to be considered seriously'.[45] A division of opinion even appeared within the Ministry, as the younger Inspectors were not prepared to fight for the nineteenth-century regulations. A.G. Hayward, the Inspector for Yorkshire, tried both tasks himself and found that he managed fairly well with stone breaking, but was soon outpaced by an experienced tramp with the oakum.[46] Chamberlain saw that oakum picking was not worth argument, and in June 1925 ordered it to be discontinued because of its penal associations. Stone breaking he retained, although admitting it was not much used.

Throughout the 1920s policy towards vagrants was devised by a body of senior officials who still believed in the principles of deterrence set up in 1882. As late as 1930 some of them still favoured labour colonies, although they realized that this was not likely to command public support. A departmental memorandum in this year could have been written at any time since 1882:

The difficulty is, of course, that we are dealing with a very mixed and entirely undependable section of the population. There are in the casual wards, the habitual vagrant at the one end and the bona fide work seeker at the other, but my own view, which doubtless would be unacceptable in certain quarters, is that most of these bona fide work seekers left home not entirely on account of chronic unemployment, but partly also because they had done something which made them feel impelled to uproot themselves; they therefore feel anxious to avoid telling the truth about themselves, and unless the inquiry was conducted on strictly C.O.S. lines we should not get much out of it.[47]

Except when attacked on a particular issue like oakum picking, successive Ministers of Health had little interest in vagrants, and Wheatley accepted the ruling of the permanent staff as readily as Chamberlain.[48] The guardians remained indifferent and the casual wards changed little. An Inspector reported in 1929 that 'it was easier to get a wireless installation in the workhouse paid for out of the Guardians' own pockets than to get baths or warmth in the casual wards paid for out of the rates.'[49] Lansbury continued almost unaided to plead for employment for casuals: Kingsley Wood, the Parliamentary Secretary, answered him with the habitual despair that overcame the Ministry when faced with the question. At least a quarter of vagrants, he said, were professional tramps ruined by drink:

They belong to a class for whom it is practically impossible to do anything that will reclaim them. If you find them employment, as has often been done, it is futile, one's efforts are wasted.[50]

Kingsley Wood may have had in mind the efforts of the Metropolitan Asylums Board, which had opened a hostel in 1923; this attempted to find employment for vagrants, to encourage them to emigrate, or to locate their families. Yet of the 9,733 men received in the hostel between 1923 and 1928, only 12 per cent had later turned up again in the London casual wards.[51]

In September of 1929 the new departmental committee was set up by the Labour government to inquire into the working of the laws concerning the casual poor, and to suggest ways of removing the genuine work seekers and any tramps with physical or mental defects. The 1929 Committee, like its predecessor, noted that casual paupers were neither rehabilitated nor deterred by the existing system, and it rejected labour colonies in favour of detention centres. It was argued that if the labour exchanges took better care of the unemployed, and helped them to move about in search of work, there would be no objection to raising the standards in the casual ward in order to reform the habitual vagrant; the Committee therefore asked that the wards be made more comfortable, the diet more varied and nutritious, smoking be permitted, and day-rooms and reading matter provided. Gruel and stone breaking, the symbols of a past age, should be abolished and the wards administered not by an inmate but a trained officer who could report any vagrants with obvious mental or physical problems. Hostels should be provided for those who wanted to return to a settled life, and local authorities should support charities which provided training for vagrants.

Some of the Committee's recommendations appeared in the Public Assistance (Casual Poor) Order of 1931, which allowed more comfort in the casual wards, an end to stone breaking except in a few cases, the disappearance of gruel, and the appearance of two ounces of meat and some vegetables for the midday dinner. Casuals were not to be detained if they held a ticket from a labour exchange. Yet the 'spike' seems to have changed little in the 1930s, and indeed the 1929 Committee had not really believed the problem could be solved:

> We look forward to a time when the need for casual wards will be no longer felt, but that time is not yet. Years must pass before we see the last of the army of wayfarers who now haunt our high-ways . . . Better treatment will give an element of self-respect, a sense of the value of cleanliness and order, and a desire for such; it can do little more.[52]

In the end it was the Second World War and the affluence of the motorized age which again changed the nature and the treatment of vagrancy, though without removing it. Perhaps the main difference was that after 1945 the tramp became less visible; he no longer travelled on foot along the highroad but hitched a lift; if he did not care for the hostels which replaced the casual wards, he took to derelict houses in slums awaiting demolition. This gave many people the comforting illusion that he had vanished. Local authorities now had a statutory duty to house the homeless, a duty they performed with varying degrees of enthusiasm.

By 1931 the most outstanding features of the nineteenth-century system of casual wards had been officially abolished: yet the treatment of casuals always ran counter to the treatment of settled inmates. Nearly all the reforms which affected the workhouse system passed by the casual wards, and deterrence was as attractive a policy to the authorities in the 1920s as it had been in the 1830s. Society could not come to terms with the casual: was he a criminal, a loafer, a pathetic wanderer, or a figure of romance? While the imagined freedom of the open road contended with the realities of the casual ward, the treatment of casuals remained an anomaly.

Conclusion

In his novel *Resurrection*, Tolstoy made his hero Nekhludov an indignant spectator of the Russian prison system, a witness to the physical and mental degradation of its inmates. Did the answer lie in prison reform? Tolstoy's answer was characteristic:

> Government officials had often told Nekhludov that the conditions which excited his indignation and which they admitted to be imperfect, would be improved as soon as prisons were built in accordance with modern methods. This explanation, however, did not satisfy Nekhludov, because he felt that the things that aroused his indignation were not caused by more or less perfect or imperfect methods. He had read about improved prisons, equipped with electric bells, where execution was done by electricity (as Tarde recommended), but this perfected system of violence disgusted him all the more.

Tolstoy's horror at the 'perfected system of violence' has been echoed in the twentieth century by Foucault, by Goffman and by Illich, and with them, growing numbers of social administrators. The demand for decarceration, ironically enough, is backed by economic considerations. Institutions, as they become 'perfected', will price themselves so highly that they ultimately arouse political controversy. It has been traditional to view the boards of guardians as myopic defenders of the public purse, but at least they were fortified by a vague belief in 'less eligibility', which made economies under the Poor Law seem acceptable. This book was written at a time when governments on both sides of the Atlantic were reacting to economic recession by substantial cuts in public spending; as ever, reduced expenditure on institutions, including schools and hospitals, is an easy resort. The government's actions are approved by the taxpayer, often protected by the very nature of enclosed institutions from seeing the results of his financial demands.

In nineteenth-century England, voices like Tolstoy's were rarely heard. Some protested about the growth of asylum treatment for lunatics, but on the whole, protest was directed at the abuse of institutions rather than their existence. Asylums and hospitals began to

267

house people of all classes, and not just the poor. Amongst these changing institutions the workhouse was uniquely unspecialized: it was a hospital for the sick and the healthy, an asylum for the sane and the insane; a prison for the deviant and the innocent. In an age of specialization it could not escape criticism.

Unlike Tolstoy, British reformers thought of amelioration rather than decarceration. They could not envisage a society without institutions, hence the workhouse must be reformed, and the reform must involve specialization. The notion of a 'workhouse' in its original meaning might be attacked, but not institutions as such. In the eyes of the Webbs, for example, the need for institutions would diminish if social problems were attacked at source, but they accepted that there would always have to be specialized institutions for the helpless or the incorrigible. The workhouse could thus be replaced by hospitals, asylums, children's homes and labour colonies. Tufnell had once hesitated to send families to separate institutions because of the threat to social order. The Webbs had no such reservations; they feared nothing from the 'residuum' for whom separation would be necessary even in the ideal world.

Ultimately the views of the Royal Commission of 1905 prevailed. Chamberlain accepted the principle of specialized institutions, but he could not withstand the continuing social and economic pressures which finally removed the threat of incarceration from the able-bodied unemployed. It took several decades for the intentions of 1929 to be realized, but under the Welfare State, and especially in the more affluent 1950s and 1960s, institutions developed rapidly. At this stage, British critics of institutions still tended to demand administrative reform, or, more usually, a change in the size of institutions. A large institution was impersonal; a small one might be a viable alternative to family life. As we have seen, warnings of a more radical and Tolstoyan kind have begun to impress social administrators, and historians like Foucault have increased the disquiet by throwing doubt on the original 'humanitarian' motives for incarceration. The workhouse, in any case, always confused the treatment of the helpless with the control of the able-bodied.

If one sees the English workhouse system, not as something unique, but as part of a larger pattern of incarceration, the workhouse loses something of its mystery. This book has tried to show that although some of the problems of the workhouse system arose from the peculiar nature of the deterrent Poor Law, many of its worst features did not come from this alone. The workhouse system had difficulties common to many kinds of residential institutions, and the life of staff and inmates was as much conditioned by the nature of the 'total institution' as by the workhouse system. For most of the nineteenth century, and long after, people feared incarceration in an asylum or home, even if these were established for the most humanitarian motives. Hospitals became more acceptable because they were seen as temporary residences, and because they offered perceptible hope of a cure after the mid-nineteenth century. The most terrifying aspect of the workhouse was its function as a long-term home for the aged, the incurably ill, and the friendless children. As a temporary expedient for the unemployed and rootless it was harsh enough, but it intimidated the helpless groups for whom conditions were constantly being ameliorated. It added insult to injury to associate the miseries of institutional life with the shame of pauperism.

If the history of the workhouse system is seen as part of a wider pattern, then its importance as an embryonic social service can also be accepted. The workhouse provided hospital treatment in many parts of the country where no other service was available; it offered an asylum for dependent people who had no other recourse. In populous areas it was already becoming specialized before the Local Government Act of 1929. The break with pauperism was not effectively made until 1948, but even then, continuity of buildings, staff and inmates could not be avoided. Governments accepted specialized institutions as a basic social service, and the workhouse had to be incorporated into this system. Many of the problems associated with it continued because they were not only the problems of pauperism, but of chronic illness and dependency. The very successes of medical treatment, and the survival of more people into old age, required more institutional places. New treatment for conditions which the nineteenth century would have designated as incurable (including mental handicaps), put further pressure on families to commit their afflicted members to the 'expert' care of professionals within a residential institution. By the end of the nineteenth century, because the workhouse began to offer a higher standard of care for the helpless than their families could afford to provide independently, it became the ancestor of many of today's institutions.

This book is a work of history rather than sociology or psychology, and so it does not pretend to offer any solution to the question of whether residential institutions are a desirable answer to a wide variety of social problems. Rather, it assumes that institutionalization became the normal answer in the nineteenth century, and that the workhouse system played a part in this. According to one point of view, if institutions are desirable in some cases, then the workhouse was an imperfect but transitional attempt to provide residential care. From another point of view, if all institutions are fundamentally undesirable, then the workhouse is reprehensible, but not uniquely reprehensible.

These arguments are far removed from the traditional interpretation of the workhouse as a unique feature of British social policy, and a typical example of the excesses of early nineteenth-century capitalism. The report of 1834, although it firmly attributed social evils to environmental rather than personal causes, was full of rancour towards the lazy, vicious, turbulent, able-bodied poor. It was characteristic of British capitalism, tempered as it was by nostalgia for the older paternalistic values and modified by the ethics of evangelical Protestantism, that it sought to modify social tension by an institution which should at once redeem and punish, relieve and shame. If the system was devised by the bourgeoisie, it was also reformed by them; reform was always demanded under the bourgeois standard of efficiency, economy and humanity, by people like Joseph Rogers, Florence Nightingale, and the Webbs themselves.

Does the workhouse myth survive historical inspection? The myth itself is composed of fragments—*Oliver Twist*, Andover, gruel, oakum-picking, starvation, callousness. Although some of this is founded on fact, physical cruelty was neither the intention nor the usual practice of the system. Where cruelty did occur, it resulted from problems which were common to all residential institutions. Physical conditions were probably worse in some of the institutions ostensibly founded for medical or humanitarian reasons, such as the lunatic asylums, where the inmates' complaints were likely to be disregarded. Understaffing, ill-chosen attendants, and undue economy could be found in charitable as well as state institutions. It was not violence, but the unrelieved tedium of institutional life, which probably afflicted the inmates most.

A myth of course, does not need to be based on fact to be powerful. It was not only the 'workhouse horrors' which explain the hatred felt by the working classes for the system, even at a time when they were with less reluctance using its hospital facilities and committing their dependent members to its care. The real horror of the workhouse was that for nearly a century it threatened the working class as the penalty for failure, whatever the cause of the failure had been. All the palliative measures, such as friendly societies, private charity, insurance and pensions, could not entirely remove the threat of this institution. To the emerging Labour Party it was a continued affront, even though many of the Labour movement came from that most solid section of the working class who were unlikely ever to become inmates. The Poor Law Commissioners had succeeded too well in founding a system based not on physical cruelty but on psychological deterrence, on shame and fear. The growing respectability of the working class made the system more intolerable. The values inculcated in the national schools stressed the primacy of family life and the duty and spiritual benefit of work. Paradoxically, the workhouse system responded to social failure by dividing the family, and by making work a punishment. The more the working class improved its position, the worse the workhouse would seem, even if its physical conditions were comfortable. The great strength of the Webbs' analysis of the Poor Law was that they recognized this inconsistency and strove to remove the social services irrevocably from the concept of pauperism.

The fundamental problem of the deterrent workhouse system was that it was practically obsolete at the time it was devised. Envisaged as a solution to rural pauperism, it was created at a time when rural poverty was to seem less significant than the effects of trade and industrial depressions. Created as an unspecialized institution, the workhouse came into being just as specialized knowledge was being applied to social problems. It was enacted just before the rapid development of the voluntary hospitals, charitable homes and other types of asylum—models with which it could never compete. In 1909, R.H. Tawney described how the Royal Commissioners of 1832 had mistakenly ascribed social distress to 'Speenhamland' poor relief, and his words may stand as a final comment on the New Poor Law:

> the student realizes, with something like horror, that three generations of men and women have been sacrificed to what, when it is examined critically, turns out to be nothing more nor less than a gigantic historical blunder.

So much for the deterrent functions of the workhouse; but it is not easy to see how its other functions could have been replaced by anything other than a different set of institutions. Such was the consequence in countries which had no comparable Poor Law. The British system took nearly a century to dissociate the problems of the helpless poor from those of the underpaid and unemployed, and while serving this dual purpose, the workhouses aroused not merely the antipathy which most institutions excited, but a peculiar revulsion. The emotion was not necessarily appropriate to the institutions themselves, which ranged from unsupervised barns to modern hospitals, never amenable to the plans of a central authority. Chadwick's legacy was not a monolithic system of deterrence, but an illusion of such a system—an illusion which he encouraged to disguise the weaknesses of his master-plan. As a result, British social policy was shaped as much by the myth of the workhouse system as by the reality.

Notes

Introduction

1 Charles Dickens, 'Wapping Workhouse', first published in *All the Year Round*, 18 Feb. 1860.
2 Paupers could not vote in general elections until 1918.
3 Always so spelt. See E. Partridge, *Dictionary of Historical Slang*.
4 E. Goffman, *Asylums* (1961).
5 The best-known exponent of the extreme line is Ivan Illich in, for example, *Medical Nemesis: the Expropriation of Health* (1975). For a discussion of the contemporary debate on the value of residential institutions, see J. Tizard, I. Sinclair and R.V.G. Clarke (eds), *Varieties of Residential Experience* (1975).
6 Goffman, *Asylums*, 17.
7 ibid, 81.
8 A. Solzhenitsyn, *The First Circle* (trans. M. Guybon, Fontana 1970), 699.
9 On hospitals see B. Abel-Smith, *The Hospitals 1800–1948* (1964); on lunatic asylums Kathleen Jones, *Lunacy, Law and Conscience 1744–1845* (1955), G.M. Ayers, *England's First State Hospitals and the Metropolitan Asylums Board 1867–1930* (1971), and A. Scull, *Museums of Madness* (1979). There are few printed sources on pauper schools, but see W. Chance, *Children Under the Poor Law* (1897) and F. Duke, 'Pauper Education,' in D. Fraser (ed.) *New Poor Law* (1976).

Chapter 1

1 S. and B. Webb, *English Local Government: English Poor Law History*, Part I. *The Old Poor Law* (1927), 83–6.
2 S.G. and E.O.A. Checkland (eds), *The Poor Law Report of 1834* (1974), 135. The original report, PP 1834 (44) xxvii, was also published in cheap editions, and again by the Royal Commission on the Poor Laws in 1905. All references here are to the Penguin edition, cited as *Checkland*.
3 ibid, 375.
4 M. Blaug, 'The Poor Law Report reexamined', *Journal of Economic History* 1964, 229 ff.
5 For detailed information on the south east see D.A. Baugh, 'The cost of poor relief in south east England, 1790–1834', *Economic History Review* 1975.
6 J.D. Marshall, *The Old Poor Law 1795–1834* (1968), 33.
7 For general comments on the Poor Law and population growth, see N. Tranter, *Population Since the Industrial Revolution* (1973), 76 ff.
8 P. Laslett, *Family Life and Illicit Love in Earlier Generations* (Cambridge, 1977), 136.

9 For a general discussion: U. Henriques, 'Bastardy and the New Poor Law', *Past and Present* (1957).

10 Compare the letters published in M. Bowley, *Nassau Senior and Classical Economics* (N.Y. 1967), 291–8, with Checkland 132, 338.

11 PP 1834 (44) xxxv, 220. Appendix (B2) part ii.

12 For details of the debate: J.R. Poynter, *Society and Pauperism: English Ideas on Poor Relief 1795–1834* (1969).

13 In the first version of the *Essay on the Principle of Population* (1798), Malthus suggested county workhouses where cases of extreme distress could be relieved and deterrent work offered the unemployed. In later versions of the *Essay*, he favoured total abolition of all poor relief.

14 Poynter, op. cit. 316.

15 Checkland, *Poor Law Report*, 334.

16 Poynter, op. cit. 119.

17 Checkland, op. cit. 484 ff.

18 ibid, 355.

19 E.P. Thompson, *The Making of the English Working Class* (Penguin 1968), 295.

20 Collected from PP 1834 (44) xxx, xxxiv. See also E.J. Hobsbawm and G. Rudé, *Captain Swing* (1969), 82.

21 PP 1834 (44) xxviii, 24.

22 A.J. Peacock, *Bread or Blood: a Study of the Agrarian Riots in East Anglia in 1816* (1965), 102.

23 Hobsbawm and Rudé, 104. Their appendix contains full details of the place and type of each riot.

24 Checkland, *Poor Law Report*, 122.

25 *Hansard*, 3rd series xxiv, 2 July 1834, 213–246.

26 The early novels of Dickens embody the same mixture of paternalism with love of 'efficiency'.

27 D. le Marchant, *Memoir of John Charles Viscount Althorp, Third Earl Spencer* 91876, 486.

28 Checkland, *Poor Law Report*, 275–6.

29 J.S. Taylor, 'The unreformed workhouse 1776–1834', in E.W. Martin (ed.), *Comparative Development in Social Welfare* (1972), 62.

30 PP 1834 (44) xxxi, 217.

31 M.E. Rose *The English Poor Law 1780–1930* (Newton Abbot, 1971), 82.

32 Webb, *Old Poor Law*, 220n.

33 Checkland, *Poor Law Report*, 30.

34 J.D. Marshall, 'The Nottinghamshire reformers and their contribution to the New Poor Law', *Ec. Hist. Rev.* 1960–1, 382 ff.

35 D. Marshall, *The English Poor in the Eighteenth Century* (1969), 138.

36 PP 1834 xxxv, B2, 83, 168, 67.

37 Checkland, *Poor Law Report*, 434.

38 G.A. Body, thesis, 167, 175.

39 E.M. Hampson, *The Treatment of Poverty in Cambridgeshire 1597–1834* (Cambridge, 1934), 74.

40 Body, thesis, 174–5.

41 Webb, *Old Poor Law*, 237.

42 Martin, *Comparative Development*, 69.

43 Poynter, *Society and pauperism*, 136.
44 Hampson, 266.
45 S. Kelly, 'The select vestry of Liverpool and the administration of the Poor Law 1821–1871', M.A. thesis, Liverpool (1971), 8, 10.
46 O.H. Hufton, *The Poor of Eighteenth-Century France 1750–1789* (Oxford 1974), ch. viii and *passim*.

Chapter 2

1 Details of these events in S. Finer, *The Life and Times of Sir Edwin Chadwick* (1952), Book 6.
2 PRO MH 32/70, 10 Jan. 1839. E.C. Tufnell.
3 D. Roberts, 'How cruel was the Victorian Poor Law?' *Historical Journal* 1963, 102.
4 Details in PP 1839 (489) xliv.
5 City Record Office, Bath. Bath Union minutes, 11 Sept. 1839, 21.
6 PRO MH 12/12459, 29 Oct. 1840.
7 Compare viewpoint in D. Fraser, *New Poor Law*, 19–20, with the more popular view in N. Longmate, *The Workhouse* (n.d.) *passim*.
8 U. Henriques, 'How cruel was the Victorian Poor Law?' *Historical Journal* 1968, 366.
9 *Second Report PLC*, PP 1836 (595) xxix, 199.
10 PRO MH 32/69, 15 March 1836. E.C. Tufnell.
11 Webb, *Poor Law History* ii, 1040. M.E. Rose, *The Relief of Poverty 1834–1914* (1972), 54.
12 Webb, ibid. 1039.
13 D. Roberts, *Origins of the British Welfare State* (New Haven, 1960), 153–5.
14 A. Brundage, 'The landed interest and the New Poor Law: A reappraisal of the revolution in Government', *English Historical Review*, 1972, 31.
15 M. Caplan, 'The administration of the Poor Law in the unions of Southwell and Basford', D. Phil. thesis, Nottingham (1967), 18–23. N. McCord, 'The implementation of the Poor Law Amendment Act on Tyneside', *International Review of Social History*, 1969, 94.
16 PRO MH 32/69, 24 April 1836. E.C. Tufnell.
17 Checkland, *Poor Law Report*, 429.
18 PRO MH 1/1, 4 Nov. 1834, 58.
19 *First Report PLC*, PP 1835 (500) xxv, 166.
20 Quoted in S. Jackman, *Galloping Head* (1958), 63.
21 Webb, *Poor Law History* i, 122 ff.
22 Finer, *Chadwick*, 93.
23 Webb, *Poor Law History* i, 130 and 130 n.
24 University College, London, Chadwick papers 23/13. Chadwick's notes on further combination of unions, 1838.
25 PRO MH 32/70, March 1838. Printed circular from Tufnell to certain Sussex guardians; and see also 19 July 1838.
26 PRO MH 32/69, 24 Feb. 1836. E.C. Tufnell.
27 The full story of Day's career is told in R.A. Lewis, 'William Day and the

Poor Law Commissioners', *University of Birmingham Historical Journal* 1963–4.

28   *Second Report PLC*, PP 1836 (595) xxix, 215.

29   *First Report PLC*, PP 1835 (500) xxxv, 415.

30   See the essay on workhouse architecture by R. Wildman in N. Longmate, *The Workhouse*, 289 ff.

31   PRO MH 1/1, 4 Nov. 1834, 73.

32   Dr Tomlinson estimates that there were 230 local prisons in the 1830s, and 113 in 1877. H. Tomlinson, thesis, 99.

33   Finer, *Chadwick*, 82–3.

34   Checkland, *Poor Law Report*, 338.

35   e.g. PRO MH 1/1, 4 Nov. 1834 and T. Mackay, *English Poor Law*, 284.

36   PRO MH 32/69, 24 Feb. and 31 May 1836. E.C. Tufnell.

37   Goffman, *Asylums, passim.*

38   Webb, *Poor Law Policy*, 62 ff.

39   PRO MH 10/1, first letter, article 2.

40   e.g. St Marylebone. A.R. Neate, *St Marylebone Workhouse and Institution* (1967), 8.

41   *Fourth Report PLB*, PP 1852 (1461) xxiii, 106–7.

42   M. Rose, 'The allowance system under the New Poor Law', *Ec. Hist. Rev.* 1966.

43   See (e.g.) Fraser, *New Poor Law*, 132–8; P. Mawson, thesis, 31 ff; M.J. Todd, thesis, 87 ff.

44   PP 1852–3 (973) lxxxiv.

45   PP 1863 (477) lii.

46   *Fourth Report PLB*, PP 1852 (1461) xxxiii, 106–7.

47   PP 1843 (483) xlv, 303.

48   Webb, *Poor Law History*, i, ch. 2. See also N.C. Edsall, *Anti-Poor Law Movement* for a fuller account.

49   PRO MH 1/1, 4 Nov. 1834, 68

50   KCA G/B1 ACa 1, 30 Nov. 1835.

51   Todd, thesis, 87 ff.

52   PRO MH 32/70, July 1838. E.C. Tufnell.

53   Edsall, op. cit. 43–4.

54   T.D. Jones, thesis, 97.

55   V.J. Walsh, 'Old and New Poor Laws in Shropshire 1820–1870', *Midland History* 1974, 235.

56   M. Caplan, thesis, 86.

57   R.A. Church, *Economic and Social Change in a Midland Town: Victorian Nottingham 1815–1900* (1966), 120.

58   P. Searby, 'The relief of the poor in Coventry, 1830–1863,' *HJ* 1977, 351.

59   R. Boyson, thesis, 292.

60   R.N. Thompson, thesis, 76, 325.

61   P. Mawson, thesis, 37, 42; N. McCord, 'The implementation of the 1834 Poor Law Amendment Act on Tyneside', *International Review of Social History* xiv, 1969, 91 ff.

62   P. Dunkley, 'The "hungry forties" and the New Poor Law: a case study', *HJ* 1974, 335 ff.

63   D. Fraser, 'Poor Law politics in Leeds, 1833–1855', *Publications of the*

Thoresby Society, Miscellany, Vol 15, part 1, 1971, 37.
64 Edsall, op. cit. 222.
65 Boyson, thesis, 263.
66 N. McCord, 'Ratepayers and social policy', in P. Thane (ed.), *British Social Policy* (1978), 23 ff.
67 PRO MH 32/69, 24 Feb. 1836. E.C. Tufnell.
68 PP 1840 (309) xxxix.
69 PP 1857–8 (337) xlix, Pt. 1.
70 PRO MH 32/69, 24 Feb. 1836. E.C. Tufnell.

Chapter 3

1 B.S. Rowntree, *Poverty: a Study of Town Life* (2nd ed. n.d.), 305.
2 *Report of the Royal Commission on the Poor Laws and Relief of Distress* (HMSO 1909), Separate Report, 701. The Report will hereafter be referred to under its two sections as *Majority Report* and *Minority Report*.
3 ibid. 743.
4 PP 1909 (4671) ciii, 743.
5 For a full account see P. Cowan, 'Some observations concerning the increase of hospital provision in London between 1850 and 1960', *Medical History* xiv, 1970.
6 This theme is developed in A. Scull, *Museums of Madness*, 102 ff.
7 Kathleen Jones, *Mental Health and Social Policy 1845–1959* (1960), 210.
8 These and following figures are from T. Mackay, *A History of the English Poor Law* (1899), 603–4, and PP 1914 (7444) xxxviii, 88 and 104.
9 PP 1914 (7444) xxviii, 88.
10 Like most Poor Law statistics, these figures refer to the 'mean number' of paupers, that is, the average of paupers on relief on the two dates 1 January and 1 July in a given year. They therefore provide only a rough guide to actual levels of pauperism during the year.
11 G. Goldin, 'Building a hospital of air: the Victorian pavilions of St Thomas' Hospital, London', *Bulletin of the History of Medicine*, xl, 534.
12 *Majority Report* ii, 180–1, and see also *Minority Report*, 195.
13 *Majority Report* i, 48.
14 PP 1920 (932) xvii, 147. This includes interest payments on loans.
15 In 1904, £752,000 was spent on new buildings, exclusive of interest charges and repairs. Of this, 44 per cent went on accommodation for the sick, 23.5 per cent for administrative buildings and nurses' homes. *Majority Report* i, 48.
16 PP 1895 (7684) xiv, 35–6.
17 PP 1908 (4202) xxxix, 226.
18 PP 1906 (2852) ciii, 59.
19 J. Manton, *Mary Carpenter and the Children of the Streets* (1976), 159.
20 *3rd Report LGB*, PP 1874 (1071) xxv, 171.
21 See, in particular, M. Foucault, *Discipline and Punish: the Birth of the Prison*, trans. A. Sheridan (1977).
22 D.J. Rothman, *The Discovery of the Asylum: Social Order and Disorder in the New Republic* (Boston 1971) *passim*.

23   J. Woodward, *To Do the Sick No Harm: a Study of the British Voluntary Hospital System to 1875* (1974), 142 ff.
24   *Reports of the Poor Law District Conferences* 1875, 214.
25   C. Dickens, *Little Dorrit*, ch. 31.
26   B. Abel-Smith, *A History of the Nursing Profession* (1960), 40–2.
27   C. Woodham-Smith, *Florence Nightingale* (Fontana, 1964), 352.
28   L. Twining, *Workhouses and Pauperism* ... (1898), 3 n.
29   E.M. Ross, thesis, 64.
30   PRO MH 12/12479, 7 Dec. 1869.
31   E.M. Ross, thesis, 129 ff.
32   R. Boyson, thesis, 384.
33   *Poor Law Officers' Journal*, 7 July 1892, 154.
34   PP 1909 (4671) ciii, 818.
35   E.M. Ross, thesis, 67.
36   Lord Meath, *The Diaries of Mary Countess of Meath* (1928), 50.
37   E. Sheppard, *Experiences of Workhouse Visitor* (4th ed. 1857), 8.
38   For a criticism of the idea of the 1880s as a 'watershed' in policy, see E.P. Hennock, 'Poverty and social theory in England; the experiences of the eighteen-eighties', *Social History* i, 1976.
39   See chapter 8.
40   *2nd Report LGB*, PP 1873 (748) xxix, 248–9: *31st Report LGB*, PP 1902 (1231) xxxv, 310–11.
41   T. Mackay, *English Poor Law*, 423.
42   H. Bosanquet, *Social Work in London 1869 to 1912* (1914), 267.
43   E. Sheppard, op. cit. 3.
44   H. Rider Haggard, *A Farmer's Year* (1906), 429.
45   C. Booth, *The Aged Poor in England and Wales: Condition* (1894), 42–3.
46   Webb, *Poor Law History* i, 375 ff.
47   ibid. 393 ff.
48   PRO MH 32/93, file for October 1898.
49   M. Rose, *The Relief of Poverty*, 55.
50   *Charity Organization Review* xviii, 1 October 1905, 194.
51   *Poor Law Conferences* 1875, 175.
52   ibid. 1878, 133; 1875, 327.
53   ibid. 1875, 298.
54   ibid. 1878, 502.
55   ibid. 1875, 167–8, and 327.
56   Webb. *Poor Law History* i, 234.
57   E.M. Rose covers the whole debate, thesis 98 ff and 240 ff; see also W. Chance, *Children Under the Poor Law* (1897), 97–8.
58   P.A. Ryan, 'Poplarism', in P. Thane (ed.), *British Social Policy*, 56 ff.
59   For a full biography see R. Postgate, *The Life of George Lansbury* (1951).
60   G. Haw, *From Workhouse to Westminster; the Life Story of Will Crooks, M.P.* (1907), 106 ff.
61   T.D. Jones, thesis 390, 407. *8th Report MoH*, PP 1927 (2938) ix, 888.
62   PRO MH 32/105, 25 July 1877.
63   S. Liveing, *A Nineteenth-Century Teacher. John Henry Bridges* (1926), 208.

64 R.M. Macleod, 'The frustration of state medicine 1880–1899', *Medical History* xi, 1967, 16–18.
65 Webb, *Poor Law History* i, 193 n, 200. For data on length of service of Inspectors see PP 1906 (350) cii, and *British Imperial Calendar*.
66 Webb, *Poor Law History* i, 359.
67 PRO MH 32/98, 17 May 1894. J.S. Davy.
68 ibid. 32/93, 21 Sept. 1895. H.B. Kennedy.
69 J. Brown, 'The appointment of the 1905 Poor Law Commission', *Bulletin of the Institute of Historical Research* xlii, 1962, 240, 242.
70 *Minority Report* 280.
71 C. Booth, *Aged Poor*, 41.
72 PP 1914 (7444) xxxviii, 88.
73 *Minority Report*, 280.
74 For a biography along these lines see J. Kent, *John Burns: Labour's Lost Leader* (1950).
75 G.D.H. Cole and R. Postgate, *The Common People* (UP ed. 1963) 426.
76 Add MSS 46323 (Burns papers) 16 April 1906.
77 ibid. 5 June 1906.
78 ibid. 27 Oct. 1906.
79 N. Mackenzie (ed.), *The Letters of Sidney and Beatrice Webb* (1978), ii, 258.
80 Add MSS 46325, 19 April 1907.
81 Kent, op. cit. 205. Add. MSS 46323, 10 March 1906.

Chapter 4

1 *Poor Law Conferences* 1903–4, 518.
2 PRO MH 57/37, 2 June 1919. Registrar General.
3 *Poor Law Conferences* 1921, 26.
4 PP 1914–16 (7808) liv, 960; PP 1928–9 (114) xvi, 746.
5 M.A. Crowther, 'The later years of the workhouse 1890–1929', in Thane, (ed.), *British Social Policy*, 39.
6 G.R. Searle, *Eugenics and Politics in Britain 1900–1914* (Leyden 1976), 104 ff.
7 *44th Report LGB*, PP 1916 (8195) xii, 608 ff.
8 Webb, *Poor Law History* ii, 1045.
9 *44th Report LGB*, PP 1916 (8195) xii, 603.
10 ibid. 557.
11 *46th Report LGB*, PP 1917–18 (8697) xvi, 148.
12 J.M. Winter, 'The impact of the First World War on civilian health in Britain', *Ec. Hist. Rev.* xxx, Aug. 1977, 502 ff.
13 Abel-Smith, *The Hospitals*, 281.
14 *1st Report MoH*, PP 1920 (932) xvii, 357, and Abel-Smith, *op. cit.* 261–2.
15 Webb, *Poor Law History* ii, 810.
16 *1st Report MoH*, PP 1920 (932) xvii, 147.
17 ibid. 387.
18 John Brown, 'The 1909 Poor Law Reports in historical perspective',

University of Glasgow Discussion Papers in Social History, no. 1, 24–5.
19 B.B. Gilbert, *British Social Policy*, 108.
20 *1st Report MoH*, PP 1920 (932) xvii, 355–6.
21 Gilbert, op. cit. 32.
22 Abel-Smith, *The Hospitals*, 353
23 *48th Report LGB*, PP 1919 (413) xxiv, 430
24 *1st Report MoH*, loc. cit. 332.
25 PRO MH 57/23, 11 June 1928. Mrs. E. Pinsent.
26 K. Jones, *Mental Health and Social Policy*. 76 ff.
27 PRO MH 57/23, 15 July 1927. F.J. Willis.
28 PP 1924 (2161) xix.
29 HMSO, *The Provision of Mental Hospital Accommodation*...(1925), 19.
30 PRO MH 57/23, 30 Dec. 1924. Unsigned memo. See also 16 July 1925, circular to boards of guardians.
31 HMSO, *Provision of Mental Hospital Accommodation*, 23: PRO MH 57/23, 29 July 1927. H.W.S. Francis.
32 PRO MH 57/23, 19 Nov. 1927. W.P. Elias.
33 ibid. 17 Nov. 1927. W.D. Bushell.
34 ibid. 11 June 1928. Mrs. E. Pinsent.
35 See Crowther, op. cit. 47–8.
36 PP 1928–9 (114) xvi, 745.
37 *1st Report MoH*, PP 1920 (932) xvii, 328.
38 José Harris, *William Beveridge, A Biography* (Oxford 1977), 402 ff.
39 Gilbert, *British Social Policy*, 211, 214.
40 Chamberlain papers, NC 2/21, 16 Oct. 1926.
41 See P.A. Ryan, 'Poplarism 1894–1930', in Thane, *British Social Policy*: I am substantially in agreement with Ms Ryan.
42 Webb, *Poor Law History* ii, 846 ff.
43 See B.J. Elliot, 'The last five years of the Sheffield guardians', *Transactions Hunterian Archeological Society* 10, 1975.
44 Quoted by K. Feiling, *Life of Neville Chamberlain* (3rd ed. 1970), 158.
45 Webb, *Poor Law History* ii, 941.
46 *7th Report MoH*, PP 1926 (2724) xi, 123, and *8th Report MoH*, PP 1927 (2938) ix, 741.
47 *8th Report MoH*, 868. See also P.A. Ryan, 'The Poor Law in 1926', in M. Morris (ed.), *The General Strike* (1976).
48 PRO MH 57/118, Feb. 1927, unsigned memo.
49 PRO MH 57/94.
50 PRO MH 57/148, 30 Nov. 1925. H.W.S. Francis.
51 PRO MH 57/94.
52 P. Ryan, 'Poor Law in 1926', 375–6: PRO MH 57/118, 1 June 1926, 31 May 1926. S.L. Scott.
53 PRO MH 57/94, scales of relief; *8th Report MoH*, PP 1927 (2938) ix, 741, 868. P. Ryan, 'Poor Law in 1926', 377.
54 PRO MH 57/109, 20 Dec. 1928. J. Pearse.
55 ibid. departmental memo accompanying Pearse's report. For the 1930s see J. Macnicol, 'Family allowances and less eligibility', in P. Thane, *op. cit.* 180.
56 PRO MH 57/97C, 17 Jan. 1928. C.F. Roundell.

Notes

57 PRO MH 57/97 C, 17 Jan. 1928. A.B. Lowry. Webb, *Poor Law History* ii, 976n.
58 PRO MH 57/146, 30 May 1927. Unsigned memo.
59 Chamberlain papers, NC 2/21, 28 March 1926.
60 Abel-Smith, *The Hospitals*, 369–70; Webb, *Poor Law History* ii, 990 for an accurate prediction of the problems of this legislation.
61 *11th Report MoH*, PP 1930–1 (3667) xiii, 947.
62 Abel-Smith, op. cit. 369.
63 PP 1938–9 (135) xxi.
64 B. Abel-Smith and R. Pinker, 'Changes in the use of institutions in England and Wales between 1911 and 1951', *Transactions Manchester Statistical Society* 1959–60, 32. The figures which Pinker and Abel-Smith use refer to inmates on a single day in 1911 and 1951; they have no information about length of stay in institutions. In mid-1963 Townsend estimated that only 4.5 per cent of the population aged 65 and over was living in institutions of *all* kinds in Britain. (P. Townsend and D. Wedderburn, *The Aged in the Welfare State*, 1965, 23). The census of 1911 gives 4.3 per cent of the same section of the population as living in workhouses *only* in England and Wales.
65 Townsend and Wedderburn, op. cit. 27–9.
66 P. Townsend, *The Last Refuge* (1962) 328 ff.
67 ibid. 415.

Chapter 5

1 *Minority Report*, 14.
2 Goffman, *Asylums*, 73 ff.
3 For a fuller discussion: M.H. Tomlinson, '"Prison Palaces:" a re-appraisal of early Victorian prisons, 1835–77', *Bulletin Inst. Hist. Research*, May 1978.
4 PRO MH 32/70, 17 Feb. 1840. E.C. Tufnell.
5 ibid. 32/56, 21 March 1827. C. Mott.
6 ibid. 32/62, 6 Nov. 1861. G. Pigott, and see subsequent letters on Pigott's resignation.
7 PRO MH 10/5, 17 Dec. 1841, 68.
8 HMSO, *First Report PLC*, 1835, 216.
9 A. Redford and I.S. Russell, *The History of Local Government in Manchester* (1940) ii, 103.
10 PRO MH 10/5, 17 Dec. 1841. Regulation 75.
11 KCA G/B1 ACa 1, 27 Sept. 1835.
12 *Minority Report*, 13.
13 KCA G/By AM 76, 25 May 1888.
14 PRO MH 12/12479, 6 Oct. 1869.
15 e.g. N. Longmate, *Workhouse*.
16 PP 1846 (663-i) v, part i, 180, 227.
17 PRO MH 10/4, 27 Sept. 1839.
18 Kept at PRO MH 9. The ones used here are provincial unions beginning with the letters A–C and H–L inclusive.

281

19 PRO MH 12/12461, 10 Nov. 1843.
20 e.g. PRO MH 12/12474, 6 April 1865; June 1866.
21 P. Dunkley, 'Hungry forties' 342. For similar evidence in East Anglia, see Digby, *Pauper Palaces*, 80.
22 e.g. in Tewksbury, PP 1852–3 (420) lxxxiv, 551.
23 PRO MH 12/12478, 2 June 1869.
24 ibid. 14 May 1869.
25 NRO PUE/3/1, 12 Feb. 1842.
26 PRO MH 32/93, Oct. 1895. N. Herbert.
27 ibid. 32/69, 29 Jan. 1836. E.C. Tufnell. 32/70, 5 July 1838.
28 ibid. 12/12479, 6 Oct. 1869.
29 idem.
30 Abel-Smith, *Hospitals*, 33.
31 See note 24.
32 PP 1849 (306) xlvii.
33 KCA G/By Am3, 17 July, 4 Sept., 6 Oct. 1846.
34 HMSO, *2nd Report PLC* (1836), 13.
35 PRO MH 32/69, 25 Oct. 1836.
36 ibid. 10/1, 4 Feb. 1836.
37 PP 1844 (231) xl.
38 PP 1862 (181) x, 151–3.
39 PRO MH 12/4865, 4 Dec. 1874.
40 KCA G/B1 ACa 4, July 1840.
41 ibid. 29 March 1843.
42 ibid. ACa 6, 27 Feb. 1849.
43 PRO MH 32/56, 5 Jan. 1848.
44 KCA G/By Am8, 141.
45 PRO MH 12/4862, 21 Jan. 1871.
46 M.H. Tomlinson, thesis, 378 ff.
47 KCA G/B1 ACa 6, 13 Aug. 1851.
48 ibid. ACa 7, 2 Jan. 1851 (misdated 1850); ACa 8, 4 May 1854.
49 PP 1862 (181) x, 82–3.
50 PRO MH 12/12477, 22 Oct. 1868.

Chapter 6

1 HMSO *Minority Report*, 15.
2 HMSO *Majority Report*, ii, 45–6.
3 *1st Report MoH*, PP 1920 (932) xvii, 147.
4 ibid. 320, also PP 1849 (306) xlvii; *Majority Report* iv, 150. Workhouse doctors who were also district officers might be counted twice.
5 Records for both unions in MH 9/3.
6 GLC La Bg 228/1–2.
7 *Minority Report*, 240.
8 ibid. 323n, and PP 1909 (4755) xl, q. 24930.
9 *Poor Law Conferences* 1881, 79.
10 PP 1902 (1366) xxxix, 15.
11 MH 55/448, 11.
12 ibid. 32/106, 28 July 1890. A.H. Downes.

13 PP 1898 (9002) li, pp vi–vii.
14 *3rd Report LGB*, PP 1874 (1071) xxv, 184.
15 PRO MH 57/62, circular 223, 5 Aug. 1921.
16 *Poor Law Conferences* 1881, 78.
17 Spoor, 103. *Poor Law Officers' Journal*, 17 March 1892, 28.
18 University of Warwick, NPLOA MSS 28/NPL/1/1/1, 12 Dec. 1893.
19 ibid. 20 NPL/1/1/3, 4 June 1898.
20 Spoor, 104. *Poor Law Officers' Journal*, 17 March 1892, 28.
21 *Majority Report* iv, 151.
22 Spoor, 105.
23 *Poor Law Officers' Journal*, 7 Jan. 1910, editorial.
24 ibid. 14 Jan. 1910, 48.
25 NPLOA MSS, 20 NPL/1/1/1, 11 July 1891.
26 *Majority Report* iv, 149.
27 PP 1909 (4684) xl, q. 19466.
28 ibid. q. 14881.
29 M.J. Smith, *Professional Education for Social Work in Britain* (1965) 44, 52, 57.
30 John Brown, 'The 1909 Poor Law Reports in historical perspective', University of Glasgow *Discussion Papers in Social History* i, 32 ff.
31 *Poor Law Officers' Journal*, 16 Jan. 1925, 63.
32 ibid. 14 Jan. 1927, 57.
33 NRO PUB/6/9, 29 March 1917.
34 *Poor Law Conferences*, 1920, 56–8.
35 ibid. 63.
36 PP 1909 (4755) xl, q. 26408.
37 Spoor, 105.
38 The history of the various schemes is in PP 1919 (329) xxiv.
39 Personal information.
40 NRO C/WE/5/45.
41 NRO MH 32/93, Oct. 1895. H. Preston-Thomas.
42 PP 1909 (4755) xl, q. 28308.
43 HMSO Board of Education: *Report upon the Educational Work in Poor Law Schools* (1908), 10.
44 Noordin, 107, 116.
45 ibid. 157.
46 *Poor Law Officers' Journal*, 2 Sept. 1927, 1101.
47 PP 1909 (4864) xl, q. 23847, 23945.
48 Tizard, Sinclair and Clarke, 4, 9–10, 44, 56, 114.
49 Townsend, *Last Refuge*, 78–9.

Chapter 7

1 *The Lancet*, 25 Dec. 1920, 1290.
2 S. and B. Webb, *The State and the Doctor* (1910), 129.
3 C. Newman, *The Evolution of Medical Education in the Nineteenth Century* (1957).
4 Webb, op. cit. 100n.
5 These figures are incomplete, as they refer only to infirmaries which were

accepted by the Ministry of Health as training schools for nurses PRO MH 55/448, appendix 1, June 1920.
6 PP 1862 (321) x, 35. See also R.G. Hodgkinson, *The Origins of the National Health Service* (1967) 432 ff.
7 *Poor Law Conferences* 1883, W. Midland 7.
8 J. Rogers, *Reminiscences of a Workhouse Medical Officer* (1889), vii.
9 PRO MH 32/71, 15 July 1842.
10 Compare PRO MH 10/5, 17 Dec. 1841, regulation 17, with the published version in *8th Report PLC*, PP 1842 (389) xix, 49.
11 Caplan, thesis, 393.
12 *Fourth Annual Report of the Registrar-General*, PP 1842 (423) xix.
13 GLC B.B.G. 30 Dec. 1891.
14 KCA G/B1 ACa 8, 13 Feb. and 7 May 1856.
15 PRO MH 12/12462, 25 Sept. 1846.
16 Kelly, thesis, 99.
17 E. Hart, *An Account of the Condition of the Infirmaries of London Workhouses* (1866), 6, 8.
18 PRO MH 12/12467, 27 June 1854.
19 E.G. PP 1850 (133) xxi.
20 Hodgkinson, op. cit. 504–6.
21 Woodward, *To Do the Sick No Harm*, 44 ff.
22 KCA G/B1 ACa 8, 20 March and 28 March 1855. A.B. Andrews.
23 Hodgkinson, op. cit. 422 ff, 682.
24 *12th Report of the Commissioners in Lunacy*, PP 1859 (228) ix, 17, 19.
25 I have argued this in more detail in 'Paupers or patients?' in J. Woodward and D. Richards (ed.), *Health Professions and the State* (forthcoming).
26 H.W. Rumsey, *Essays on State Medicine* (Arno reprint, N.Y. 1977) 278.
27 F.E. Anstie, 'Workhouse infirmary reform', *MacMillan's Magazine* xiii, 1865–6, 481–2.
28 Abel-Smith, *The Hospitals*, 44.
29 e.g. PRO MH 12/12466, 21 Nov. and 24 Nov. 1853.
30 B. Abel-Smith, *A History of the Nursing Profession* (3rd ed. 1966), 12 ff.
31 Webb, *Poor Law Policy*, 120n.
32 Twining, *Workhouses and Pauperism*, quoted p. 201.
33 Anstie, op. cit. 480.
34 Pinker, *English Hospital Statistics*, 52, 61, 75.
35 Quoted in Webb, *Poor Law History* i, 319.
36 e.g. J.L. Brand, *Doctors and the State* (Baltimore 1965); Abel-Smith, *The Hospitals*, 81.
37 PP 1877 (147) lxxi.
38 Brand, *Doctors and the State*, 103.
39 Webb, *State and Doctor*, 93.
40 PP 1909 (4573) xlii, 45–6.
41 PP 1909 (4835) xli, q. 39013.
42 *Lancet*, 31 July 1920, 275.
43 Only 10 members attended the first annual general meeting to be held in the provinces. *BMJ* 1908 ii, 231.
44 *BMJ* 1911, ii, 466: 1912 i, supp. 469: 1914 i, 1388.
45 ibid. 1913 ii, 1517.

46   *Poor Law Conferences* 1901–2, 762.
47   PP 1909 (4625) xxxix, q. 103 (5–8).
48   ibid. q. 10459.
49   PP 1872 (310) li.
50   See R.M. MacLeod, 'The anatomy of state medicine: concept and application', in F.N.L. Poynter (ed.), *Medicine and Science in the 1860s* (1968), 218 ff.
51   Webb, *State and Doctor*, 238.
52   PP 1909 (4835) xli, q. 39013.
53   G. Cuttle, *The Legacy of the Rural Guardians* (Cambridge 1934), 62.
54   Abel-Smith, *The Hospitals*, 190.
55   *Poor Law Conferences* 1883, 6, 8.
56   ibid. 1901–2, 767.
57   Webb, *State and Doctor*, 98 and n.
58   I disagree here with Hodgkinson, *op. cit.* 422 ff, and Brand, *op. cit.* 89.
59   G/By AM46, 11 April 1911.
60   PP 1909 (4625) xxxix, q. 10732–4.
61   *Poor Law Conferences* 1901–2, 767.
62   PP 1909 (4573) xlii, 49.
63   PRO MH 32/67, 15 April 1867, 12.
64   Twining, *Workhouses and Pauperism*, 212.
65   ibid. 202.
66   PP 1902 (1366) xxxix, 15.
67   PRO MH 32/106, March 1890.
68   PRO MH 57/178, 11 April 1917. A.H. Downes.
69   PP 1902 (1366) xxxix, 8.
70   *Poor Law Conferences* 1903–4, 111.
71   ibid. 1881, 185.
72   PP 1909 (4853) xli, q. 37927.
73   GLC La Bg 74/1, 31 Jan. 1906, 67.
74   PRO MH 57/178, 25 May 1913. N. Herbert.
75   PP 1909 (4755) xl, q. 33118.
76   A. Newsholme, *International Studies on the Relationship between the Private and Official Practice of Medicine...* (1931) iii, 99.
77   *Poor Law Conferences* 1901–2, 190, 770.
78   Abel-Smith, *The Hospitals*, 269.
79   KCA G/By AM51, 7 Sept. 1915.
80   *The Hospital*, 25 March 1916, 570: 30 Oct. 1915, 104.
81   from the *Medical Directory*.
82   A. Newsholme, *The Last Thirty Years in Public Health* (1936), 70.
83   A. Newsholme, *International Studies* iii, 98.
84   PRO MH 57/20, 4 July 1923.
85   *2nd Report MoH*, PP 1921 (1446) xiii, 141.
86   PRO MH 57/20, 13 April 1922, 30 May 1922.
87   *Poor Law Officers' Journal*, 21 Jan. 1927, 86.
88   *BMJ* 1927 ii, 519.
89   *Lancet*, 16 Aug. 1919, 292.
90   P.J. Watkin, *Lambeth Hospital Fifty Years Retrospect* (n.d.) 13.
91   GLC B.B.G. 418, 13 June 1929.

92 HMSO, *Annual Report of the Chief Medical Officer of the Ministry of Health for the year 1924* (1925), 166, 169.
93 *5th Report MoH*, PP 1923–4 (2218) ix, 865.
94 PRO MH 55/448, June 1920. J.H. Turner,
95 ibid. 4.
96 ibid. 25.
97 *5th Report MoH*, PP 1924 (2218) ix, 865.
98 *Poor Law Officers' Journal*, 14 Jan. 1927, 59.
99 ibid. 28 Jan. 1927, 108.
100 Abel-Smith, *Nursing Profession*, 274.
101 HMSO, *Ministry of Health, Costing returns year ending 31st March 1933* (1934) pt. i, 4.
102 *Poor Law Conferences 1901–2*, 193–4.
103 *The Hospital*, 23 April 1921, 70.
104 A. Newsholme, *Medicine and the State* (1932), 80.
105 Pinker, *English Hospital Statistics*, 121, 135.
106 B. Aronovitch, *Give it Time: An Experience of Hospital* (1974), 69. See also F.B. Smith, *The People's Health 1830–1910* (1979).

Chapter 8

1 C. Dickens, 'A walk in a workhouse', *Household Words*, 25 May 1850, 204–5.
2 Quoted in Townsend, *Last Refuge*, 30.
3 H.O. Barnett, *Canon Barnett, His Life, Work, And Friends* (1919), i, 201.
4 Kelly, thesis, 81–2.
5 *3rd Report LGB*, PP 1874 (1071) xxv, 196.
6 F. Thompson, *Lark Rise to Candleford* (World's Classics 1954), 314.
7 PRO MH 10/4, 9 March 1839.
8 NRO PUE 3/1, 1 June 1839.
9 PRO MH 12/12467, 31 July 1854. J.E. Palmer. 4 Aug. 1854, clerk.
10 PRO MH 32/93, 13 Dec. 1898, J.S. Davy.
11 Goffman, *Asylums*, 220–1.
12 Checkland, *Poor Law Report*, 450–1.
13 PRO MH 32/103, 21 June 1873. H. Longley.
14 KCA G/B1 ACa 4, 2 Sept. 1842. W. Dunbar.
15 PRO MH 12/12462, 2 June 1846. J. McDonnell.
16 *Poor Law Conferences*, 188, 182.
17 PRO MH 32/67, 21 April 1871.
18 PRO MH 32/103, 7 Feb. 1871.
19 Townsend, op. cit. 80–2.
20 Muir Gray, 'The dilemma of residential care', *Community Care* 27 Oct. 1976, 25.
21 For more recent examples see Townsend, op. cit. 125–7.
22 Checkland, *Poor Law Report*, 430, 437.
23 HMSO, *2nd Report PLC* (1836), 35.
24 PRO MH 10/7, 31 Jan. 1837.
25 HMSO, *2nd Report PLC* (1836), 209.

26 R. Johnson, 'Educational policy and social control in early Victorian England', *Past & Present*, Nov. 1970.
27 A. Digby, *Pauper Palaces* (1978), 180 ff.
28 ibid. 183.
29 ibid. 183, 185.
30 *4th Report PLB*, PP 1852 (1461) xxxiii, 99. *Majority Report* ii, 64.
31 PP 1862 (321) x, 83.
32 KCA G/B1 ACa 5, 19 Oct. 1848. H. Church.
33 PRO MH 32/60, 12 Oct. 1839. H.W. Parker. R. Boyson, thesis, 324–6.
34 Chadwick papers, 23, 14 Feb. 1841. A. Austin.
35 PRO MH 32/108, 31 Jan. 1867. H. Bowyer.
36 ibid. 29 March 1864.
37 PP 1909 (4671) ciii, 818.
38 PRO MH 32/108, 29 March 1864. H. Bowyer.
39 ibid. 25 Jan. 1864.
40 HMSO, Board of Education: *Report upon the Educational Work in Poor Law Schools* ... (1908), 17.
41 KCA G/Bl ACa 6, 28 Nov. 1849. R. Coleman.
42 A.M. Ross, thesis, 114.
43 *Poor Law Officers' Journal*, 16 Jan. 1925, 65.
44 PRO MH 32/106, 17 Nov. 1894. A.H. Downes. 11 Dec. 1894. W.E. Knollys.
45 ibid. 10/9, ? 1840.
46 PP 1843 (63-ii) xlv, 373. The figures did not take account of paupers who were tried twice, and there may have been summary discharges which were not recorded.
47 PP 1901 (659) lxxxix, 118–9.
48 PP 1843 (63-i) xlv, 344.
49 PP 1862 (181) x, 155, 160.
50 KCA G/F WRm 1, 21 Feb. 1840.
51 ibid. 28 Dec. 1838.
52 NRO PUE 3/1, 2 Oct. 1841.
53 PRO MH 32/93, Oct. 1895. N. Herbert.
54 KCA G/B1 ACa 11, 22 Nov. 1866. J. Martin.
55 Haw, *Workhouse to Westminster*, 11.
56 'Three months in a London workhouse', *Chambers' Journal*, 16 May 1903, 381–2.
57 PRO MH 32/69, 24 Feb. 1836.
58 S.K. Allen, 'Crime and punishment in the Ashford Division of Kent 1830–1850', University of Kent Social Sciences extended essay 1969, appendix 4.
59 Boyson, thesis, 363–4, 367, 374
60 T.C. Barker, D.J. Oddy, J. Yudkin, *The Dietary Surveys of Dr Edward Smith 1862–3* (1970), 27 ff.
61 PP 1850 (133) xxi, 782, 784.
62 PP 1872 (275) li, 6.
63 PRO MH 32/106, Oct. 1891. A.H. Downes.
64 ibid. 32/67, 3 Sept. 1866.
65 Rowntree, *Poverty* 86: M.F. Davies, *Life in an English Village* (1909),

215 ff. For a similar comparison at an earlier date see F. Purdy, 'On the earnings of Agricultural Labourers in England and Wales 1860', *Jnl. Statistical Soc.* xxiv (1861).

66 D.J. Oddy, 'A nutritional analysis of historical evidence: the working-class diet, 1880–1914', in D.J. Oddy and D.S. Miller (eds), *The Making of the Modern British Diet* (1976), 216.

67 Barker, *Edward Smith*, 31, 41.

68 PRO MH 32/60, 9 July 1842.

69 PRO MH 32/93, 8 Oct. 1895.

70 R. Noordin, *Through a Workhouse Window*, 27.

71 R. Asher, 'Clinical sense', in *Talking Sense* (1972), 8.

72 PRO MH 32/91, 30 Dec. 1873. W.J. Sendall.

73 KCA G/Bl ACa 5, 22 Nov. 1848. R. Hall.

74 *Conference of Managers of Reformatory and Industrial Institutions* 1869, 106.

75 *3rd Report LGB*, PP 1874 (19017) xxv, 311 ff.

76 PRO MH 32/24, 16 Jan. 1862. H.B. Farnall. PP 1862 (494) xiv.

77 Townsend, *Last Refuge*, 367.

Chapter 9

1 KCA G/AW WRm 1, 15 Jan. 1916.

2 PRO MH 32/103, 7 Nov. 1873.

3 PP 1874 (1071) xxv, 173. PP 1909 (337) lxxi, 5.

4 *Minority Report* i, 73n.

5 M. Vicinus, *The Industrial Muse* (1974), 275.

6 Copy in the Johnson Collection, Bodleian Library, Oxford.

7 PRO MH 12/12469, 26 Oct. 1855.

8 PRO MH 12/12470, 13 June 1856. J. Logan.

9 Church, *Victorian Nottingham*, 116, 121; Dunkley, 'Hungry forties', 340n; Digby, *Pauper Palaces*, 103; Mawson, 'South Shields', 42, 61; McCord, 'Poor Law Amendment Act on Tyneside', 107; Fraser, *New Poor Law*, 145.

10 PP 1861 (490) lv.

11 These and subsequent figures for Holborn are from GLC Ho Bg 542/1. Although the documents are filed as 'Holborn workhouse', the workhouse seems to have been the old workhouse of the parish of St James, Clerkenwell, which became part of Holborn union in 1869.

12 Hufton, *The Poor of Eighteenth-Century France*, ch. III, esp. p. 126.

13 L. Chevalier, *The Labouring Classes and the Dangerous Classes in Paris During the First Half of the Nineteenth Century* (trans. F. Jellinek 1973), 5 ff.

14 D. Philips, *Crime and Authority in Victorian England. The Black Country 1835–1860* (1977), 289. See also V.A.C. Gatrell and T.B. Hadden, 'Criminal statistics and their interpretation', in E.A. Wrigley (ed.), *Nineteenth-Century Society* (Cambridge, 1972).

15 From surviving workhouse admission and discharge registers, KCA and GLC.

16 GLC La Bg 172/1. Lambeth Master's Journal.

17 *Majority Report* ii, 42.
18 ibid. ii, 43.
19 ibid. iv, 185.
20 Selected from KCA G/Br WIa. The method used here is simple indexing. The admissions books would no doubt yield more to computer techniques.
21 Abel-Smith and Pinker, 'Changes in the use of institutions', 32.
22 Townsend, *Last Refuge.*
23 PRO MH 32/69, 2 Oct. 1836.
24 M. Anderson, *Family Structure in Nineteenth-Century Lancashire* (Cambridge, 1971), 143.
25 R. Roberts, *The Classic Slum* (Pelican 1973), 45, 50, 53–4. P. Thompson, *The Edwardians* (Paladin 1977), 54 ff.
26 Caplan, 'Southwell and Basford', 495; KCA G/AW AM2, 20 Jan. 1840.
27 KCA G/Me WIr 1.
28 PRO MH 12/12460, 8 Oct. 1841. R. Watmore.
29 *South London Press*, 3 Jan. 1880, 10.
30 Digby, *Pauper Palaces*, 228. These Norfolk labourers inserted themselves into the workhouse without going through admission formalities; but the Bromley labourers who earlier did the same thing (see p. 237) formally admitted and discharged themselves regularly.
31 *The Autobiography of Joseph Arch* (1898. MacGibbon & Kee reprint 1966) 98–9. See also Roberts, *Classic Slum*, 74 n.
32 KCA G/B1 ACa 9, 30 March 1859.
33 Roberts, *op. cit.* Ch. 1.
34 Booth, *Aged Poor*, 330.
35 E. Sellers, 'Shifting scenes in rural workhouses', *Nineteenth Century* 54, 1903, 1000.
36 PRO MH 32/93, 5 Oct. 1895. J.S. Davy.
37 *Autobiography of Joseph Arch*, 101.
38 M.K. Ashby, *Joseph Ashby of Tysoe* (Merlin ed. 1974), 191–2.
39 PP 1906 (2891-ii) ciii, 189. Will Crooks.
40 KCA G/F WRm1, 21 Feb. 1840; G/B1 WI, 26 Nov. 1897.
41 Haw, *Workhouse to Westminster*, 109.
42 Townsend, *Last Refuge*, 118 ff, 315 ff.
43 PRO MH 10/1, October 1836.
44 KCA G/By AM 5, 25 May 1855.
45 PP 1850 (1228) xxi.
46 There is an example of one of these in the museum of Pembroke castle. See also R.A. Church and B.M.D. Smith, 'Competition and monopoly in the coffin furniture industry, 1870–1915', *Ec. Hist. Rev.* xix 1966, 923.
47 See also J. Hurley, *Rattle His Bones* (Dulverton 1974) 33 ff.
48 PP 1910 (5074) lii, 4.
49 PP 1909 (4835) xli, q 47. J. Spottiswoode Cameron.
50 PRO MH 10/1, 17 Dec. 1834.
51 Digby, *Pauper Palaces*, 226.
52 Church, *Victorian Nottingham*, 295.
53 PRO MH 32/98, 13 Feb. 1879. J.S. Davy.
54 T.D. Jones, 'Merthyr Tydfil Union', 296 ff.
55 *Poor Law Conferences* 1878, 502–6.

56 ibid. 59.
57 Webb, *Poor Law History* ii, 836 ff.
58 GLC La Bg 274/1, 28 March 1906, 181.

Chapter 10

1   PRO MH 10/9, 15 Feb. 1841.
2   PP 1906 (203) ciii, vol. iii, 25.
3   D. Hudson (ed.), *Munby, Man of Two Worlds* (1972), 198.
4   J. London, *People of the Abyss* (1903), ch. ix; G. Orwell, *Down and Out in Paris and London* (1933), chs. 27, 34. For a harsh view of tramp life see F. Gray, *The Tramp, His Meaning and Being* (1932), and for a romantic view F.L. Jennings, *Tramping with Tramps* (1932).
5   R. Vorspan, 'Vagrancy and the New Poor Law in late-Victorian and Edwardian England', *English Historical Review* 92, 1977, 73.
6   M.E. Rose, *The English Poor Law*, 211 ff.
7   PRO MH 32/9, 27 Nov. 1865.
8   C.J. Ribton-Turner, *A History of Vagrants and Vagrancy and Beggars and Begging* (1887), 296, 302.
9   For an extended discussion of this, see D.J.V. Jones, ' "A dead loss to the community": the criminal Vagrant in mid-nineteenth-century Wales', *Welsh Historical Review* 1977, 312 ff.
10 PP 1906 (2852) ciii, 16 ff.
11 Sources: PP 1906 (203) ciii, vol iii, 20: *Annual Statement of the Number of Paupers Relieved* (PP): B.R. Mitchell and P. Deane, *Abstract of British Historical Statistics* (Cambridge 1962), 64–5.
12 Advice on this technique was given me by Dr J.M. Crowther, who referred to G.E.P. Box and G.M. Jenkins, *Time Series Analysis Forecasting and Control* (San Francisco 1970), 371–77.
13 W.H. Beveridge, *Unemployment: a Problem of Industry* (1930 ed.), 12–12.
14 Webb, *Poor Law History* i, 403.
15 PRO MH 32/67, 26 Nov. 1867. Poor Law Board.
16 PP 1906 (203) ciii, vol iii, 80 and PRO MH 57/62, 5 July 1924.
17 PP 1906 (2852) ciii, vol i, 19; PP 1929–30 (3640) xvii, 15.
18 PP 1906 (2852) ciii, vol i, 18. Professor Vorspan (op. cit. p. 60), notes that 'at least 85 per cent of vagrants were demonstrably adult men under sixty-five years of age', but this does not recognize the problem of the older workers.
19 PP 1929–30 (3640) xvii, 15. The sample was of 2,582 casuals.
20 PRO MH 57/78, 26 July 1920. W.D. Bushell. For the alleged youthfulness of post-war casuals see F. Gray, *op. cit.* 56.
21 PP 1906 (2852) ciii, vol i, pp 26, 57.
22 PP 1908 (4202) xxxix, 316.
23 ibid. 317.
24 PP 1929–30 (3460) xvii, 8, 27.
25 PP 1906 (2852) ciii, vol i, 121, 91, 120.
26 H. Preston-Thomas, *The Work and Play of a Government Inspector* (1909), 349.

27 J. Harris, *Unemployment and Politics*, 187.
28 PP 1901 (659) lxxxix, 51. PP 1930–1 (3853) xxxii, 68–9.
29 PP 1901 (659) lxxxix, 51.
30 PRO MH 57/61, 29 Sept. 1924. C.F. Roundell.
31 PP 1924 (2267) xix, 8. There is a difference between these figures and the Ministry's unpublished extract PRO MH 57/62, 5 July 1924, which gives 229 'good', 204 'medium' and 119 'bad'.
32 PRO MH 56/62, 24 May 1923. A.H. Wagstaff.
33 PRO MH 57/62, 18 Dec. 1882.
34 PP 1906 (203) ciii, vol iii, 80. On the other hand, about 4 per cent of unions indulged vagrants with unsanctioned luxuries like tea, coffee or milk.
35 PRO MH 57/62, 23 Sept. 1914.
36 ibid. 22 June 1921.
37 ibid. 56/67, 1 Sept. 1913.
38 PP 1906 (203) ciii, vol iii, 80. PRO MH 57/68, 4 June 1924.
39 PRO MH 57/92, 16, Jan. 1930. J. Summer Dury.
40 PRO MH 57/62, 3 May and 14 July 1923. The officers' associations had been asked to comment on the order before it appeared.
41 ibid. 9 June 1923.
42 ibid. undated draft minute with the Casual Poor (Relief) Order 1925.
43 *Manchester Guardian*, 7 May 1925.
44 *Hansard*, 5th ser. clxxxviii, 564, 19 Nov. 1929.
45 PRO MH 57/68, 4 June and 25 May 1925.
46 ibid. 28 May 1925.
47 PRO MH 57/80, 3 Feb. 1930. L.N. Ure.
48 e.g. *Hansard*, 5th ser. clxxii, 1347, 16 April 1924.
49 PP 1929–30 (3640) xvii, 21.
50 *Hansard*, 5th ser. ccxiv, 2192, 5 April 1928.
51 *10th Report MoH*, PP 1929–30 (3362) xiv, 150. The hostel, however, did select the 'better' class of London casuals.
52 PP 1929–30 (3640) xvii, 50. See also pp. 8, 27.

Select Bibliography

A. Manuscript Sources

Burns papers, British Library
Chadwick papers, University College, London
Chamberlain papers, University of Birmingham
Kent Poor Law records, County Hall, Maidstone
London Poor Law records, County Hall, London
Ministry of Health records, Public Record Office, London
Nottinghamshire Poor Law records, County House, Nottingham
Poor Law Officers' Association records, University of Warwick

B. Unpublished theses (university of origin shown in brackets)

BODY, G.A. 'The administration of the Poor Laws in Dorset 1760–1834', Ph.D. 1965 (Southampton)

BOYSON, R. 'The history of Poor Law Administration in north east Lancashire, 1843–1871', M.A. 1960 (Manchester)

CAPLAN, M. 'The administration of the Poor Law in the unions of Southwell and Basford: 1836–71', D. Phil. 1967 (Nottingham)

DUNKLEY, P.J. 'The New Poor Law and County Durham', M.A. 1971 (Durham)

FROSHAUG, A. 'Poor Law administration in selected London parishes 1750–1850', M.A. 1969 (Nottingham)

HUZEL, J.P. 'Aspects of the Old Poor Law, population and agrarian protest in early nineteenth-century England with particular reference to the county of Kent', Ph.D. 1975 (Kent)

JONES, T.D. 'Poor Law and public health administration in the area of Merthyr Tydfil Union 1834–1894', M.A. 1961 (Wales)

KELLY, S. 'The select vestry of Liverpool and the administration of the Poor Law 1821–1871', M.A. 1971 (Liverpool)

MAWSON, P. 'Poor Law administration in South Shields 1830–1930', M.A. 1971 (Newcastle)

ROSS, A.M. 'The care and education of pauper children in England and Wales 1834 to 1896', Ph.D. 1955 (London)

ROSS, E.M. 'Women and Poor Law administration 1857–1909', M.A. 1956 (London)

THOMPSON, R.N. 'The New Poor Law in Cumberland and Westmorland 1834–1871', Ph.D. 1976 (Newcastle)

TODD, M.J. 'The operation of the New Poor Law of 1834 in Kent and Middlesex', Social Sciences extended essay 1969 (Kent)

TOMLINSON, M.H. 'Victorian prisons: administration and architecture 1835–1877', Ph.D. 1975 (London)

WHITE, R. 'The development of the Poor Law nursing service and the social, medical and political factors that influenced it; 1848 to 1948', M.Sc. 1975 (Manchester)

C. Periodicals

British Parliamentary Papers
British Medical Journal
The Hospital
The Lancet
The Poor Law Officers' Journal
Reports of the Poor Law District Conferences.

D. Contemporary printed sources (published in London, unless otherwise stated)

WYTHEN BAXTER, G.R. *The Book of the Bastiles* (1841)
BOOTH, C. *The Aged Poor in England and Wales: Condition* (1894)
BOSANQUET, H. *Social Work in London 1869 to 1912. A History of the Charity Organization Society* (1914)
CHANCE, W. *Children Under the Poor Law* (1897)
CHECKLAND S.G. and E.O.A. (eds.), *The Poor Law Report of 1834* (Pelican reprint 1974)
DAVENPORT-HILL, F. *Children of the State* (2nd ed. 1889)
GRAY, F. The Tramp, *His Meaning and Being* (1931)
HAW, G. *From Workhouse to Westminster: The Life Story of Will Crooks, M.P.* (1907)
MACKAY, T. *A History of the English Poor Law from 1834 to the Present Time* (1899)
NEWSHOLME, A. *The Last Thirty Years in Public Health* (1936)
PRESTON-THOMAS, H. *The Work and Play of a Government Inspector* (1909)
RIBTON-TURNER, C.J. *A History of Vagrants and Vagrancy and Beggars and Begging* (1887)
ROGERS, J. *Reminiscences of a Workhouse Medical Officer* (1889)
ROWNTREE, B. SEEBOHM *Poverty: a Study of Town Life* (1901)
TWINING, L. *Workhouses and Pauperism* (1898)

E. Secondary sources

ABEL-SMITH, B and PINKER, R. 'Changes in the use of institutions in England and Wales between 1911 and 1951', *Trans. Manchester Statistical Soc.* 1959–60
ABEL-SMITH, B. *The Hospitals 1800–1948* Heinemann 1964
ABEL-SMITH, B. *A History of the Nursing Profession* 3rd ed. Heinemann 1966
BLAUG, M. 'The myth of the Old Poor Law and the making of the New', *Jnl. of Economic History* 1963
BLAUG, M. 'The Poor Law Report reexamined', ibid. 1964
BRAND, J.L. *Doctors and the State: The British Medical Profession and*

Government Action in Public Health 1870–1912 Baltimore, Johns Hopkins 1965

BRUNDAGE, A. *The Making of the New Poor Law 1832–39* Hutchinson 1978

DIGBY, A. *Pauper Palaces* Routledge and Kegan Paul 1978

DUNKLEY, P. 'The hungry forties and the New Poor Law: a case Study', *HJ* 1974

EDSALL, N.C. *The Anti-Poor Law Movement 1834–44* Manchester University Press 1971

FINER, S.E. *The Life and Times of Sir Edwin Chadwick* Methuen 1952

FRASER D. (ed.), *The New Poor Law in the Nineteenth Century* Macmillan 1976

GILBERT, B.B. *British Social Policy 1914–1939* Batsford 1970

GOFFMAN, E. *Asylums: Essays on the Social Situation of Mental Patients and Other Inmates* Pelican 1968

HARRIS, J. *Unemployment and Politics* Oxford University Press 1972

HENRIQUES, U. 'How cruel was the Victorian Poor Law?' *HJ* 1968

HODGKINSON, R.G. *The Origins of the National Health Service. The Medical Services of the New Poor Law, 1834–1871* Wellcome 1967

JONES, G. STEDMAN *Outcast London* Oxford University Press 1971

JONES, KATHLEEN, *Lunacy, Law and Conscience 1744–1845* Routledge and Kegan Paul 1955

JONES, KATHLEEN, *Mental Health and Social Policy 1845–1959* Routledge and Kegan Paul 1960

LOCHHEAD, A.V.S. (ed.), *A Reader in Social Administration* Constable 1968

LONGMATE, N. *The Workhouse* History Book Club, n.d.

MARSHALL, D. *The English Poor in the Eighteenth Century* 2nd ed. Routledge and Kegan Paul 1969

MARSHALL, J.D. *The Old Poor Law 1795–1834* Macmillan 1968

MARTIN, E.W. (ed.), *Comparative Development in Social Welfare* Allen & Unwin 1972

McCORD, N. 'The implementation of the 1834 Poor Law Amendment Act on Tyneside', *International Review of Social History* 1969

McLEOD, R.M. 'The frustration of state medicine 1880–1899', *Medical History* 1967

MORRIS, M. (ed.), *The General Strike* Pelican 1976

NEATE, A.R. *St Marylebone Workhouse and Institution* St Marylebone Society 1967

PARRY, N. and PARRY, J. *The Rise of the Medical Profession* Croom Helm 1976

PETERSON, M.J. *The Medical Profession in Mid-Victorian London* Berkeley, University of California Press 1978

PINKER, R. *English Hospital Statistics 1861–1938* Heinemann 1966

POSTGATE, R. *The Life of George Lansbury* Longman 1951

POYNTER, J.R. *Society and Pauperism. English Ideas on Poor Relief 1795–1834* Routledge and Kegan Paul 1969

ROBERTS, D. *Victorian Origins of the British Welfare State* New Haven, Yale University Press 1960

ROBERTS, D. 'How cruel was the Victorian Poor Law?' *HJ* 1963

ROBERTS, R. *The Classic Slum* Pelican 1973

Rose, M.E. 'The allowance system under the New Poor Law', *Ec. Hist. Rev.* 1966

Rose, M.E. *The English Poor Law 1780–1930* Newton Abbot, David & Charles 1971

Rose, M.E. *The Relief of Poverty 1834–1914* Macmillan 1972

Rothman, D.J. *The Discovery of the Asylum: Social Order and Disorder in the New Republic* Boston, Little, Brown & Co. 1971

Scull, A.T. *Museums of Madness* Allen Lane 1979

Smith, F. *The Life and Work of Sir James Kay-Shuttleworth* Murray 1923

Smith, F.B. *The People's Health 1830–1910* Croom Helm 1979

Spoor, A. *White-Collar Union: Sixty Years of NALGO* Heinemann 1967

Thane, P. (ed.), *Origins of British Social Policy* Croom Helm 1978

Tizard, J.A., Sinclair, I. and Clarke, R.V.G. (eds.), *Varieties of Residential Experience* Routledge and Kegan Paul 1975

Townsend, P. *The Last Refuge: a Survey of Residential Institutions and Homes for the Aged in England and Wales* Routledge and Kegan Paul 1962

Vorspan, R. 'Vagrancy and the New Poor Law in late-Victorian and Edwardian England', *English Historical Review* 1977

Webb, S. and B. *The State and the Doctor* Longmans 1910

Webb, S. and B. *English Poor Law Policy* Cass reprint 1963

Webb, S. and B. *English Poor Law History, Part I: the Old Poor Law* Cass reprint 1963

Webb, S. and B. *English Poor Law History, Part II: the Last Hundred Years* 2 vol Cass Reprint 1963

Woodward, J. *To Do the Sick No Harm: a Study of the British Voluntary Hospital System to 1875* Routledge and Kegan Paul 1974

Young, A.F. and Ashton, E.T. *British Social Work in the Nineteenth Century* Routledge and Kegal Paul 1956

Index